JUGENDSTIL WOMEN AND THE MAKING OF MODERN DESIGN

CULTURAL HISTORIES OF DESIGN

Series editors:
Grace Lees-Maffei of the University of Hertfordshire, UK
Kjetil Fallan of the University of Oslo, Norway

The Cultural Histories of Design series presents rigorous and original research on the role and significance of design in society and culture, past and present. From a vantage point in the heart of the humanities, the series explores design as the most significant manifestation of modern and contemporary culture.

In the series:
Modern Asian Design, D. J. Huppatz
Norman Bel Geddes: American Design Visionary, Nicolas P. Maffei
Soviet Critical Design: Senezh Studio and the Communist Surround, Tom Cubbin
The New Typography in Scandinavia: Modernist Design and Print Culture, Trond Klevgaard
Open Plan: A Design History of the American Office, Jennifer Kaufmann-Buhler
Atari Design: Impressions on Coin-Operated Video Game Machines, Raiford Guins
Jugendstil Women and the Making of Modern Design, Sabine Wieber

Forthcoming titles:
Art Botany in British Design Reform, 1835–1865, Sarah Alford
The Professionalization of Window Display in Britain, 1919–1939: Modern Styles, Design and Education, Kerry Meakin
Mid-century Molecular: Design and X-ray Crystallography in Britain, Emily Candela
Cultural Meanings of Design: Key Concepts, Mads Nygaard Folkmann

JUGENDSTIL WOMEN AND THE MAKING OF MODERN DESIGN

Sabine Wieber

BLOOMSBURY VISUAL ARTS
LONDON • NEW YORK • OXFORD • NEW DELHI • SYDNEY

BLOOMSBURY VISUAL ARTS
Bloomsbury Publishing Plc
50 Bedford Square, London, WC1B 3DP, UK
1385 Broadway, New York, NY 10018, USA
29 Earlsfort Terrace, Dublin 2, Ireland

BLOOMSBURY, BLOOMSBURY VISUAL ARTS and the Diana logo are trademarks of
Bloomsbury Publishing Plc

First published in Great Britain 2022
Paperback edition published 2024

Copyright © Sabine Wieber, 2024

Sabine Wieber has asserted her right under the Copyright, Designs and Patents Act, 1988, to be identified as Author of this work.

For legal purposes the Acknowledgements on p. xiv constitute an extension of this copyright page.

Cover design: Louise Dugdale
Cover image: Josef Rudolf Witzel – Cover of the art and literary magazine "Jugend", issue no. 16/1896. Courtesy Heidelberg University Library, Germany.

All rights reserved. No part of this publication may be reproduced or transmitted in any form or by any means, electronic or mechanical, including photocopying, recording, or any information storage or retrieval system, without prior permission in writing from the publishers.

Bloomsbury Publishing Plc does not have any control over, or responsibility for, any third-party websites referred to or in this book. All internet addresses given in this book were correct at the time of going to press. The author and publisher regret any inconvenience caused if addresses have changed or sites have ceased to exist, but can accept no responsibility for any such changes.

A catalogue record for this book is available from the British Library.

A catalog record for this book is available from the Library of Congress.

ISBN: PB: 978-1-3504-2796-9
HB: 978-1-3500-8852-8
ePDF: 978-1-3500-8854-2
eBook: 978-1-3500-8853-5

Series: Cultural Histories of Design

Typeset by Deanta Global Publishing Services, Chennai, India
Printed and bound in Great Britain

To find out more about our authors and books visit www.bloomsbury.com and sign up for our newsletters.

To the extraordinary women at the heart of this book

CONTENTS

List of illustrations x
Acknowledgements xiv

INTRODUCTION: A NEW STYLE FOR A NEW AGE? 1

I.1 Modern women 2
I.2 The cultural geography of Munich around 1900 5
I.3 Munich–Berlin 7
I.4 Prince Regent Luitpold 9
I.5 The term 'Jugendstil' 10
I.6 Summary of chapters 14

1 MAKER: MARGARETHE VON BRAUCHITSCH AND THE UNITED WORKSHOPS 25

1.1 Introducing Margarethe von Brauchitsch 28
1.2 The Vereinigte Werkstätten für Kunst im Handwerk 32
1.3 The *Kunstsalon* Littauer 1896 33
1.4 The 'Seventh International Art Exhibition' at the Munich Glaspalast 34
1.5 The United Workshops and Margarethe von Brauchitsch 36
1.6 A new direction for embroidery 38
1.7 The materiality of Margarethe von Brauchitsch's embroideries 40
1.8 Interiors and textiles 42
1.9 Machine embroidery 45
1.10 Embroidery and Jugendstil historiography 46
1.11 Was Margarethe von Brauchitsch a Jugendstil woman? 47
1.12 Relegated to the sidelines 49

2 ACTIVISTS: THE ELVIRA PHOTOGRAPHY STUDIO AND MUNICH FEMINIST POLITICS 57

- 2.1 August Endell's first commission 59
- 2.2 August Endell and Munich Jugendstil 61
- 2.3 The building and its façade 62
- 2.4 The interior 66
- 2.5 The patrons: Anita Augspurg and Sophia Goudstikker 69
- 2.6 Studio photography in Munich around 1900 71
- 2.7 The Photo-Studio Elvira and Munich's women's movement 74
- 2.8 The Association for Women's Interests (1894) 75
- 2.9 Going their separate ways 78
- 2.10 Jugendstil experimentation and political advocacy 80
- 2.11 Postscript 82

3 STUDENTS: EDUCATING WOMEN AT THE DEBSCHITZ SCHOOL 89

- 3.1 The Debschitz School at Dresden 91
- 3.2 Hermann Obrist (1862–1927) 93
- 3.3 Wilhelm von Debschitz (1871–1948) 95
- 3.4 The *Lehr- und Versuchs-Ateliers für angewandte und freie Kunst* 96
- 3.5 The curriculum 98
- 3.6 Women at the Debschitz School 102
- 3.7 Art and design education in Munich around 1900 104
- 3.8 The Royal Applied Arts School (1868) 104
- 3.9 The *weibliche Abteilung* at the Royal School of Applied Arts (1872) 105
- 3.10 The Munich Women Artists' Association 106
- 3.11 Women at the Debschitz School 108
- 3.12 Emilie Butters (1879–1961) 110
- 3.13 Modernism's paradox 111

4 PATRON: FASHIONABLE TASTE AT ELSA BRUCKMANN'S SALON 119

- 4.1 Elsa Bruckmann (1865–1946) 121
- 4.2 Munich–Vienna: The Todesco Palais 122
- 4.3 Marrying into a publishing empire 124
- 4.4 The Bruckmanns' new headquarters 125
- 4.5 Munich–Glasgow: The dining room 126
- 4.6 Munich–London: Hermann and Anna Muthesius 130
- 4.7 Elsa Bruckmann's debut as salonnière 132
- 4.8 A brief history of salon culture 134
- 4.9 The Mackintosh dining-room-cum-salon 136
- 4.10 Salon culture and gender 137
- 4.11 Elsa Bruckmann's 'enhanced independence' 137

5 REFORMERS: DRESSING THE PART 147

- 5.1 What is Artistic Dress? 149
- 5.2 Artistic Dress and German dress reform 150
- 5.3 Dress and function 153
- 5.4 Fashion/anti-fashion 155
- 5.5 Maria van de Velde and Alfred Mohrbutter 158
- 5.6 Artistic Dress and Jugendstil interiors 159
- 5.7 Health and beauty 161
- 5.8 German life reform 162
- 5.9 Dress reform and Germany's women's movement 163
- 5.10 Jugendstil women and dress reform 164
- 5.11 Anna Muthesius and Else Oppler 165
- 5.12 Artistic Dress and the department store 167
- 5.13 The Kaufhaus Oberpollinger and the Warenhaus Hermann Tietz 169
- 5.14 Shopping 172

6 CONCLUSION 183

Bibliography 195
Index 216

ILLUSTRATIONS

Figures

1 'Cabinet 25' at the Seventh International Art Exhibition, Munich Glaspalast 1897, in *Kunst und Handwerk* 47 (1898–9): 43 6
2 Johannes Bernhard, 'Castle Neuschwanstein under Construction', 1882–5 8
3 W. Fleck, 'The Gothic Reception Room at the German House', Chicago World's Fair, 1893, in *Kunstgewerbeblatt* 5, 3 (1894): 6 13
4 C. F. Weysser, 'Street View of the new Hofbräuhaus', Munich, 1897, in *Kunst und Handwerk* 47 (1898): 392 26
5 Richard Riemerschmid, 'Upper Coat Check', Munich, 1900–1, in *Kunst und Handwerk* 51 (1901): 286 26
6 Margarethe von Brauchitsch and Richard Riemerschmid, 'Curtain for the Munich Schauspielhaus', 1900–1, in *Kunst und Handwerk* 51 (1901): 288 27
7 'Margarethe von Brauchitsch', in *Dekorative Kunst* 11 (1903): 69 29
8 Margarethe von Brauchitsch, 'Two Embroideries on Linen', Darmstadt Applied Arts Exhibition, 1900, in *Deutsche Kunst und Dekoration* 3 (1898–9): 123 30
9 Margarethe von Brauchitsch, Illustration in *Die Jugend* 4, Bd. 2, no. 51 (1899): 836 31
10 Margarethe von Brauchitsch, 'Back Pillow', 1907, in *Deutsche Kunst und Dekoration* 21 (1907): 32 31
11 'Cabinet 25' at the Seventh International Art Exhibition at the Munich Glaspalast, 1897, in *Kunst und Handwerk* 47 (1897–8): 43 35
12 Margarethe von Brauchitsch, Interior with Furniture and Embroidery Work: A Ladies' Toilette, in *Deutsche Kunst und Dekoration* 15 (1904–5): 258 39
13 Margarethe von Brauchitsch, Interior with Furniture and Embroidery Work: Dressing Room, in *Deutsche Kunst und Dekoration* 15 (1904–5): 261 41

14	Georg Pettendorfer, Von-der-Tann Strasse with view towards the English Garden 58	
15	Georg Pettendorfer, Photo-Studio Elvira c. 1937 without the façade 58	
16	August Endell, Photo-Studio Elvira, Munich 1898, in *Dekorative Kunst* 6 (1900): 298 60	
17	Reinhold Kirsch, ironwork at main entrance, Photo-Studio Elvira, 1898, in *Dekorative Kunst* 6 (1900): 299 64	
18	Müller, Radiator Covers, Photo-Studio Elvira, 1898, in *Dekorative Kunst* 6 (1900): 304 65	
19	August Endell and J. Müller, Stairways, Photo-Studio Elvira, 1898, in *Dekorative Kunst* 6 (1900): 301 67	
20	Photo-Studio Elvira, Garden House with Sophie Goudstikker on the lower balcony, Königin-Street 3a, c. 1900, in *Dekorative Kunst* 6 (1900): 305 67	
21	August Endell, Entrance Hall, Photo-Studio Elvira, 1898, in *Dekorative Kunst* 6 (1900): 300 68	
22	Reinhold Kirsch, oak doors with ironwork, Photo-Studio Elvira, 1898, in *Dekorative Kunst* 6 (1900): 302 68	
23	Verein für Fraueninteressen Munich, photograph, 1896 74	
24	Martha von Kranz and Laura Lange (Debschitz School), three-part photo-frame with photographs of Anita Augspurg, 1911, in *Kunst und Handwerk* 62 (1911–12): 52 79	
25	Photo-Studio Elvira, Lou Andreas-Salome, photograph, c. 1897 80	
26	Main Boulevard, 'Bavarian Trade, Industry and Art Exhibition', Nuremberg 1906, in *Schweizerische Bauzeitung* 48, no. 11 (1906): 130 90	
27	Map of the 'Bavarian Trade, Industry and Art Exhibition', Luitpoldhain, Nuremberg 1906, in *Schweizerische Bauzeitung* 48, no. 11 (1906): 129 90	
28	Applied Arts Pavilion, Nuremberg 1906, Concept by Friedrich Adler, in *Dekorative Kunst* 14 (1906): 345 92	
29	Debschitz School, Silver Work, Nuremberg 1906, in *Dekorative Kunst* 14 (1906): 362 92	
30	Dora Polster; Friedrich Adler, Gravestone, Nuremberg 1906, *Dekorative Kunst* 14 (1906): 351 93	
31	Hermann Obrist and Berthe Ruchet, Whiplash, silk embroidery on linen, 1896, in *Pan* 5 (1896): 325 95	
32	Wilhelm von Debschitz, Bedroom Furniture, 1898, in *Kunst und Handwerk* 49 (1898–9): 177 96	
33	Wilhelm von Debschitz, oak husk, 'Eine Methode des Kunstunterrichts', in *Dekorative Kunst* 12 (1904): 213 101	
34	Laura Lange, Debschitz School, sketch, in *Dekorative Kunst* 12 (1904): 212 102	

35	Charles Rennie Mackintosh, dining room, Bruckmann Villa Munich, 1899, in *Dekorative Kunst* 4 (1899): 78 120
36	Charles Rennie Mackintosh, dining room, Bruckmann Villa Munich, 1899, in *Dekorative Kunst* 4 (1899): 79 120
37	Salon at the Palais Tedesco, photograph, Vienna, c. 1900 123
38	Charles Rennie Mackintosh, smoker's cabinet, 1899, in *Dekorative Kunst* 4 (1899): 79 127
39	Margaret Macdonald, Repoussé Panel for the Bruckmann dining room, 1899. *Dekorative Kunst* 4 (1899): 79 128
40a/b	Else Oppler in one of her *Künstlerkleider*, c. 1900, in *Deutsche Kunst und Dekoration* 10 (1902): 366 148
41a/b	Henry van de Velde, tea gown, c. 1900, in *Deutsche Kunst und Dekoration* 10 (1902): 371 151
42	Alfred Mohrbutter, Dress, c. 1900, in Heinrich Pudor, *Die FrauenReformkleidung* (1903): 42 152
43	Margarethe von Brauchitsch, street dress 1902, in *Deutsche Kunst und Dekoration* 10 (1902): 365 154
44	Clara Möller and Else Oppler, three women in formal dress, 1904, in *Deutsche Kunst und Dekoration* 14 (1904–5): 455 154
45	Margarethe von Brauchitsch, formal dress, c. 1900, in *Album moderner, nach Künstler-Entwürfen ausgeführten Damenkleider*, 1900: plate 22 155
46	Maison Jeulin, Paris, promenade costume, 1902, in *Deutsche Kunst und Dekoration* 10 (1902): 386 157
47	Paul Schultze-Naumburg, reform dress, *Deutsche Kunst und Dekoration* 11 (1902): 168 162
48	Frances McNair in formal dress, in Anna Muthesius, *Das Eigenkleid der Frau* 1903 166
49	Else Oppler, summer street dress, in *Deutsche Kunst und Dekoration* 14 (1904): 456 168
50	Max Littmann, department store Tietz, in *Deutsche Bauzeitung* 39, no. 53 (1905): 326 170
51	Max Littmann, department store Oberpollinger, *Deutsche Bauzeitung* 39, no. 54 (1905): 338 170
52	Max Littmann, department store Tietz, Lichthof, *Deutsche Bauzeitung* 39, no. 53 (1905): 335 171
53	Madame Poiret modelling clothing designed by her husband Paul Poiret, 1913 174
54	Poster for the 'Third National Applied Arts Exhibition' in Dresden, 1906, *Deutsche Kunst und Dekoration* 18 (April–September 1906): 463 186

55 Richard Riemerschmid, 'Affordable Dining Room Furniture', Raumkunst at the 1906 Dresden Exhibition, *Deutsche Kunst und Dekoration* 18 (April–September 1906): 640 188

Plates

1 Munich Hofbräuhaus, postcard *c.* 1900
2 Josef Rudolf Witzel, title page for *Die Jugend* 1, no. 16 (18 April 1896)
3 Margarethe von Brauchitsch in her embroidery studio, photograph *c.* 1910
4 Margarethe von Brauchitsch, tablecloth and pillows, 1909, in *Dekorative Kunst* 18 (1909–10): 27
5 Photo-Studio Elvira, Grand Duchess Regent of Luxemburg, Maria Anna of Portugal with her children, 1903
6 Postcard of the Applied Arts Pavilion at the 'Bavarian Trade, Industry and Art Exhibition', Nuremberg 1906
7 Debschitz School, metal workshop, 1905
8 Ernst Heilemann, Studentinnen, in *Simplicissimus* 4, no. 41 (6 January 1900): 332
9 Emilie Butters, vase, glazed and painted earthenware, Keramische Werkstätten Munich-Herrsching, 1912
10a Hugo Bruckmann, Staatsbibliothek München, Handschriften Sammlung, Nachlass Elsa und Hugo Bruckmann (Bruckmanniana)
10b Atelier Elisabeth, Gladbeck, Elsa Bruckmann, photograph, *c.* 1895
11 Martin Dülfer, Bruckmann villa, Munich, 1898–9
12 Charles Rennie Mackintosh, smoker's cabinet, drawing, 1899
13 Anna and Hermann Muthesius, drinking tea at the Priory, Hammersmith, London 1896
14 Bruno Paul, 'Der Münchner Jugendbrunnern', *Simplicissumus* 2, no. 10 (5 June 1897): 76

ACKNOWLEDGEMENTS

This book has been long in the making and brings to life actors and design practices that I first encountered during the writing of my doctoral dissertation on Munich Historicism almost twenty years ago. At the time, it was not possible to include this material in my argument, and I am very happy that I can finally draw attention to these women's rich life stories and professional careers. Any book with this prolonged an incubation period is indebted to too many individuals and institutions to name. However, I must thank a number of specific institutions and people without whom this book would not have been possible.

I owe thanks to archivists, curators and librarians at the Bayerische Staatsbibliothek, the Bayerische Nationalmuseum, the Münchner Stadtmuseum, the Münchner Stadtarchiv and the Monacensia Sammlung, the Bayerische Hauptstaatsarchiv, the Staatliche Graphische Sammlung in Munich, the Museum für Kunst und Gewerbe, Hamburg and the Folkwang Museum, Essen. In this context, I thank Rüdiger Joppien, Hans Ottomeyer and Michael Koch and acknowledge their pioneering work on Jugendstil design. The University of Glasgow supported crucial research for this book, and I am privileged to work in such an intellectually stimulating academic environment. My colleagues and students at Glasgow continue to challenge my thinking and make me want to hone my analytical skills. Particular thanks are due to Debra Strickland, Sally Tuckett, Debbie Lewer, Clare Willsdon and Robyne Calvert. I also benefited from too many colleagues to name across the UK, Europe and North America who critically engaged with aspects of the book – I am in their debt. I want to express particular gratitude to Allison Morehead and Leslie Topp for their exemplary scholarship, their invaluable friendship and their unfaltering belief in the importance of this book. It has been a true pleasure to work with the patient, critically astute and professional team at Bloomsbury Academic Press: my commissioning editors Grace Lees-Maffei and Kjetil Fallan (*Cultural Histories of Design*) and editorial assistant Libby Davies. I am also deeply grateful for the thoughtful feedback from my book's anonymous reviewers who read my manuscript with such care; any remaining errors are my own.

INTRODUCTION

A NEW STYLE FOR A NEW AGE?

Every image of the past that is not recognised by the present as one of its own concerns threatens to disappear irretrievably.

WALTER BENJAMIN (1942)[1]

I write this Introduction in the midst of the 2020-1 Covid-19 pandemic, and Walter Benjamin's evocative proposal of an interconnection between past and present resonates more strongly than ever before.[2] As the world experiences a prolonged period of lockdowns, individuals of certain socio-economic backgrounds across Europe and North America have once again taken up crafting to fill their time and soothe their anxieties. Countless blogs and newspaper articles trace personal journeys of making, dole out advice and recommend suitable supplies. Unsurprisingly, many of these endeavours are driven by, and geared towards, middle-class women who experience lockdown from within the comforts of their homes.[3] *The Times* newspaper published an article on this phenomenon in early 2021, titled 'By Georgian! Needlework and Piano Keep Lockdown Lizzies Busy'.[4] It described Britain's third lockdown (January–March 2021) as being characterized by an unprecedented uptake of embroidery, sewing, reading and playing the piano. This revival of traditional pastimes was in part fuelled by the representation of the historical upper-middle class in recent TV series like Netflix's successful Regency drama *Bridgerton* (2020).[5] 'A third national lockdown is making many of us feel like we're living in an Austen novel ourselves', *The Times* author asserted, and Britons are rediscovering 'tech-free hobbies'.[6] The class and gender implications of these trends are unmistakable and Covid-19 forces us to, once again, rethink the cultural, socio-economic and political structures of capitalist society. This brings me back to Walter Benjamin's opening quote because as a design historian,

I 'recognise as one of my own concerns' the formative role of material objects in cultural reform and the construction of gender identities. Observing the socioculturally conditioned gender preferences in recent Covid-19-lockdown craft practices offers a particularly timely and interesting connection to the topic of this book.

Jugendstil Women and the Making of Modern Design investigates the complex historical gender dynamics operating within German design reform discourses and practices known as Jugendstil (1895–1914). The case studies presented in this book shed new light on the diverse roles women played within the production, dissemination, reception and consumption of Jugendstil design and thus contribute to ongoing efforts by gender historians to map women's lived experiences back onto the German Empire's sociocultural landscape (1871–1918).[7] This undertaking responds to Teresa de Lauretis's call to write a 'theory of culture with women as subjects – not commodities but social beings producing and reproducing cultural products, transmitting and transforming cultural values'.[8] Writing during the Covid-19 pandemic, it seems just as important as ever to pay heed to Michel Foucault's diktat that any history of the past must be written in terms of the present.[9] This book seeks to encourage readers to reflect on the ways in which history and, more specifically, the writing of design history are implicated in contemporary discussions around gender equality and offers a different history of Jugendstil that explores the complex relationship between design and gender as one way of shedding light on the relationship between the past and present.

I.1 Modern women

The women at the centre of this book lived in late-nineteenth-century Munich, knew one another and moved in the same social circles, but they did not form a cohesive group. They were modern, middle- and upper-middle-class women who experienced turbulent sociopolitical times and, each in her own way, challenged the German Empire's tightly policed class and gender relations. Without necessarily calling themselves 'New Women', a term coined by the Irish writer Sarah Grand in 1894 to describe women who pushed against the gender hierarchies of their day, they each deployed culture to negotiate a place of increased personal, socio-economic and/or political power.[10] They consciously aligned themselves with Jugendstil as Germany's most progressive design discourse of the day and thereby tapped into the 'transformative and creative possibilities of modernity'[11] to assert control over (at least some aspects of) their own lives. This book presents four case studies that explore how specific Jugendstil women harnessed a moment of great cultural change and hoped to carve out a 'place of their own' in a dynamic urban context.[12] The late nineteenth century was a time of great historical change and mobility that opened up unprecedented opportunities for German women, but they also had to endure considerable backlash from the German Empire's conservative quarters.¹³ As I investigate in greater detail, Jugendstil offered Germany's distinctive response to calls from progressive cultural figures across Europe and parts of North America for a modern style fit for a modern age that has since been firmly engrained in histories of modern art, architecture and design under the rubric of 'International Art Nouveau'. Despite its important link to international debates over design reform and the development of a modern style, a number of international exhibitions and scholarly monographs recently demonstrated that scholarship on German Jugendstil features its own trajectory and historiography.¹⁴

Women regrettably remain largely absent from even the most revisionist accounts of German Jugendstil art, architecture and design. And yet, they actively participated in the cultural and socio-economic exchanges that generated this distinctly German design response to European modernism. This book explores the diversity of women's contributions to modern German culture as creative partners, collectors, consumers, critics, designers, educators/students, patrons and salonnières. *Jugendstil Women and the Making of Modern Design* offers an interdisciplinary analysis of this vibrant moment in German design history that illuminates the rich manifestations of female agency without creating ahistorical categories for women. Hannah Arendt famously described the 'human condition of plurality' in her investigation of *vita activa* (labour, work, action).¹⁵ This book endeavours to reshape the contours of Jugendstil historiography by examining women's lived experiences against dominant ideologies that organized social relations and circumscribed historical experiences. This demands a shift away from analysing the design and production of Jugendstil objects and instead focus on their dissemination, reception and consumption – processes in which women played active parts.

The year 2019 marked the 100-year anniversary of Walter Gropius's founding of the Staatliche Bauhaus (1919–33) in Weimar; without a doubt, a pivotal moment in European modernism. Within this context, a number of exhibitions, publications and films turned their attention to the role of women in Bauhaus design.¹⁶ These activities offered a long-overdue corrective to the considerable body of scholarship on the Bauhaus, but they also underscored just how much historical work on design still needs to be done in response to Linda Nochlin's pioneering essay 'Why Have There Been No Great Women Artists?' published around half a century ago!¹⁷ How can we still find ourselves in a position in which so many women designers need to be painstakingly retrieved from obscurity and their lives and careers are only now being brought into view through monographs and exhibitions? While this kind of 'memory work' represents a crucial aspect of feminist scholarship, it also runs the risk of creating a 'separate spheres model' within design history that is no longer viable. Art historian Julie Johnson recently argued in a Viennese context that women artists were deeply embedded in the city's institutional landscape during the early twentieth century: 'women artists were not part of a separate sphere but integrated into the art exhibitionary complex of Vienna' and have only been written out of this world by twentieth-century historiography.[18] Equally, the women at the centre of *Jugendstil Women and the Making of Modern Design* wanted to be taken seriously within the cultural fabric that generated Germany's first modern design style, and they actively participated in contemporary discourses and practices that constituted modernism. Writing about successful women artists in the Weimar Republic (1918–33), art historian Marsha Meskimmon reminds us that women 'were professional artists and they examined the crucial debates of their time within their practice. If we cannot see this work, this is the fault of our methods, our paradigms, and our theoretical disposition.'[19]

Meskimmon's observation holds very much true for the Jugendstil women discussed here. Most of these women were not actually practicing designers, but they played an integral part in the wider cultural networks through which Jugendstil came into being. They did not strive to create a culture of their own. Rather, they strategically operated within Munich's rich cultural fabric and deployed their political networks and social connections to position themselves within progressive elements of German society. They adopted modernist discourses to articulate and construct a progressive identity. The philosopher Nelson Goodman argued that 'truth cannot be defined or tested by agreement with "the world"; for not only do truths differ for different worlds but the nature of agreement between a version and a world apart from it is notoriously nebulous.'[20] This opens up a productive point of entry into Jugendstil's historiography that offers a more inclusive cultural history and celebrates the many different roles played by historical women (who, of course, did not represent a homogeneous category) in the production, dissemination and consumption of Germany's first truly modern design language.

It cannot be stressed enough that Jugendstil women were very much present in late-nineteenth-century Munich and left archival records – no matter how difficult these might be to uncover. Archives have to be read against the grain, meaning that traces of these historical women's lived experiences have to be unearthed in unlikely places and archives. Today, the concept of 'gender' describes a more varied landscape than the binary female–male.[21] During the period investigated within the parameters of this book, however, gender represented a socially constructed system that coded attitudes and behaviours as either female or male according to 'normative conceptions of attitudes and activities appropriate for one's sex category.'[22] Social systems are never static, and gender is constantly in the making. As an analytical category, 'gender' offers historians a productive entry into the complex, and often hidden, mechanisms, norms, structures and symbols that designated historical bodies as feminine or masculine. This book presents a series of case studies to investigate how Jugendstil women used their support of progressive design practices to subvert normative gender roles operating in late-nineteenth- and early-twentieth-century Munich and how, in turn, critical debates and practices at the heart of Jugendstil design either questioned or reinforced these very norms.

But first, a brief word about the use of the term 'design' that is employed throughout this study. 'Design' is a distinctly twentieth-century concept that some readers might object to being used in discussing Munich Jugendstil because it had no currency at the time. I cannot disagree with this observation, but the English language does not offer the same kind of nuanced meanings as the multiple German terms deployed in critical debates of the time: *Kunsthandwerk, Kunstgewerbe, Kunstindustrie, Dekorative Kunst, Wohnkultur, Raumkunst* and so on. For this reason, I draw on Frederic Schwartz's definition in his book on the German Werkbund that defined design as a fusion of art and technology.[23] The support or rejection of this fusion seems to have driven late-nineteenth-century debates on design reform and offers a more inclusive category than the terms 'applied arts' or 'decorative arts'. Furthermore, Munich Jugendstil designers had a very different relationship to machine production than, for example, the British Arts and Crafts movement. As a committed socialist, William Morris (1834–1896) exalted the aesthetic and moral values of hand craftsmanship but simultaneously employed Jacquard looms, for example, at his Merton Abbey Mills. *Jugendstil Women* purposely employs the term 'design' to signal a specifically German desire to embrace new technology in the service of making tasteful goods of high quality. In 1906, Richard Riemerschmid's promotion of serial furniture (*Maschinenmöbel*) pushed this credo to its natural conclusion by striving to make good design available to hitherto overlooked sections of the German population.[24]

I.2 The cultural geography of Munich around 1900

Munich has long been acknowledged by design historians as the cradle of German Jugendstil.[25] At the 'Seventh International Art Exhibition' held at Munich's famous Glaspalast exhibition venue in 1897, a group of progressive artists, architects and designers presented two small cabinets as aesthetically integrated, modern environments (Figure 1). The prelude and reverberations of this exhibition are discussed in the first chapter of this book. But for now, this episode begs the question, why Munich, a fairly small and barely industrialized provincial town in the German Empire's south, provided such fertile grounds for the germination of Germany's first truly modern design language? How did Munich become one of central Europe's main artistic centres in terms of private and state-led training opportunities, purpose-built exhibition spaces for contemporary art, art dealers and critics as well as public collections?[26] Its rich institutional fabric attracted artists from across Europe and North America, and Munich had more artists per

FIGURE 1 'Cabinet 25' at the Seventh International Art Exhibition, Munich Glaspalast 1897, in *Kunst und Handwerk* 47 (1898–9): 43. Universitätsbibliothek Heidelberg, urn:nbn:de:bsz:16-diglit-68434.

capita than any other German city, including the Wilhelmine Empire's capital Berlin.[27] The painter and sometime critic Ernst Wilhelm Bredt (1869–1938) described Munich in 1907 as follows: 'In no other city in the world is the artist so connected with all circles of society or is art so unpretentiously, unobtrusively or quietly involved in general economic activity as in Munich.'[28]

Munich's reputation as Germany's premier art city traces back to the reign of King Ludwig I (1825–48), who was a great sponsor of art and architecture. Ludwig was well educated, a liberal and a fervent nationalist. His politics turned more conservative when he came to the throne in 1825, but his cultural ambitions remained truly visionary. He commissioned leading architects of his day such as Leo von Klenze (1784–1864) to design several public museums that have since become pillars of Munich's cultural landscape. Germany's first public museum, the Glyptothek (1830), housed Ludwig's extensive collection of antiquities, the Alte Pinakothek (1836) exhibited the Wittelsbach collection of Old Masters and the Neue Pinakothek (1853) was built for Ludwig's personal collection of nineteenth-century art.[29] He generously supported the Munich Academy of Fine Arts and served as patron of the Munich *Kunstverein* (Art Club), a private initiative aimed at fostering contemporary art through travelling exhibitions, lectures and publication.[30] In 1837, the Bavarian historian Johann Michael Soeltl (1797–1888) hailed Ludwig with these words: 'Through him, Munich rises in such splendour that its buildings and institutions garner admiration throughout Europe. Through him, the great art connoisseur, art awoke and took its proper seat in Munich.'[31]

Soeltl alluded to Ludwig's grand urban building programme that established Munich's reputation as central Europe's *Isar-Athen* (Athens on the River Isar) or the Monaco of Bavaria.[32]

Ludwig's ambitious patronage was controversial because he drew heavily on state funding without consulting his parliament. As Europe was ravaged by the 1848 Revolutions, his excessive spending combined with a very public extramarital affair with the Irish dancer and actress Lola Montez (1821–1861) forced his abdication.[33] He was succeeded by his son Maximilian II (1811–1864), who completed his father's projects but focused his attention more closely on day-to-day politics. Maximilian knew very well that he could not compete with his father's legacy and supported literature and the sciences instead.[34] He was much beloved by the Bavarian people because he restored stability to Bavaria after the 1848 upheavals, but his outlook was less international than his father's, which might explain his commitment to founding a Bavarian National Museum in 1855. This institution eventually became one of the first German museums to collect Jugendstil furniture and objects.[35] It was also during his reign that the *Bayerische Kunstgewerbe Verein* (Bavarian Applied Arts Association) was created in 1851.[36] Its members supported the applied arts and were committed to educating Bavarian producers and consumers in matters of style and taste through lectures, publications and design exhibitions. This initiative was a direct response to the negative reception of Germany's applied arts sections at the 1851 Universal Exposition in London and represented a concerted effort to compete on international markets.[37] The Association put applied arts debates onto the radar of German critics and advocated the revival of historical styles that were eventually targeted by Jugendstil designers and their supporters.

I.3 Munich–Berlin

When Germany was finally declared a nation-state in 1871 (as a direct result of the Franco-Prussian War 1870–1), Berlin became the empire's new seat of government.[38] This unleashed centripetal cultural–political forces that actively endeavoured to turn Berlin into the empire's new art capital.[39] In reaction, Bavarian artists, politicians and critics made concerted efforts to underscore Munich's rich cultural heritage and bolster its reputation as central Europe's premier art centre.[40] As so often happens in history, art and culture were once again deployed as political weapons. Ironically, Bavaria's complicated bid for political influence through cultural supremacy was actually supported by the German constitution because it granted Bavaria legislative authority over schooling (including universities), culture (*Kulturhoheit*) and church affairs (with certain restrictions). This constitutional framework created a cultural battlefield that ignited numerous political conflicts.[41] Ludwig II (1845–1886), who came to the Bavarian throne in

1864 and was one of Europe's most dazzling monarchs of his day, declared in 1875 that 'it is the job of Bavarian politics to preserve Munich's status as a *Kunststadt*', though he contributed neither time nor money for this endeavour.[42] Ludwig II was obsessed with the composer Richard Wagner's (1813–1883) epic operas like his iconic *Der Ring der Nibelungen* (Ring of the Nibelung, 1876) and tried his best to lure Wagner to Munich. He promised the composer a new opera house to be designed by the prominent German architect Gottfried Semper (1803–1879) but his bid was rejected by Munich's city council and the composer famously settled in Bayreuth instead. Deeply disappointed and with mental illness looming, Ludwig recused himself from royal patronage and escaped into building his fairy castles (Neuschwanstein, Linderhof and Herrenchiemsee) in the foothills of the Bavarian Alps (Figure 2). This proved to be a huge financial windfall for Munich's building industry (e.g. architects, engineers, interior decorators) and craftsmen (e.g. furniture makers, gilders, muralists, silversmiths, textile producers).[43] At the same time, the '*Erste Deutsche Kunst und Kunstindustrie Ausstellung*' (First German Art and Art Industry Exhibition) was held at the Glaspalast in 1876 and advocated a Neo-Northern Renaissance style as the German Empire's new national style. This exhibition put Munich on the map as Germany's unrivalled applied arts centre and premier production site for historicist design objects that revived past styles.[44] This exhibition was superseded by the 'German-National Applied Arts Exhibition' of 1888, also organized at the Glaspalast, which advocated a Neo-Baroque and Neo-

FIGURE 2 Johannes Bernhard, 'Castle Neuschwanstein under Construction', 1882–5. http://images.zeno.org/Fotografien/I/big/PHO02532.jpg.

Rococo style.⁴⁵ By this point in time, historicism had transmuted into eclecticism and was ripe for Jugendstil's eventual attack as a random copying of design styles that had no relevance to the modern age.

Historian Robin Lenman argued in his groundbreaking 1997 study of the German Empire's art market that the final decades of the nineteenth century witnessed Munich's transformation from a *Kunststadt* (art city) supported by state and royal patronage into a *Künstlerstadt* (artists' city) propelled by a market economy.⁴⁶ This observation is borne out by the prominent German art historian and museum director Alfred Lichtwark (1852–1914), who, upon visiting the 1883 Salon in Berlin, observed that 'it is a noticeable occurrence that the Berlin salon still has not managed to carve out a central and commanding position in Germany's artistic life. Munich, which claims this leadership, succeeded in securing art exhibitions and the art market'.⁴⁷ Lichtwark's assessment had crucial implications for the emergence of Munich Jugendstil in the 1890s. It generated an art system that was powered by networks between artists, architects and designers, critics, patrons and collectors as well as private institutions, all of whom rejected historicism and called for design reform in the service of generating of a truly modern style that was no longer anchored in vacuous revivals of the past. One of the principal arguments of the book is that it was precisely Munich's art economy and demand for innovation that carved out a novel sphere of influence for women who were still largely excluded from the German Empire's official art institutions. Academies, Salons, Artists' Associations and even the progressive Secession (1892) continued to cater almost exclusively to men. Women, on the other hand, would become the paragon of change in the German design world.

I.4 Prince Regent Luitpold

Historians of the period inevitably quote Thomas Mann's famous description of late-nineteenth-century Munich as a 'radiant city', which he evoked in his novella *Gladius Dei* (1902).⁴⁸ Although Mann described some of the historical conflicts that potentially troubled this image (liberalism and laissez-faire attitudes regularly collided with conservative politics and Catholicism), his story celebrates the remarkable presence of the visual arts in the Bavarian capital.⁴⁹ Munich Jugendstil emerged during this very moment. The historical period is called the *Prinzregenten* era (1886–1912) because Bavaria was governed by Prince Regent Luitpold (1821–1912), who had stepped into politics after his nephew King Ludwig II was declared mentally incompetent in 1886.⁵⁰ This was a time of great cultural, socio-economic and political transition that was driven by Germany's relatively late, but rapid, industrialization (1850s) and the country's unification in 1871. As a result of the familiar epiphenomena of industrialization (economic expansion, technical innovation, medical discoveries, wealth re-distribution, urbanization), Munich's population increased from just over 260,000 in 1885 to almost 500,000 in 1900.[51] This small provincial capital had grown into a bustling metropolis and consumer society over the course of fifteen years.[52]

The *Prinzregenten* era tends to be remembered as a time of peace, liberal governance and a slower pace of life that engendered a typically Bavarian sense of *Gemütlichkeit* (contentment) and wit that was sanctioned by relatively relaxed censorship laws.[53] Art and culture played an important role in Munich's tourist-oriented economy that emerged from the 1850s onwards. Then, as now, the city and its alpine surroundings represented a popular tourist destination.[54] An astute observer writing in one of Germany's leading daily newspapers noted in 1872 that 'art turned Munich into a metropolis, a magnet for so many thousands, and if a capital investment ever paid off for the national economy, then it was the great sums of money Ludwig put into the arts'.[55] This holds true well into the present because Ludwig I's museums combined with his urban renewal projects, attract as many international tourists as Ludwig II's fairy castles, Munich's historicist beer halls and the annual Oktoberfest (Plate 1).[56] Internationally, the city and its idyllic environs are regularly seen to represent German culture at large.

I.5 The term 'Jugendstil'

In 1896, Josef Rudolf Witzel (1867–1927) created a cover design for the weekly magazine for art and literature *Die Jugend: Illustrierte Wochenschrift für Kunst und Leben* (The Youth), published from 1896 to 1940 (Plate 2).[57] This illustration features on the cover of this book on Jugendstil Women because it beautifully illustrates two young women dressed in billowing gowns without the constraints of a corset and with flowing hair, climbing a tree without a care in the world. Only the face of one of the two protagonists is visible, but she seems utterly happy and perhaps coaxing her friend to climb even higher. The tree not only frames the scene, but it also represented a potent symbol of cyclical renewal and growth. During this time, young trees can be found in the iconography of modern artists and designers right across Europe, and they symbolize a break with the past and a welcome of the future. *Die Jugend* was published by Georg Hirth (1841–1916), who owned one of Germany's most liberal publishing houses and supported applied arts reform and modern design.[58] The magazine positioned itself against the sociopolitical stronghold of the Bavarian Catholic Church and provided a platform for progressive artists and thinkers to showcase their work.[59] International in outlook, the publication played a key role in the emergence of German modernism and its rich visual and literary archive deserves our attention – least of all because it became the eponym for Jugendstil.[60]

Scholars regularly posit a close connection between Munich's liberal magazine culture and progressive design practices. They argue that Munich Jugendstil was characterized by strong graphic lines, flat pictorial spaces and a rhythm of basic geometric forms *precisely* because so many Munich Jugendstil artists and designers supplied graphic designs for *Die Jugend* and its more politically oriented sister publication *Simplicissimus* (1896–1967). This conceptualization holds some weight in that Munich Jugendstil artists made an important contribution to the graphic arts through magazines, posters, theatre and exhibition programmes.[61] But it also runs the danger of homogenizing a complex set of aesthetics, visual cultures and material practices that accommodated a wide range of experimentation ranging from Hermann Obrist's organic forms inspired by the natural world to Bruno Paul's disciplined abstract patterns based on geometric shapes. Kathryn Bloom Hiesinger described this dynamic in her pioneering exhibition 'Art Nouveau in Munich' (1988) as follows:

> However, even as they combined advanced thinking with self-appointed purposefulness, the leading artists of Munich Jugendstil were themselves divided between expressive and rational styles that were related to, but independent of, the international Art Nouveau movements in France and Belgium, and the Arts and Crafts movement in England. [...] It is in the mix of these two styles in Munich, where they were oriented toward a more restrictive, specifically German culture that the aesthetics of the modern machine-made product were founded.[62]

An in-depth discussion of the roots, trajectories and historiography of Munich Jugendstil is misplaced here because this book is not about the history of Jugendstil in and of itself. This terrain has been well covered by many prominent design historians.[63] Instead, this study aims to shine a light on the multifarious engagement of modern women with Jugendstil design across diverse spheres of actions to argue that this first modern German design language would not have come into being without this larger sociocultural network of women in place. In other words, women acted as key protagonists (as advocates, educators and students, makers, patrons and reformers) in making Munich Germany's late-nineteenth-century capital of modern design. However, a few basic observations that ground the cultural–historical meaning of the term 'Jugendstil' and its subsequent reception in design history are warranted at this point.

It has already been established that the term 'Jugendstil' emerged from its practitioners' close affiliation with the Munich journal *Die Jugend*. But how did a group of progressive architects, artists and designers working in Munich between 1895 and 1914 become affiliated with this 'label'? And is Jugendstil a movement or a style – and does it matter? The short answer is that it was a style that participated in a cross-European movement known as International Art Nouveau and yes, it does matter. Style is a central yet problematic tool in design history. 'International Art Nouveau' is a disputed term because it tends to homogenize a complex phenomenon that has distinct national, if not regional, manifestations. Stylistic identification is critical because it enables historians to allocate specific artefacts to distinct historical contexts and it thus forms the basis of interpretation. But any classification of objects is fraught because it is based on a subjective interpretation of material properties.[64] This basic realization opens up productive ways to think about style as an 'important means whereby social groups project their constructed identities and stake their claims in the world' – in the instance of this book, modern women who engaged with Jugendstil in fascinating, and often incongruous, ways to carve out an identity for themselves within the German Empire's sociopolitical spaces.[65] It also matters because historical stakeholders – makers, critics, patrons, collectors, consumers – actually deployed the term 'style' to advocate for a modern design language that endeavoured to infiltrate all aspects of everyday life.

The prominent Munich designer and key actor within Jugendstil circles Hans Eduard von Berlepsch-Valendas (1849–1921) wrote a consequential essay called '*Endlich ein Umschwung!*' (At Long Last, a Turnabout!) in the inaugural issue of the journal *Deutsche Kunst und Dekoration* (1897–1932) published by Alexander Koch in Darmstadt.[66] Berlepsch-Valendas took the two Jugendstil rooms exhibited at the 1897 Glaspalast exhibition as his point of departure to discuss the state of Europe's applied arts in general and to praise his fellow Munich designers for introducing exhibition visitors to powerful examples of what modern design could or should look like. Berlepsch-Valendas raised two noteworthy points. First, he stressed that applied arts reform must liberate contemporary design from its 'Cinderella' status vis-à-vis the fine arts.[67] A truly modern style could no longer be confined to art and architecture but must permeate everyday objects. Taking his cue from the British Arts and Crafts movement, which was carefully followed in Germany through the circulation of magazines like *The Studio* and the *Yellow Book* as well as the Arts and Crafts Exhibition Society's regular exhibitions, progressive Munich designers and their supporters called for a 'unity of all arts' that abolished academically entrenched hierarchies between the fine arts ('major arts') and the decorative arts ('minor arts').[68] One of Munich's most innovative Jugendstil designers, Otto Eckmann (1865–1902), serves as a case in point. He actually trained as a painter but dispersed the entire contents of his studio in a fire sale in 1894 to solely focus on applied arts.[69]

The aesthetically unified interior, derived from Richard Wagner's 1849 articulation of a *Gesamtkunstwerk* (total work of art), provided Jugendstil designers with a theoretical platform to formulate this marriage of fine arts and applied arts, which, once achieved, was intended to infuse every single component of quotidian life with an aesthetic vision: 'The ball has finally been set into motion and nothing can stop it now!'[70] Second, Berlepsch-Valendas argued that a decisive break from nineteenth-century revivals of past styles was mandatory before a truly modern interior (*Wohnkultur*) could be realized.[71] By 1897, historicism had run its course and mutated into a kind of eclecticism that was characterized by a pastiche of styles drawn at will from different historical periods (Figure 3). Berlepsch-Valendas conceded that it was not the past in and of itself that posed a problem, but the way in which an inflexible evocation of 'tradition' impeded innovation and progress: 'Where are children without father or mother? But it is a mistake to block development towards a future goal by positing that which has already been achieved as the only desirable objective.'[72]

Without advocating an outright break with the past, Berlepsch-Valendas and his supporters instead championed a modern style that was firmly anchored in close observation of the natural world: 'let us study the ornaments of other epochs, but let us do so alongside gardens, aquariums, terrariums, places where living nature repeatedly offers an inerasable inspiration.'[73] The word 'inspiration' is crucial here because nature was not to be copied but mined for its inexhaustible formal possibilities and underlying structural principles. Much has been written on Jugendstil's 'cult of nature' and within the context of this book it must suffice to say that Charles Darwin's (1809–1882) and Ernst Haeckel's (1834–1919) evolutionary theories radically impacted late-nineteenth-century Munich.[74] Catholicism had commanded Bavarian cultural life for centuries and the idea that mankind was inextricably bound into natural and cosmical cycles toppled the conventional world views of many.[75] New scientific discoveries and technologies

FIGURE 3 W. Fleck, 'The Gothic Reception Room at the German House', Chicago World's Fair, 1893, in *Kunstgewerbeblatt* 5, 3 (1894): 6. Universitätsbibliothek Heidelberg, urn:nbn:de:bsz:16-diglit-35851

such as the microscope offered rich visual sources for Jugendstil design and Haeckel's beautiful portfolio *Kunstformen der Natur* (Artforms of Nature; 1899–1904) made a significant contribution to its visual idiom.[76] But these advances in the material sciences also propagated a renewed interest in monism, spiritism and the occult. Carl du Prel (1839–1899), one of Germany's most prominent high priests of spiritism, for example, was living in Munich and had many followers among Munich's progressive upper-middle classes.[77] His theories around the unity of body/material world and soul/spiritual world were particularly appealing to women who also played a key role in Munich occult circles.[78]

I.6 Summary of chapters

This book offers an expanded conceptualization of Munich Jugendstil by critically examining the diverse roles historical women played in this key moment of German modernism. In short, it presents a cultural history of Jugendstil from a gender perspective. Rather than solely reviving these women as makers, their roles in the *inception* of Munich Jugendstil are examined through a series of case studies. This method opens up a broader understanding of their crucial agencies within a wider range of activities and cultural–political networks. This book is about how and why these progressive women got involved in Jugendstil and illuminates the different ways in which they were intrinsically involved in bringing about this new and modern style. Jugendstil women did not merely follow a fashion trend, but they believed in the revolutionary potential of this modern style. The case study approach is regularly employed in the sciences because it allows 'in-depth, multi-faceted explorations of complex issues in their real-life settings'.[79] The last point about 'real-life settings' is important here because this book demonstrates the multiple ways in which historical actors engaged with and, in turn, experienced an important episode in design history. For the women at the centre of this book, Jugendstil was a 'real-life setting' and, to recall Walter Benjamin, it is the design historian's tantalizing task to 'navigate both the past and the present in an intricate balancing act to form a coherent bridge of understanding between these two worlds'.[80]

Jugendstil Women and the Making of Modern Design presents five case studies that are organized in approximate chronological order. The book opens with a discussion of the 'Seventh International Art Exhibition' at the Munich Glaspalast in 1897 that engendered the birth of Jugendstil and generated the founding of one of its key production sites, the *Vereinigte Werkstätten für Kunst im Handwerk* (United Workshops for Art in Handcraft), in 1898. The chapter analyses the United Workshops' key influences, design initiatives and philosophies, such as the aesthetically unified interior based on Richard Wagner's *Gesamtkunstwerk*. Women were actively involved in the production of key objects for the United

Workshops, but their creative voices have largely been silenced due to a misguided critical focus on designers rather than makers as is often found to be the case. Historically rooted gender norms not only curtailed women's artistic opportunities but also shaped future scholarship on Jugendstil and are in part to blame for the lack of archival records on these women in the first place.[81] Chapter 1 introduces Margarethe von Brauchitsch (1865–1957), who was a versatile and prominent female designer/maker of her day. An analysis of her practice and contemporary reception offers new insights into the United Workshops as a key agent of Munich Jugendstil by drawing long-overdue attention to the German Empire's larger sociopolitical contexts, which not only governed the progressive reform initiative of the United Workshops but also produced a story of modern German design that excluded key actors like Margarethe von Brauchitsch.

Chapter 2, 'The Elvira Photography Studio and Munich feminist politics', turns to one of Munich Jugendstil's most iconic buildings and earliest examples of the United Workshops' design aesthetic, the photography studio *Hof-Atelier Elvira* (1898). The building façade and interior were designed by August Endell (1871–1925) for its proprietors Anita Augspurg (1857–1943) and Sophia Goudstikker (1865–1924). The two women were business partners and key figures in Munich's women's movement whose members fought for equal access to education and voting rights. It remains unclear if they were romantically involved with one another, but they lived and worked under the same roof for many years. Their relationship therefore presents an intriguing spin on what Bibiana Obler recently labelled an 'intimate collaboration', that is, an artistic and personal relationship that drove aesthetic innovation in late-nineteenth-century Germany.[82] This chapter scrutinizes the multiple identities of these two professional women and explores their extensive artistic and political networks throughout Germany. This not only further historicizes the avant-garde's construct of artistic collaboration but also questions its assumed heteronormativity. Augspurg and Goudstikker believed that they could bring about a more just society through their 'visionary feminism'.[83] An analysis of their complicated private and professional relationships thus offers new insights into the rich cultural–political entanglements of late-nineteenth-century gender politics with Jugendstil design.

Chapter 3, 'Educating women at the Debschitz School', discusses Jugendstil women's important roles as educators and students. In the German Empire, women were mostly prohibited from enrolling in fine arts academies and had only limited access to applied arts academies until 1919.[84] As a result, a thriving system of private tuition in artists' studios especially geared towards middle-class women offered lucrative income opportunities for academy-trained artists and designers. The so-called Debschitz School, short for *Das Lehr- und Versuchs-Ateliers für angewandte und freie Kunst* (Teaching and Experimental Studio for Applied and Fine Arts), was founded in this vein by Hermann Obrist (1862–1927) and Wilhem von Debschitz (1871–1948) in 1902. It represented an important pedagogical experiment and an opportunity for women with serious artistic ambitions to receive an education. While mindful of a simplistic teleology, this chapter introduces readers to an educational experiment that trialled a number of pedagogies (such as the famous *Vorkurs*, or foundation course) that are more commonly viewed as Bauhaus innovations. The Debschitz School's progressive curriculum and pedagogy offered rare employment opportunities for female educators. Although gender equality was far off the Debschitz School's radar, it carved out a niche for Jugendstil women as both students and teachers.

Chapter 4, 'Fashionable taste at Elsa Bruckmann's salon', explores the fascinating interplay between iconic Jugendstil objects and the wider cultural forces that shaped their dissemination and consumption. Elsa Bruckmann's first Munich salon offers a multilayered case study that unveils the cultural dynamics underpinning Jugendstil's success. Bruckmann (1865–1946) was married to one of Munich's most renowned art publishers, Hugo Bruckmann, and a liberal supporter of modern art. The couple spearheaded Munich's cultural and intellectual elite. They lived in a Jugendstil villa designed by Martin Dülfer (1859–1942) in Munich's prestigious Nymphenburg district. The villa's interiors were decorated by the Scottish architect Charles Rennie Mackintosh (1868–1928) and his wife Margaret Macdonald (1864–1933) as aesthetically unified interiors, and this chapter introduces some of Jugendstil's international dimensions. These interiors provided the physical settings for Elsa Bruckmann's weekly salons and played an important role in her politics of taste. Salon culture has not received due attention for its important contributions to modern identity formation in late-nineteenth-century Germany. Archival research reveals that one of Munich's premier salonnières was not an overtly political actor nor can she be considered a New Woman in the strictest sense of the term. But as a well-educated, upper-class individual with a devoted husband, a beautiful home, impeccable appearance, taste and great sociocultural influence, Elsa Bruckmann embodied a type of late-nineteenth-century femininity that made her a Jugendstil woman.

Chapter 5, 'Dressing the part', presents new research on the complicated interrelationship between modern design, fashion and women as the German Empire's new consumers. Dress reform occupied the minds of many applied arts reformers and women's rights activists during the final decades of the nineteenth century. This chapter investigates how artistically inspired dress became one of the most successful conduits of Jugendstil design and reveals its links to German *Lebensreform* (life reform). A number of exhibitions and noteworthy publications such as Anna Muthesius' *Das Eigenkleid der Frau* (Woman's Own Dress; 1904) popularized a new silhouette that rejected Parisian fashion dictates (wasp-waists and mono-bosoms) in favour of looser-fitting gowns with empire waists and made from soft natural fabrics such as cotton. Women played formative roles in these debates as both theoreticians publishing key tracts and as designers of reform dress. This chapter links Margarethe von Brauchitsch's embroideries discussed in

Chapter 2 with the late-nineteenth-century phenomenon of the department store, which represented a key outlet for female Jugendstil designers and consumers alike. Women like Margarethe von Brauchitsch supplied department stores with her garments, Else Oppler-Legband (1875–1965) managed the new reform-dress department at one of Germany's premier department stores (Westheim, Berlin) and fashionable patrons of Jugendstil like Elsa Bruckmann could freely socialize and peruse the latest trends in progressive design and fashion.

In summary, this book collates a series of case studies that each explores specific roles of women during one of Germany's most vibrant episodes in the emergence of modern architecture and design. It offers a thematic, rather than a strictly chronological, account of the history of Munich Jugendstil from the iconic 1897 Glaspalast exhibition to the founding of the Werkbund in 1907. In the process, largely forgotten historical actors are resurrected and well-known artefacts are placed into new critical frameworks. But most importantly, this book interrogates crucial cultural debates that operated in turn-of-the-last-century Germany and that still inform the reception of Jugendstil art, architecture and design today.

Notes

1. Walter Benjamin, 'Theses on the Philosophy of History', in *Illuminations*, ed. Hannah Arendt (London: Fontane, 1942), 247. Benjamin actually stipulated that a 'true image of the past' could be captured only through a state of full *Geistesgegenwart* (presence of mind). See Matthias Fritsch, *The Promise of Memory: History of Politics in Marx, Benjamin and Derrida* (Albany: State University of New York Press, 2006), 28.
2. The Covid-19 pandemic is/was caused by the virus SARS-CoV-2 and first identified in Wuhan, China, in December 2019. The World Health Organization declared the outbreak a 'Public Health Emergency of International Concern' in January 2020 and upgraded it to a pandemic on 11 March 2020. As of February 2021, 105 million cases have been confirmed worldwide and over 2.31 million deaths have been attributed to Covid-19. 'World Health Organisation', accessed 07 February 2021, https://www.who.int/emergencies/diseases/novel-coronavirus-2019.
3. New terms like 'Covid-Quilter' or 'Covid Knitter' have been coined across North America and Europe to describe individuals who have taken up these crafts during lockdown.
4. Louis Eccles, 'By Georgian! Needlework and Piano Keep Lockdown Lizzies Busy: Hobbies Familiar to Jane Austen Heroines Are Making a Comeback as Families Swap Screens for Cross Stitch', *The Times and Sunday Times* 24 January 2021, accessed 25 January 2021, https://www.thetimes.co.uk/article/by-georgian-needlework-and-piano-keep-lockdown-lizzies-busy-fqqx35b6b.
5. Shonda Rhymes, *Bridgerton*, Netflix 2020.
6. Eccles, According to this article, one of the UK's leading suppliers of craft supplies reported that sale of cross-stitch kits is up by 545 per cent in January 2021. See also Lois Alter Mark, 'Knitting Has Become the Cool Activity during the Coronavirus Crisis', *Forbes* 21 May 2020, accessed 4 February 2021, https://www.forbes.com/sites/l

oisaltermark/2020/03/27/knitting-has-become-the-cool-activity-during-the-coronavirus-crisis/?sh=29de8d6f921c.

7 Renate Berger, *Malerinnen auf dem Weg ins 20. Jahrhundert: Kunstgeschichte als Sozialgeschichte* (Cologne: DuMont, 1982).

8 Teresa de Lauretis, *Technologies of Gender: Essays on Theory, Film and Fiction* (Bloomington: Indiana University Press, 1987), 93.

9 In his study of prisons, Foucault asked: 'Why write a history of the prison? Simply because I am interested in the past? No, if one means by that writing a history of the past in terms of the present. Yes, if one means writing the history of the present.' This famously engendered his shift from conceiving historical research as 'archaeology' to 'genealogy'. Michel Foucault, *Discipline and Punish: The Birth of the Prison* (New York: Pantheon, 1977), 31.

10 Sarah Grand, 'The New Aspect of the Woman Question', *North American Review* 158 (1894): 270–6.

At the turn of the nineteenth century the concept of the New Woman, or Neue Frau, accommodated a range of political positions from radical feminism to middle-class liberalism. The term realized its full transgressive potential only during the Weimar Republic when Germany's Neue Frauen pushed hard against heteronormative gender roles. See for example Marsha Meskimmon and Shearer West, *Visions of the Neue Frau: Women and the Visual Arts in Weimar Germany* (Aldershot: Ashgate, 1995) and Maria Makela, 'New Women, New Men, New Objectivity', in *New Objectivity: Modern German Art in the Weimar Republic,* ed. Stephanie Barron (Los Angeles: Los Angeles County Museum of Art, 2015), 51–63.

11 Rebecca Houze, *Textiles, Fashion, and Design Reform in Austria-Hungary before the First World War* (Farnham: Ashgate, 2015), 4.

12 Virginia Woolf, *A Room of One's Own* (London: Hogarth Press, 1929).

13 Lynn Abrams and Elisabeth Harvey, *Gender Relations in German History: Power, Agency and Experience from the Sixteenth to the Twentieth Century* (Durham: Duke University, 1997).

14 For example, Sabine Schulze, *Jugendstil: Die Grosse Utopie* (Hamburg: Museum für Kunst und Gewerbe, 2015); Nicola Bröcker, Gisela Moeller and Christine Salge, *August Endell, 1871-1925: Architekt und Formkünstler* (Imhof: Petersberg, 2012); *Hermann Obrist: Sculpture, Space, Abstraction around 1900,* ed. Museum Bellerive (Chicago: University of Chicago Press, 2017).

15 Hannah Arendt, *The Human Condition* (Chicago: University of Chicago Press, 1958).

16 The Bauhaus was Germany's first state school to admit women and its inaugural cohort featured more female students than male (84 versus 79). And yet, despite Gropius' famous declaration that there should be 'no difference between the beautiful and the strong sex' – a statement that already revealed his deeply entrenched gender biases – women continued to be relegated to the weaving shed, the ceramics workshop and the toy-making studio because, according to Gropius, they were unable to think in three dimensions. Gropius in Weltge, *Women's Work: Textile Art from the Bauhaus* (San Francisco: Chronicle Books, 1992), 41.

For some of the Bauhaus celebrations that specifically focused on women see Ann Coxon, *Anni Albers* (Munich: Hirmer Verlag, 2018); Patrick Rössler, *Vier Bauhausmädels* (Dresden: Sandstein Verlag, 2019); Elisabeth Otto and Patrick

Rössler, *Bauhaus Women: A Global Perspective* (London: Bloomsbury/Herbert Press, 2019), as well as *Bauhaus Bodies: Gender, Sexuality, and Body Culture in Modernism's Legendary Art School* (London: Bloomsbury Academic, 2019); Ulrike Müller, *Bauhaus Women: Art, Handicraft, Design* (Paris: Flammarion, 2015); Ursula Muscheler, *Mutter, Muse und Frau Bauhaus* (Berlin: Berenberg, 2018); *Lotte am Bauhaus*, ARD, 13 February 2019, written by Jan Braren, directed by Gregor Schnitzle; Bauhausfrauen, ARD, 3 September 2019, directed by Susanne Radelhof.

17 Linda Nochlin, 'Why Have There Been No Great Women Artists?', *Art News* (January 1971): 22–39 and 67–71.

18 Julie Johnson, *The Memory Factory: The Women Artists of Vienna 1900* (West Lafayette: Purdue University Press, 2012), 4–5.

19 Marsha Meskimmon, *We Weren't Modern Enough: Women Artists and the Limits of German Modernism* (London: I.B. Tauris, 1999), 3.

20 Nelson Goodman, *Ways of Worldmaking* (Indianapolis: Hackett Publishing, 1978), 17.

21 The UK government defines gender as 'a social construction relating to behaviours and attributes based on label of masculinity and femininity; gender identity is a personal, internal perception of oneself and so the gender category someone identifies with may not match the sex they were assigned at birth. Where an individual may see themselves as a man, a woman, as having no gender, or as having a non-binary gender – where people identify as somewhere on a spectrum between man and woman'. Accessed 28 January 2021, https://www.ons.gov.uk/economy/environmentalaccounts/articles/whatisthedifferencebetweensexandgender/2019-02-21.

22 Candance West and Don H. Zimmerman, 'Doing Gender', in *The Social Construction of Gender*, ed. Judith Lorber and Susan Farrell (Newbury Park: Sage Publications, 1999), 16. See also Joan Wallach Scott, 'Gender: Still a Useful Category of Analysis?', *Diogenes* 57, no. 1 (October 2010): 7–14 and Judith Butler's iconic book *Gender Trouble: Feminism and the Subversion of Identity* (New York: Routledge, 1990).

23 Frederic J. Schwartz, *The Werkbund: Design Theory and Mass Culture Before the First World War* (New Haven: Yale University Press, 1996), 1.

24 Riemerschmid first exhibited his *Maschinenmöbel* at the Third German Applied Arts Exhibition in Dresden, where they were widely praised by critics as an 'epoch-making innovation' that rejected superfluous ornament in lieu of a 'style that grew from the spirit of the machine'. Paul Schumann, 'Die dritte deutsche Kunstgewerbeausstellung Dresden 1906', *Kunstgewerbeblatt* 17, no. 10 (1906): 191.

25 See for example Paul Greenhalgh, *Art Nouveau: 1890–1914* (London: Victoria and Albert Museum, 2000); Kathryn Bloom-Hiesinger, *Art Nouveau in Munich* (Munich: Prestel, 1988); Jeremy Howard, *Art Nouveau: International and National Styles in Europe* (Manchester: Manchester University Press, 1996); Helmut Selig, *Jugendstil: Der Weg ins 20. Jahrhundert* (Heidelberg: Keyser, 1959).

26 No other German city had as spectacular an exhibition venue for contemporary art as the Munich Glaspalast, and international buyers and collectors regularly travelled to the Bavarian capital to gain a sense of the latest national and international trends in contemporary art.

27 'By 1895, around 1180 painters and sculptors – over 13 percent of the total number in Germany – lived in Munich. That same year there were only 1159 painters and

sculptors working in Berlin, which was by then more than four times as populous as the Bavarian capital.' Maria Makela, *The Munich Secession: Art and Artists in Turn-of-the-Century Munich* (Princeton: Princeton University Press, 1990), 14–15. See also Leopold Gmelin, *Deutsche künstlerisches Handwerk zur Zeit der Weltausstelling in Chicago 1893* (Munich: Bayerischer Kunstgewerbe Verein, 1893).

28 Ernst Wilhelm Bredt, *München als Kunststadt* (Berlin: Marquardt, 1907), 13.

29 Only works made after 1800 were shown and until the inauguration of Berlin's *(Alte) Nationalgalerie* in 1876, the *Neue Pinakothek* was Germany's sole contemporary art museum.

30 York Langenstein, *Der Münchner Kunstverein im 19. Jahrhundert, Miscellanea Bavarica Monacensia* (Munich: Uni Druck, 1983); Sabine Wieber, 'German Art Academies and Their Impact on Artistic Style', in *A Companion to Nineteenth-Century Art,* ed. Michelle Facos (Hoboken: John Wiley & Sons, 2017), 103–21.

31 Johann Michael Soeltl quoted in Marita Krauss, *Wirtshäuser in München um 1900* (Munich: Buchendorfer Verlag, 1997), 316.

32 This included the Ludwig Strasse that was lined with shops, the university and that the state library as well as the Königsplatz, one of Munich's grandest public squares designed by Karl von Fischer (1817) and completed by Leo von Klenze (1862). The square is formed by the Propylaea, the Glyptothek and the State Museum of Classical Art. See Makela; Carola Friedrichs-Friedlaender, *Architektur als Mittel politischer Selbstdarstellung im 19. Jahrhundert: Die Baupolitik der Wittelsbacher,* Miscellanea Bavarica Monacensia (Munich: Stadtarchiv, 1980).

33 Bruce Seymour, *Lola Montez: A Life* (New Haven: Yale University Press, 1996).

34 Like his father before him, Maximilian also built a boulevard named after him the connected the royal palace with the Maximilianeum, an elite educational institution and art gallery. Hans Rall, 'Wie der König Max II die Kultur förderte', *Das Bayernland* 55 (1953): 27–32.

35 Michael Koch, *Jugendstil im Bayerischen Nationalmuseum* (Dresden: Arnoldsche Art Publishers, 2010).

36 Sabine Wieber, 'Designing the Nation: Neo-Northern Renaissance Interiors and the Politics of Identity in late Nineteenth-Century Germany, 1876-1888' (PhD Dissertation, The University of Chicago, 2004).

37 Sabine Wieber, 'Between Invention and Tradition: In Search of a Modern Style', in *Atlas of Furniture Design*, ed. Mateo Kreis and Jochen Eisenbrand (Weil am Rhein: Vitra Design Museum, 2019), 26–50.

38 German unification was finally achieved in 1871 as a direct result of the Franco-Prussian War and the Prussian king was declared Emperor Wilhelm I in Versailles' Hall of Mirrors on 18 January 1871. This momentous event was commemorated by several paintings by Anton von Werner (1843–1915). Thomas W. Gaehtgens, *Anton von Werner: Die Proklamierung des Deutschen Kaiserreichs* (Frankfurt: Fischer, 1990).

39 Emperor Wilhelm I (1797–1888) had a powerful ally and supporter in Anton von Werner, who was not only the director of the Prussian Academy of Fine Arts but soon became Berlin's shrewdest art politician who could make or break artistic careers. Dominik Bartmann, *Anton von Werner* (Munich: Hirmer, 1993); Nicolaas Nicolaas Teeuwisse, *Vom Salon zur Secession* (Berlin: Deutscher Verlag für Kunstwissenschaft, 1986).

40 Douglas Klahr, 'Munich as Kunststadt, 1900-1937: Art, Architecture and Civic Identity', *Oxford Art Journal* 34, no. 2 (2011): 179–201; Horst Ludwig, *Kunst, Geld und Politik um 1900 in München* (Berlin: Gebr. Mann Verlag, 1986); Isabel Balzer, 'Exhibiting Unified Germany: 1871-1889' (PhD Dissertation, Northwestern University, 1997).

41 The so-called *Kulturkampf* (1872–78) was a conflict between the Prussian government and the Roman Catholic Church, and reverberated throughout the closing decades of the nineteenth century. Rebecca A. Bennette, *Fighting for the Soul of Germany: The Catholic Struggle for Inclusion after Unification* (Harvard: Harvard University Press, 2012).

42 Ludwig II quoted in Robin Lenman, *Die Kunst, die Macht und das Geld: Zur Kulturgeschichte des kaiserlichen Deutschlands* (Frankfurt: Campus Verlag, 1994), 70.

43 Neuschwanstein (1886), Linderhof (1886) and Herrenchiemsee (1878). Over the years, Ludwig II exhibited increasing signs of schizophrenia, which contributed to his withdrawal from public life.

44 Wieber, 'Designing the Nation'; Stefan Muthesius, 'Das Münchner Kunstgewerbe und das künstlerische Wohn-Interieur: Gabriel von Seidl und Georg Hirth', in *Schön und Gut: Positionen des Gestaltens seit 1850*, ed. Christoph Hölz (Munich: Deutscher Kunstverlag, 2002), 155–66.

45 Hölz, *Schön und Gut*, 28–43.

46 Robin Lenman, *Artists and Society in Germany, 1840-1914* (Manchester: Manchester University Press, 1997).

47 Alfred Lichtwark, 'Die Ausstellung der Akademie III', *Gegenwart* 23 (1883): 366. Lichtwark soon became one of Germany's most progressive museum professionals and the Hamburg Kunsthalle acquired many important and, at the time, quite controversial works of modern art during his tenure (1886–1914). He was also an avid supporter of design reform.

48 One of the novella's central plots revolves around a monk who discovers what he considered to be an indecent painting of Mary and Baby Jesus in a shop window of one of Munich's many art dealers. He subsequently embarks on a mission to rid Munich of its filth and sees himself as the sword of God (Gladius Dei). Thomas Mann, 'Gladius Dei', in *Stories of Three Decades*, trans. H. T. Lowe-Porter (New York: Knopf, 1946), 181–93. For a critical analysis of *Gladius Dei* see Helmut Spelsberg, *Thomas Manns Durchbruch zum Politischen in seinem kleinepischen Werk* (Marburg: N. G. Elwert, 1972).

49 Geoff Eley, Jennifer L. Jenkins and Tracie Matysik, *German Modernities from Wilhelm to Weimar: A Contest of Futures* (London: Bloomsbury Academic, 2016).

50 Ludwig II was removed from the throne by the Bavarian Parliament on 10 June 1886 and died in Lake Starnberg on 13 June. His younger brother Otto was in line to take over the Bavarian throne, but he had been declared mentally ill and was already relieved of any public duties in 1883. See Max Spindler, *Bayerische Geschichte im 19. und 20. Jahrhundert* (Munich: C. H. Beck Verlag, 1978).

51 Ludwig Hollweck, *Was war wann in München: Stadtgeschichte in Jahresporträts* (Munich: Wilhelm Umverhau, 1972), 137 and 150.

52 Stefan Fisch, 'Die Prinzregentenstrasse: Moderne Stadtplanung zwischen Hof, Verwaltung und Terraininteressen', in *München: Museenstadt mit Hinterhöfen*, ed.

Prinz and Kraus (Munich: C.H. Beck, 1988), 82–9; Verena Winiwarter, Gertrud Haidvogl and Michael Bürkner, 'The Rise and Fall of Munich's Early Modern Water Network: A Tale of Prowess and Power', *Water History* 8 (2016): 277–99.

53 Norbert Götz and Clementine Schack-Simitzis, *Die Prinzregentenzeit* (Munich: C. H. Beck, 1988); Karl Möckl, *Die Prinzregentenzeit: Gesellschaft und Politik während der Ära des Prinzregenten Luitpold in Bayern* (Munich: R. Oldenbourg, 1972).

54 Robin Lenman, 'Art and Tourism in Southern Germany, 1850–1930', in *The Arts, Literature and Society*, ed. Arthur Marwick (London: Routledge, 1990), 163–80.

55 'Die localen Verhältnisse der Münchner Akademie der Künste', *Allgemeine Zeitung* (28 November 1872): 1.

56 Munich's Jugendstil heritage plays an important role in Munich's tourism sector, even though many key sites were destroyed before or during the Second World War.

57 Hoelzel started his career as a German Impressionist and was closely acquainted with Wilhelm von Uhde. He played a key role in establishing the famous Dachau Art Colony, which was located in an idyllic rural setting in the Dachauer Moos, 30 kilometres from Munich. Later in his career, Hoelzel moved towards abstraction and taught at the Stuttgart Academy of Fine Arts (1905–19), where his students included Oskar Schlemmer, Willi Baumeister and Johannes Itten – all key agents in German modernism. Sharon Reeber, 'What Hoelzel learned from European Sacred Art', *Zeitschrift für Kunstgeschichte* 76, no. 2 (2013): 243–60.

58 Hirth arrived in Munich in 1872 and married into the city's prominent publishing family Knorr. He subsequently became the editor of Knorr's *Münchner Neueste Nachrichten* and was a protagonist in the founding of the Munich Secession in 1892. Makela, *Munich Secession*.

59 Peter Brooker et al., *Oxford Critical and Cultural History of Modernist Magazines* (Oxford: Oxford University Press, 2013).

60 Hirth employed 275 illustrators during the 7 years of the magazine's publication. *Die Jugend*, accessed 29 May 2020, https://www.ub.uni-heidelberg.de/helios/fachinfo/www/kunst/digilit/artjournals/jugend.html.

 A second important magazine, *Simplicissumus,* was founded in Munich by Albert Langen in April 1896. It also provided crucial employment opportunities for some of Munich's Jugendstil artists and designers but it was more oriented towards political satire. As well, with the exception of Bruno Paul who delivered illustrations for both magazines, a different group of Munich Jugendstil artists worked for *Simplicissimus* (e.g. Gulbransson, Heine) than for *Die Jugend* (e.g. Eckmann, Endell, Riemerschmid).

61 This line of argument was first articulated by the first scholar of German Jugendstil, Friedrich Ahlers-Hestermann, *Stilwende: Aufbruch der Jugend um 1900* (Berlin: Gebrüder Mann, 1941). This narrative was taken up by future scholars such as Jost Hermand, *Jugendstil* (Darmstadt: Wissenschaftliche Buchgesellschaft, 1971).

62 Bloom-Hiesinger, *Art Nouveau in Munich*. This impressive exhibition and its comprehensive catalogue represented one of the first serious engagements with Munich Jugendstil in the English-speaking world and inspired important future research endeavours.

63 Sonja Günther, *Interieurs um 1900* (Munich: Fink Verlag, 1971); Hans Ottomeyer, *Jugendstil Möbel* (Munich: Prestel, 1998); John Heskett, *German Design 1870–1918* (New York: Tapliner, 1986).

64 Whitney Davis, 'Style and History in Art History', in *Replications: Archaeology, Art History, Psychoanalysis*, ed. Richard W. Quinn and Whitney Davis (University Park: Pennsylvania State University Press, 1996), 182.

65 Martin J. Powers, 'Art and History: Exploring the Counterchange Condition', *Art Bulletin* 77, no. 3 (September 1995): 384.

66 Hans Eduard von Berlepsch-Valendas studied architecture under Gottfried Semper in Zurich and moved to Munich in 1875 to study painting at the Academy of Fine Arts. He was a member of the Secession and engaged with the applied arts from the 1880s onwards as both a critic and a designer. He was closely involved in organizing the two Jugendstil rooms at the 1897 Glaspalast exhibition and exhibited at major international decorative arts exhibition such as Paris 1900 and Turin 1902. He was a fascinating figure but has not received his due attention. Christina Melk-Haen, *Hans Eduard von Berlepsch-Valandas: Wegbereiter des Jugendstils in München und Zürich* (Zurich: Denkmalpflege Amt, 1993).

67 Hans Eduard von Berlepsch-Valendas, 'Endlich ein Umschwung', *Deutsche Kunst und Dekoration* 1 (1897/98): 3.

68 The dissemination of British Arts and Crafts ideals across Europe was greatly supported by the emergence of a vibrant magazine culture during the second half of the nineteenth century that harnessed new printing technologies and distribution networks (railways).

69 Michaela Rammert-Götz, *Das Abstrakte Ornament im Münchner Jugendstil: Theorien und Gestaltung* (Munich: Quick Druck, 1994); Gisela Fiedler-Bender, *Otto Eckmann* (Krefeld: Kaiser-Wilhelm Museum, 1977).

70 Berlepsch-Valendas, 'Endlich ein Umschwung', 3.

71 The term *Wohnkultur* literally means 'culture of living' but a more apt translation is 'interior'.

72 Berlepsch-Valendas, 'Endlich ein Umschwung', 2.

73 Ibid., 11.

74 Paul Greenhalgh, 'The Cult of Nature', in *Art Nouveau: 1890–1914,* ed. Paul Greenhalgh (London: V&A Publications, 2000), 54–71; Siegfried Wichmann, *Jugendstil Art Nouveau: Floral and Functional Form* (Boston: Little Brown, 1984).

75 Barbara Larson, *The Art of Evolution: Darwin, Darwinism and Visual Culture* (Chicago: Chicago University Press, 2016).

76 Stacy Hand, 'Embodied Abstraction: Biomorphic Fantasy and Empathy Aesthetics in the Work of Herman Obrist, August Endell and their Followers' (PhD Dissertation, University of Chicago, 2008).

77 Priska Pytlik, 'Okkultismus und Moderne: Ein kulturhistorisches Phänomen und seine Bedeutung für die Literatur um 1900' (PhD Dissertation, Universität Paderborn, 2005).

78 Zeynep Çelik Alexander, 'Jugendstil Visions: Occultism, Gender and Modern Design Pedagogy', *Journal of Design History* 22, no. 3 (September 2009): 203–26.

79 Sarah Crowe et al., 'The Case Study Approach', *BMC Medical Research Methodology* 11, no. 100 (2011), accessed 29 May 2020, https://doi.org/10.1186/1471-2288-11-100.

80 Gregory A. Barton, 'The Historian's Task', *British Scholar* 2, no. 1 (September 2009): 1.

81 This archival lacuna widened even further after the Allied bombing of Munich in April 1944, which reduced 70 per cent of the city to rubble and destroyed many archives and their holdings.

82 Bibiana K. Obler, *Intimate Collaborations: Kandinsky and Münter, Arp and Taeuber* (New Haven: Yale University Press, 2014).

83 Harriet Anderson, *Utopian Feminism: Women's Movements in Fin-de-Siècle Vienna* (New Haven: Yale University Press, 1992).

84 This depended in part on the policies and patrons in different states of the Wilhelmine Empire. The Grossherzoglich-Sächsische Hochschule für Bildende Kunst in Weimer, for example, did admit women. See Anne-Kathrin Herber, 'Frauen an deutschen Kunstakademien im 20. Jahrhundert. Ausbildungsmöglichkeiten für Künstlerinnen at 1919 unter besonderer Berücksichtigung der süddetuschen Kunstakademien' (PhD Dissertation, Universität Heidelberg, 2009), especially chapter 1 'Künstlerinnen in Deutschland', 22–57.

1 MAKER

MARGARETHE VON BRAUCHITSCH AND THE UNITED WORKSHOPS

The machine has become the hand of the artist.

OTTO SCHULZE (1907)[1]

In 1900, Carl Riemerschmid, a member of Munich's prominent liqueur manufacturing family by the same name, commissioned local architect Max Littmann (1862–1931) to design a private theatre, the *Schauspielhaus*, on a piece of land he had recently acquired on Munich's prestigious Maximilians Strasse.[2] Littmann was one of Munich's most renowned architects of the day and had just completed the famous *Hofbräuhaus* beerhall that is still an immensely popular tourist destination (Figure 4). He returns to this story in Chapter 5 as the architect of Munich's two largest department stores: the Kaufhaus Oberpollinger (1905) and the Warenhaus Hermann Tietz (1905).[3] Riemerschmid awarded the contract for the *Schauspielhaus* under the condition that his brother, the burgeoning Jugendstil architect and designer Richard Riemerschmid (1868–1957), be commissioned to design its interiors. Money was no object and Richard Riemerschmid produced a Jugendstil décor of the first order.[4] When opening its doors in 1901, Riemerschmid's interior was hailed in the German press as a truly modern *Nutzbau* – that is a space with a clearly defined function that was naturally embedded in its design.[5] The *Schauspielhaus* offered an intimate setting; the stage was a mere 8 metres deep and the auditorium sat just over 700 people and yet, the back-of-house featured some of Europe's most up-to-date staging technologies. The interior was moulded like a bowl with walls painted in a vibrant coral red and drop-shaped light bulbs mounted into a light-green ceiling made to look like a celestial sphere (Figure 5).

FIGURE 4 C. F. Weysser, 'Street View of the new Hofbräuhaus', Munich, 1897, in *Kunst und Handwerk* 47 (1898): 392. Universitätsbibliothek Heidelberg, urn:nbn:de:bsz:16-diglit-68434.

FIGURE 5 Richard Riemerschmid, 'Upper Coat Check', Munich, 1900–1, in *Kunst und Handwerk* 51 (1901): 286. Universitätsbibliothek Heidelberg, urn:nbn:de:bsz:16-diglit-68434.

Most strikingly, Riemerschmid's elegant proscenium arch, decorated with stucco work in the shape of stylized volutes and trailing plants, framed an extraordinary stage curtain, which serves as a key aesthetic and practical feature in any theatre space. The curtain was embroidered with circles that gave the impression of flower petals cascading downwards as though they were falling off an invisible tree before merging with larger, multicoloured circles at the bottom of the curtain. The embroidery was done in metallic thread that would have subtly refracted the artificial light in the space (Figure 6). The original curtain does not survive but a replica was commissioned when the space was renovated in 1971. The original curtain had been made by Margarethe von Brauchitsch (1873–1939), who was one of the founding members of the Munich design cooperative *Vereinigte Werkstätten für Kunst im Handwerk* (United Workshops for Art in Handicraft) and in charge of its women's department for ornamental design.[6] She also ran her own successful commercial sewing and embroidery studio that employed sixteen female members of staff and took on large commissions such as the *Schauspielhaus* curtain as well as smaller custom work for private clients ranging from home décor to fashion accessories and garments.[7]

This chapter explores Margarethe von Brauchitsch's embroidery practice as a point of entry into larger debates around the role of women makers within

FIGURE 6 Margarethe von Brauchitsch and Richard Riemerschmid, 'Curtain for the Munich Schauspielhaus', 1900–1, in *Kunst und Handwerk* 51 (1901): 288. Universitätsbibliothek Heidelberg, urn:nbn:de:bsz:16-diglit-68434.

Munich's progressive design circles and German applied arts reform.[8] For much of the twentieth century, historians were reluctant to acknowledge women's contributions to the United Workshops because their inherent biases privileged male designers over female makers. In her work on the German Werkbund (founded in 1907), architectural historian Despina Stratigakos recently argued that gendered design values not only curtailed women's artistic opportunities at the time but also shaped the critical reception of modern German design culture for generations to come.[9] These cultural–historical prejudices are increasingly scrutinized by design historians who take their cues from gender studies, material culture studies, the agency of objects and actor-network theory.[10]

And yet, most of the Jugendstil women in this book – be they designers, makers, patrons, teachers or consumers – remain in the shadows. This chapter engages archaeologist Mary C. Beaudry's remit that 'material culture is not just something people create but an integral component of our personalities and our social lives [and] deeply implicated in how we construct social relationships'[11] to bring these women back into the light. Beaudry's observation raises the question of how Margarethe von Brauchitsch used her needlework to navigate the complex sociocultural terrain of late-nineteenth-century Munich. Her oeuvre needs to be placed into dialogue with contemporary debates around the issues of design reform and modern identity in order to reveal some of the deeply gendered dimensions of Jugendstil's historical context (early-twentieth-century Munich) and subsequent historiography (design history). This approach reinstates von Brauchitsch's multifaceted output into design historical discourse and shows that this Jugendstil designer was 'actively engaged in meaning-making practices that involved the construction, circulation and maintenance of knowledge'. [12]

1.1 Introducing Margarethe von Brauchitsch

Margarethe von Boltenstein was born in 1865 on the Baltic island of Rügen as one of ten children (Figure 7). Her parents were Prussian aristocrats and owned a sizable estate.[13] Not much is known about her upbringing, but it is safe to assume that she was raised within the gendered conventions of her elite social class that offered only limited educational opportunities for girls who were either tutored at home or left school after primary/middle education (see Chapter 3). She married the photographer Ernst von Brauchitsch (1856–1932) in 1888, and their son Johannes was born the following year. She moved to Leipzig in 1890 to study painting under Max Klinger (1857–1920), where she stayed until 1895. In her groundbreaking exhibition on Munich Jugendstil, Kathryn Hiesinger suggested that von Brauchitsch also worked under Koloman Moser (1868–1918) in Vienna,

FIGURE 7 'Margarethe von Brauchitsch', in *Dekorative Kunst* 11 (1903): 69. Bayerische Staatsbibliothek München, 4 Art. 49 sk-11, urn:nbn:de:bvb:12-bsb00087520-5.

but, despite obvious stylistic affiliations between the two designers' output, this claim cannot be substantiated by archival evidence.[14] In an unconventional move for her day, Margarethe von Brauchitsch divorced her husband in 1898 but kept his name and raised their son.[15] She became headmistress at a private art school for women in Halle (on the River Saale), where she started to explore hand-embroidery and applique work.[16]

Embroidery was Margarethe von Brauchitsch's most accomplished technique, but a survey of contemporary design journals reveals that she worked across a wide range of media that included tapestry, stained glass, ironwork, ceramics (tiles), wallpaper design and furniture design. She came to the attention of progressive German applied arts circles in 1897, when she won first place for a wallpaper design submitted to Alexander Koch's popular design competitions in his eminent journal *Deutsche Kunst und Dekoration* (German Art and Decoration), one of central Europe's leading applied arts publications of the day. The following year, von Brauchitsch exhibited some of her early embroideries at the '*Erste Kunst- und Kunstgewerbe Ausstellung*' (First Art and Applied Arts Exhibition) in Darmstadt (Figure 8).[17] This was an important, and critically acclaimed, exhibition supported by Princess Victoria Melita of Saxe-Coburg and Gotha (1876–1936), who was a great collector and patron of embroidery. Princess Victoria was married to Grand Duke Ernst Ludwig von Hessen (1868–1937) and closely involved in the founding of one of Europe's most important artists' colonies, Darmstadt's *Mathildenhöhe*

FIGURE 8 Margarethe von Brauchitsch, 'Two Embroideries on Linen', Darmstadt Applied Arts Exhibition, 1900, in *Deutsche Kunst und Dekoration* 3 (1898–9): 123. Universitätsbibliothek Heidelberg, urn:nbn:de:bsz:16-diglit-63833

(1899–1914).[18] Von Brauchitsch then secured a stand-alone feature of two applique panels for a decorative door-curtain in Koch's second illustrated journal for interior decoration *Innendekoration* (1890–1944). This exposure across important exhibitions and design publications cemented von Brauchitsch's reputation as one of the German Empire's premier embroidery artists. It should be noted that von Brauchitsch designed *and* executed her embroideries, which was quite unusual since most of her fellow designers commissioned crafts(wo)men to convert their paper designs into material form.

These combined successes brought von Brauchitsch to the attention of the United Workshops in Munich whose members were keen to secure her modern design vision and technical expertise for their design cooperative. Von Brauchitsch moved to Munich in 1900 and took over the United Workshops' *Damenabteilung für ornamentales Entwerfen* (Women's Studio for Ornamental Design). In addition, she opened her own (in other words, independent) embroidery studio-cum-tailoring shop the following year, which made soft furnishings and garments for private clients while carrying out design work that was either commissioned by the United Workshops or, if designed by von Brauchitsch herself, sold through its premises. She also regularly produced graphic work in the form of decorative borders for journals like *Die Jugend* (The Youth; Figure 9). Von Brauchitsch thus reconciled a number of different, yet equally important, artistic roles – pedagogue, designer, entrepreneur, maker and applied arts reformer. The fascinating

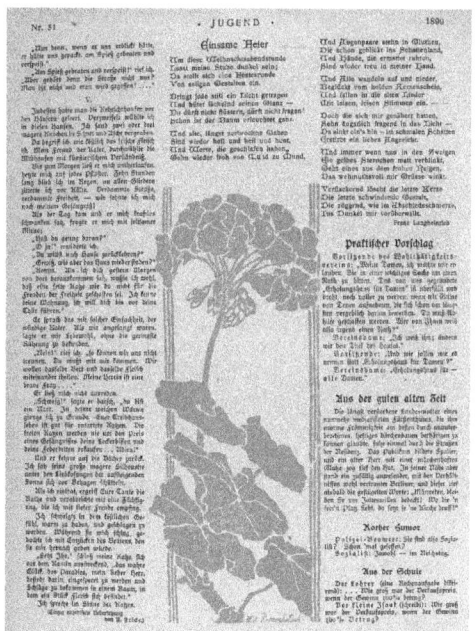

FIGURE 9 Margarethe von Brauchitsch, Illustration in *Die Jugend* 4, Bd. 2, no. 51 (1899): 836. Universitätsbibliothek Heidelberg, urn:nbn:de:bsz:16-diglit-35654.

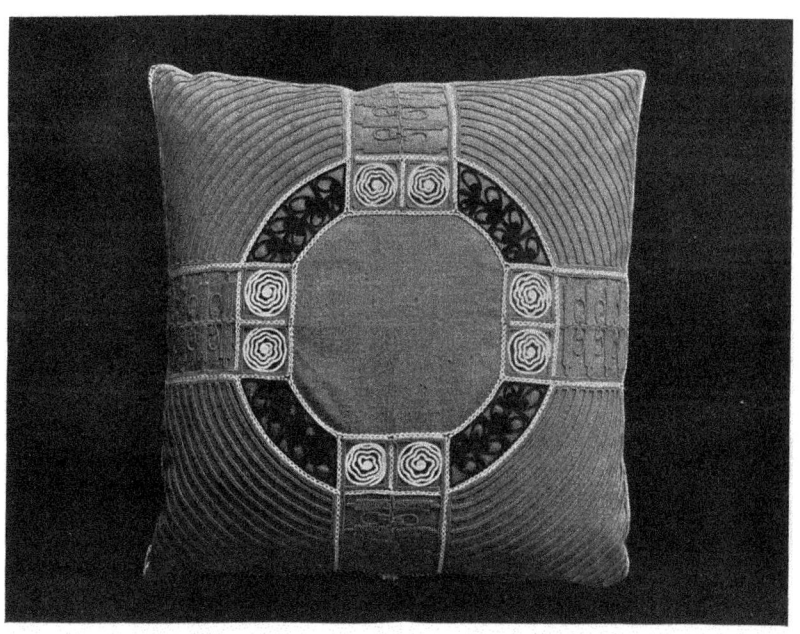

FIGURE 10 Margarethe von Brauchitsch, 'Back Pillow', 1907, in *Deutsche Kunst und Dekoration* 21 (1907): 32 Universitätsbibliothek Heidelberg, urn:nbn:de:bsz:16-diglit-63833.

intersections between her multiple professional identities open up new critical insights into the ways in which a specific female designer tried to carve out a critical and economic position in a world that was still firmly in the hands of male critics, designers, collectors, patrons and even teachers. Von Brauchitsch's multidimensional affiliation with the United Workshops marked a crucial point in her artistic career. Its progressive cultural–political milieu opened up professional opportunities that were quite unprecedented for even as exceptional and talented a designer as Margarethe von Brauchitsch. During her time at the United Workshops, von Brauchitsch developed an aesthetic vision that evolved from floral embroideries inspired by nature to a more restrained geometrical design language that became her signature style (Figure 10). This was possible only because the United Workshops and their progressive clients offered Jugendstil women like Margarethe von Brauchitsch a rare space for experimentation, education and, ultimately, an economically viable career as a designer.

1.2 The Vereinigte Werkstätten für Kunst im Handwerk

The United Workshops were founded as a Limited Company on 6 April 1898 and registered on Erzgiesserei Strasse 18 in Munich's district of Maxvorstadt. The painter and designer Franz August Otto Krüger (1868–1938) acted as the United Workshops' first director and a Who's Who of German Jugendstil designers sat on its first board: Richard Riemerschmid, Bruno Paul (1874–1968), Bernhard Pankok (1872–1943), August Endell (1871–1925) and Hermann Obrist (1862–1927). A number of its original founders had trained as painters, but they renounced their burgeoning fine arts careers in favour of the applied arts. The Viennese architect and acerbic observer of contemporary life Adolf Loos (1870–1933) observed in 1897 that

> In Germany, painters, sculptors, architects are leaving their comfortable studios, to give up art and to position themselves in front of the anvil, the loom, the pottery wheel, the kiln and the planning bench! Away with all drawing, away with all paper-based art! . . . art is something that has to be overcome.[19]

Their motivations were manifold and, at times, conflicting but they shared a deep commitment to applied arts reform. They dedicated themselves to finding a distinctly German modern style that was rooted in everyday objects and rejected historicism, inferior mass production and its inherent alienation of makers and consumers. Although they strove to reconcile artistic design with fine craftsmanship and quality manufacture, they did not follow their British counterpart's (Arts and Crafts Movement) more restricted relationship with modern tools or machine production.

Members of the United Workshops put art and design on an equal footing and vowed to disseminate aesthetically valuable objects across all aspects of everyday life. The company statutes outlined how these aims were to be attained:

(1) organizing exhibitions of the new arts and crafts;

(2) promoting artistic design;

(3) (a) the purchase and exemplary execution of artistic designs, (b) their direct commercial distribution under the most favourable possible conditions [. . .], c) the education of artistic workers in handicraft techniques;

(4) establishing an information centre in Munich. [20]

Educating consumers and craft communities was at the top of the United Workshops' pedagogical mission and its members were keen to forge links between artists, designers, crafts(wo)men and consumers. Although the United Workshops organized regular sales exhibitions within their own premises, its members also regularly contributed to major applied arts exhibitions across Germany and Europe (Darmstadt, Dresden, Berlin, Turin, Vienna, etc.). Members of the United Workshops were committed to translating outstanding designs into beautiful, functional and modern objects. Its board courted editors and publishers of some of the German Empire's recently founded modern design journals. The latter supported the United Workshops by featuring their members' work and offering employment opportunities in the graphic arts. Progressive design journals like *Deutsche Kunst und Dekoration, Innendekoration* and *Dekorative Kunst* as well as more established publications such as the Bavarian Applied Arts Association's journal *Kunst und Handwerk* were among their clients. But they also worked for progressive literary magazines such as *Die Jugend, Pan, Simplicissimus, Die Insel* and *Der Kunstwart*. And yet, looking through these publications today, readers are struck by how few women feature in these publications and/or are credited by name.

1.3 The *Kunstsalon* Littauer 1896

Two key events predated the founding of the United Workshops in 1898. These were an embroidery exhibition at the *Kunstsalon* Littauer in 1896 and Munich's 'Seventh International Art Exhibition' at the Glaspalast in 1897. The *Kunstsalon* Littauer was located in the heart of Munich's most fashionable shopping district around the Odeons-Square. It was a book dealership that hosted regular soirées during which writers from Munich's most progressive literary circles such as the George-Kreis (*c.* 1892–1933), mingled with intellectuals, university professors and Munich's educated upper classes.[21] Literary historian Reinhard Wittmann suggests that the *Kunstsalon* Littauer was one of Germany's most important promoters of Symbolism and stocked a wide range of international avant-garde journals and books.[22]

The *Kunstsalon* Littauer represented a new kind of bookstore that came to prominence around 1900: the so-called *Bücher- und Lesestube* (book and reading room). This set-up allowed customers to browse the bookshelves instead of having to ask for a particular book at a counter and strongly resembled our present-day bookshop culture. Their proprietors organized readings by popular authors and offered tables and chairs for customers to browse new books and magazines.[23] The *Kunstsalon* Littauer carried a large inventory of the latest art books and organized regular exhibitions of contemporary art. One such exhibition in 1896 showcased thirty-five embroideries (silk on linen) designed by Hermann Obrist and executed by his business partner Berthe Ruchet. The exhibition will be discussed in greater detail in Chapter 3, but it should be noted that the event unequivocally put *Kunststickerei* (art embroidery) on the radar of applied arts reformers as a potent vehicle for the articulation of a modern style. It could even be argued that the exhibition, which subsequently travelled to London for the annual showcase by the Arts and Crafts Exhibition Society (1897), registered modern embroidery on the map – full stop. It is not known if von Brauchitsch visited the exhibition at the *Kunstsalon* Littauer, but it made such a splash across Germany's art and design historical press that it is unlikely that she failed to take notice. The famous art historian and Berlin museum curator Wilhelm von Bode (1845–1929), for example, wrote an in-depth and lavishly illustrated essay about the exhibition in Meier Graefe's avant-garde journal *Pan*.[24] Interestingly, von Brauchitsch moved to Munich the following year and abandoned her artistic training to fully dedicate herself to embroidery.

1.4 The 'Seventh International Art Exhibition' at the Munich Glaspalast

The second seedbed for the founding of the United Workshops was Germany's 'Seventh International Art Exhibition' jointly hosted from June to October 1897 by Munich's *Künstlergenossenschaft* (Artists' Association) and the recently constituted *Verein Bildender Künstler* (Secession).[25] The exhibition was staged in one of the German Empire's premier exhibition spaces, the Munich Glaspalast, and attracted visitors from across Europe and North America. Despite its obvious focus on the visual arts, the exhibition featured several sections on the applied arts, which were listed in the catalogue as *Kleinkunst* (minor arts), and included two historicist and two modern interiors.[26] The latter were conceived by a group of progressive local designers who were keen to showcase recent progress vis-à-vis the formation of a modern design language. The exhibition jury set aside two small rooms, Cabinets

24 and 25, on the outmost periphery of the vast Glaspalast but refused any monetary support towards the cost of mounting the exhibits. These discouraging measures did not deter the young designers who arranged their allocated space as modern interiors in which each design element chimed with its surroundings and with the space as a whole.

To everyone's surprise, these two far-flung and supposedly insignificant cabinets became one of the exhibition's main successes and have since entered design history as 'the cradle of German Jugendstil' or even its 'germ cell'.[27] The cabinets were conceived by two architects: Martin Dülfer (1859–1942), who also designed the Bruckmann's new home/publishing headquarters discussed in Chapter 4, and Theodor Fischer (1862–1938), who was one of Munich's leading advocates of vernacular forms in architecture and supporter of workers' housing developments.[28] Dülfer and Fischer issued a call for submissions asking for 'the best that modern applied arts has accomplished' with an emphasis on 'originality of invention and on the perfect artistic and technical execution of such artistic objects as to fulfil the requirements of our modern life'.[29] Cabinet 25 was designed as a modern salon complete with dark-blue/green wooden panelling, a border with delicately painted flowers, a large wall mural featuring a dramatic riverscape and Richard Riemerschmid's easel painting *Cloud Ghosts* (Figure 11). The space was rounded off by August Endell's dramatic stucco frieze depicting fantasy-like dragons that would soon recur in his design work for the Photo-Studio Elvira's façade and interiors (1898–9) discussed in the next chapter. Endell also designed

FIGURE 11 'Cabinet 25' at the Seventh International Art Exhibition at the Munich Glaspalast, 1897, in *Kunst und Handwerk* 47 (1897–8): 43. Universitätsbibliothek Heidelberg, urn:nbn:de:bsz:16-diglit-68434

the exotic door-curtain that was embroidered with an Asian-inspired snake design, next to which stood Riemerschmid's sideboard with a tablecloth and ceramics by Max Läuger (1864–1952). Wilhelm von Bode reviewed the two cabinets for the journal *Pan* and effusively praised the room's harmonious painterly effects.[30] The notion of the *malerische* (atmospheric/painterly) became an important design principle for Jugendstil interiors because it was seen to form the material base for its beholder's emotional experience of the space.[31]

The two cabinets at the 1897 exhibition were realized as aesthetically unified interiors. The underlying concept was drawn from Richard Wagner's notion of a *Gesamtkunstwerk* (total work of art), which he formulated in his famous 1849 essays 'Art and Revolution' and 'The Artwork of the Future'.[32] Dülfer and Fischer presented exhibition visitors with two domestic spaces – albeit within the somewhat contrived setting of an exhibition – that literally materialized Wagner's notion of a *Gesamtkunstwerk* within the parameters of interior decoration. Today, we are well familiar with such staged interiors from international exhibitions, department stores and museum period rooms. But in Germany, Dülfer's and Fischer's display strategy had only recently been popularized by members of Munich's Applied Arts Association on the occasion of the German Empire's 'First National Art and Applied Arts Exhibition' also held at the Munich Glaspalast in 1876.[33] This landmark exhibition first introduced display units that conjured up formal and functional relationships between groups of objects rather than placing individual objects according to category, period or geography. Contemporary critics labelled these displays as *Gesamtarrangements* (total arrangements) because they were seen to create aesthetically unified spaces in which each element stylistically cohered with every other component in its vicinity.[34] The 1876 exhibition advocated a Neo-Northern Renaissance style as the German Empire's new national style. Cabinets 24 and 25 at the 1897 Glaspalast exhibition firmly rejected the earlier exhibition's historicist revival but adapted its innovative display strategy of presenting modern paintings, sculptures and the applied arts within stylistically unified architectural environments – which were yet to be labelled Jugendstil.

1.5 The United Workshops and Margarethe von Brauchitsch

The 1897 exhibition entered design history as the genesis of Jugendstil because it instigated a series of events and initiatives that cemented Cabinet 24's and 25's design principles and stylistic language as Germany's unique contribution to Europe's search for a modern style fit for a modern age (International Art Nouveau). The same year, Obrist, Endell, Pankok and Riemerschmid, who had all contributed to the Glaspalast cabinets, formed the *Ausschuss für Kunst im*

Handwerk (Committee for Art in Handicraft). This affiliation morphed into the United Workshops the following year. As already discussed, this body was conceived as a cooperative of artists, designers and craftsmen who pledged to stem the flooding of German and international markets by poorly designed and mass-produced applied arts objects. This enterprise was modelled on British Arts and Crafts principles embodied by Morris & Company (1861) and C.R. Ashbee's Guild of Handcraft (1888).[35] German applied arts reformers and their supporters were keenly aware of recent developments across the Channel. Key designers as well as the Arts and Crafts Exhibition Society's regular exhibitions at London's New Gallery were widely discussed in Germany's art and design historical press. Although German observers were inspired by William Morris' credo of the simplicity of design and integrity of materials, they tended to ignore his insistence on the joy of craftsmanship and the revival of traditional techniques. Despite the word 'handicraft' featuring prominently in their name, the United Workshops' statutes unequivocally encouraged the use of modern materials, techniques and machinery to manage production costs without sacrificing aesthetic value.

Hermann Muthesius (1861–1927), who served as the German Empire's cultural attaché in London from 1896 to 1904, summarized the Arts and Crafts movement's pitfalls as follows: 'William Morris and the English artist-socialists have given us an "art of the people for the people" that, ultimately, made such expensive things that only the very upper echelons [of society] consider buying them.'[36] William Morris and his followers advocated design reform that was driven by an utopian socialism that essentially retreated from the harsh realities of capitalist society. Members of the United Workshops, on the other hand, anchored their advocacy of a modern style in a potentially more realistic assessment of capitalism's socio-economic realities. This did not go unnoticed by contemporary design reformers who praised the United Workshops for promoting 'the manufacture of artistic applied arts on the basis of modern industrial business organisation and . . . modern technology'.[37] Some even went as far as to argue that handicraft had no place in modern applied arts.[38] Much ink was spilled over these pressing binaries of machine versus handicraft, artistic value versus industry and national identity versus economic viability. Unsurprisingly, the role of women in the design, production and distribution of modern applied arts did not trouble any of these writers despite rising calls from women's advocacy groups for better educational opportunities, equal property rights and universal suffrage. And yet, the United Workshops' embrace of the machine inadvertently created new employment possibilities for women designer/makers like Margarethe von Brauchitsch.

Von Brauchitsch's affiliation with the United Workshops was complex. She was the head of the *Damenabteilung für ornamentales Entwerfen* (Ladies' Department for Ornamental Design) as well as the proprietor of her own business on Theresien Strasse 75/1 (not far from the United Workshops); she embroidered her own designs and was subcontracted by members of the United Workshops; she taught female students how to design and her studio staff how to embroider; she sold her work through the United Workshops' store and her own premises; and she took on commissioned work outside of the United Workshops. This complicated set-up raises the question if von Brauchitsch needed the two opportunities for economic reasons or if this arrangement offered greater creative and professional freedom. It was probably a combination of the two potential scenarios, but readers should keep in mind that van Brauchitsch was divorced and raising her son as a single parent, which means that economic considerations were probably at the forefront of her mind.[39]

1.6 A new direction for embroidery

In the growing field of dress and textile histories, von Brauchitsch has been perfunctorily acknowledged for pushing embroidery into new directions in terms of stylistic innovation.[40] This valuation of von Brauchitsch originates in her own time when critics praised her embroideries as playing an important role within Munich Jugendstil's move away from a floral design language inspired by the sinuous lines of French Art Nouveau to a more restrained geometric *Stilkunst* associated with the German Werkbund, of which she would become a founding member (see Conclusion). Von Brauchitsch's oeuvre certainly supports this design historical narrative. Her early work bore witness to a close study of organic forms inspired by nature. But even her early embroideries, such as a tablecloth she submitted to the 'Collective Exhibition of the Munich Women Artists' Association' in 1900, already foreshadowed the distillation and abstraction of natural plant shapes that was soon to characterize her work. In an essay dedicated to her decorative embroideries published in the art history journal *Die Kunst*, an anonymous reviewer introduced von Brauchitsch as 'a talented and determined artist, who drew on her own initiative to reach her current achievements'.[41] Her embroideries were described as being focused on a *Gesamtwirkung* or overall effect that was achieved through von Brauchitsch's nuanced colour choices and her effective alteration between embroidered spaces and voids.[42] Von Brauchitsch exhibited a number of embroideries in the German section in one of the Applied Arts Pavilions at the 1900 World's Fair in Paris, which were housed in the two Industrial Halls on the Esplanade des Invalides and organized according to medium and technique.[43] Hermine Bartesch, who regularly commented on needlework and dressmaking in Germany's progressive design press, offered a lengthy discussion of *Kunststickerei* (art embroidery) at the Paris World's Fair.[44] In her essay, she specifically mentioned von Brauchitsch's embroideries alongside those of Hermann Obrist, who, at the time, was much better known. Bartesch stressed the innovative employment of ornament and colour in both their embroideries and praised their 'large and simple forms, soft and gradual colours that avoid smallness and fragmentation while creating a harmonious whole'.[45] International Art Nouveau made a huge splash at the 1900 World's Fair and for Margarethe von Brauchitsch to be discussed within its parameters was a huge achievement for the young designer who had only fairly recently turned her attention to embroidery.

Von Brauchitsch consciously aligned herself with the United Workshops' progressive design ethos and practices such as the aesthetically unified interior. Her critical engagement with interior design is even more noteworthy when recalling insidious attitudes of the day that questioned, or even outright denied, women the ability for spatial perception and projection.[46] As briefly mentioned in this book's Introduction, Walter Gropius still embraced this view when he founded the Bauhaus in 1919. Von Brauchitsch refused to be pigeonholed into these exclusionary gender roles and pushed for the recognition of women designers in the German Empire's male-dominated interior design world through her aesthetic vision, her pedagogy, her technical skills and her business acumen. A richly illustrated article published in 1905 by the prominent writer and tireless promoter of modern culture Wilhelm Michel (1877–1942) in *Deutsche Kunst und Dekoration* showcased some of von Brauchitsch's most recent embroidery work within the context of a modern overall-designed interior (Figure 12).[47] The dressing room pictured in this photograph represented an idealized space designed as a showpiece rather than as a lived-in environment. Nonetheless, it contextualized her embroideries as integral elements of an aesthetically unified interior rather than mere decoration.

FIGURE 12 Margarethe von Brauchitsch, Interior with Furniture and Embroidery Work: A Ladies' Toilette, in *Deutsche Kunst und Dekoration* 15 (1904–5): 258. Universitätsbibliothek Heidelberg, urn:nbn:de:bsz:16-diglit-63833.

1.7 The materiality of Margarethe von Brauchitsch's embroideries

Von Brauchitsch used a restrained palette of monochrome black, green, brown and grey threads that drew attention to the basic shapes of her embroidery designs. Von Brauchitsch was singled out as Germany's most promising modern embroidery artist in a review of German needlework exhibited at Berlin's *Königliches Kunstgewerbemuseum* (Royal Applied Arts Museum) that was published in the English design journal *The Studio* in 1908. In it, her embroideries were described as follows: '[she] cultivates a geometrical style of design. She chooses strong and simple colours, violet and green, black and green, brown and white, for her linen ground. She can be graceful or strong, rich and sparing, but she appears always reliable and uniform.'[48] Von Brauchitsch preferred to work with undyed linen as her material foundation because its looser weave structure was more conducive to embroidery and its natural colour produced a more harmonious effect once paired with her black and grey silk or waxed linen threads. Von Brauchitsch used a basic satin stitch but did not follow a strict horizontal line when placing her stitches. Instead, she deployed what is sometimes called an atlas stitch, which allowed embroiderers to place their stitches without a specific direction and thus create painterly effects through divergent reflections of light.[49] Retired senior curator of textiles at the Victoria & Albert Museum in London Jennifer Wearden beautifully sums up embroidery's immense aesthetic potential when describing some of the samplers in the collection:

> Given technical ability, the effects that can be created through embroidery are almost limitless. While each stitch or group of stitches have their own qualities and characteristics, it is the embroiderer's ability to select and exploit them that will transform a plain piece of fabric into a pleasing and unique work of art. The power to perform magic with a needle comes through the embroiderer's familiarity with stitches: with their structure, with hand movements required to make them and with their seemingly infinite variation.[50]

Margarethe von Brauchitsch made full use of the range of possibilities for embroidery and pushed the medium out of the dusty corners of a nineteenth-century hobby into the spotlight as an exciting canvas for avant-garde experimentation.

The tablecloth in this photograph beautifully illustrates another important design principle regularly employed by von Brauchitsch (Figure 13). She liked to strategically place empty spaces within the overall design scheme of her embroideries. A contemporary reviewer praised von Brauchitsch's successfully plotted relationship between background and decoration: 'no more space than strictly necessary was dedicated to the decorative elements, because their sole

FIGURE 13 Margarethe von Brauchitsch, Interior with Furniture and Embroidery Work: Dressing Room, in *Deutsche Kunst und Dekoration* 15 (1904–5): 261. Universitätsbibliothek Heidelberg, urn:nbn:de:bsz:16-diglit-63833.

purpose was to decorate (*zieren*).'[51] The strict lines in the tablecloth's borders and the geometric pattern in its corners pay tribute to this strategy. They delineate the pattern while drawing attention to the three completely vacant central fields. Michel's aforementioned discussion of Margarethe von Brauchitsch's embroideries also drew attention to the fact that she also designed the furniture of this Jugendstil interior. This is extraordinary because it evidences her broad design vision and her bravery in tackling different media even if she, contrary to her embroideries, did not actually make the furniture. Michel compared von Brauchitsch's white furnishings – a table, a dressing table, a cupboard and a number of smaller side tables-cum-cabinets – to the Viennese Workshops' geometric style and praised von Brauchitsch for her versatility and aesthetic vision:

> The embroideries' motifs could not be simpler and more beautiful ... And the furniture, painted white, breathes a bit of Viennese spirit [and embodies] ... the elegant, aesthetic, and light impression of the whole that we have come to love in products from the city on the Danube.[52]

The fact that von Brauchitsch designed all elements of this aesthetically unified interior should not come as a surprise given her extensive portfolio of artistic endeavours mentioned earlier. But Michel's repeated employ of words such as 'harmony', 'discipline', 'beautiful effects' and 'atmosphere' firmly embedded von Brauchitsch's embroideries within the context of a modern interior.[53] This is significant on a number of levels because it gave a woman designer unparalleled agency and carved out a place for textiles within the discourse of modern design. Michel acknowledged that Jugendstil women were capable of designing, making and orchestrating a modern *Gesamtarrangement* (complete arrangement). For much of the nineteenth century, German women had been taxed with the responsibility of making a beautiful and comfortable home. But interiors showcased at exhibitions and in design journals were virtually always curated by male architects and designers. Michel's discussion of von Brauchitsch's work cleverly posited interconnections between textiles, furniture and the room as a whole:

> Margarete von Brauchitsch now has her own sophisticated design language . . . A highly disciplined sense of colour allows her to achieve beautiful effects on particular things, such as pillows, table runners, blankets, but makes her capable of composing an entire room in terms of colour and atmosphere.[54]

Textiles played a crucial role in domestic interiors since the Renaissance and signalled social aspiration and wealth.[55] Arguably, textiles and soft furnishings took on added significance in these spaces interiors of the latter half of the nineteenth century when oriental rugs, brocade curtains, heavy drapery and upholstery were used to imbue historicist interiors with atmosphere and *Stimmung* (mood).[56] Although Jugendstil designers rejected the overcrowded and stifling Victorian parlour as harbingers of germs and disease, they continued to employ textiles in their aesthetically unified interiors. Richard Wagner had argued that the material elements of a theatre production – such as stage design, music, acting and movement, and light – only become a *Gesamtkunstwerk* within the experiential realm of the viewer/beholder.[57] Margarethe von Brauchitsch's embroideries actively participated in this formulation of a modern interior because she integrated individual pieces of furniture into the kind of emotionally vested *Gesamtarrangement* that had been advocated by Wagner almost fifty years prior. The subtle interplay of textures, shapes and patterns, colours and surfaces evoked an experience of space (*Raumgefühl*) that anchored its beholder in time and space.

1.8 Interiors and textiles

For too long, design historians failed to acknowledge the importance of textiles in interior design initiatives across the ages. In this context, Robin Schuldenfrei recently argued that materiality, and indeed luxury, must be re-inscribed into histories of Bauhaus architecture. She reminds readers that 1920s modernism was a 'material style' that embraced material choices as 'meaningful in their expression of modernism'.[58] Viewed from this perspective, von Brauchitsch embroideries embodied a distinctly modernist approach to material and design that lay at the core of German Jugendstil. Her linear designs embroidered in natural tones on crisp linen formed part and parcel of what design historians – at the time and throughout the twentieth century – cast as a distinctly German response to International Art Nouveau that was 'orderly', 'simple' and 'truthful'.[59] By extension, von Brauchitsch's embroideries created and defined modern space through their clever interplay between colour, surface and texture. Her work was therefore both an integral part of the whole – indeed, brought it into being as such – and retained its individual identity as embroidery. Von Brauchitsch's champion Wilhelm Michel described this dynamic as follows:

> The artist proved that she can think in a practical manner and conceive and realise an interior as a unified aesthetic whole. The exhibited pillows evidence a diverse aesthetic effect and a rich interchange of means. In addition to the linear effects achieved by her [embroideries'] ornamental forms, she [von Brauchitsch] also considers the colour of the ground and the needlework technique. One moment, the impression is one of discretion, reserve, elegance; the next, small objects reveal bright and warm colours, [but everything is] infused by the principles of contrast or harmony. A felicitous and assured sense of good taste is clearly evidence across all pieces.[60]

Roszika Parker's seminal work on needlework argued that from the Renaissance onwards, 'embroidery constructed stereotypes of femininity' and by the nineteenth century, 'women embroidered because they were naturally feminine and were feminine because they naturally embroidered'.[61] What was once men's and women's work had by then been gendered as feminine and 'the same characteristics were ascribed to both [embroidery and women] ... mindless, decorative and delicate'.[62] But despite her sobering assessment of embroidery's collusion in the construction of binary gender roles that supported patriarchal ideologies, Parker showed how the material culture of needlework was used by women throughout history to negotiate the constraints of patriarchy, carve out spaces of agency and meaning of their own and even subvert oppressive stereotypes. Even though historians tend to privilege text over object, needlework offers great scope to address fundamental historical questions. Mary C. Beaudry has demonstrated through her wonderful exploration of surviving artefacts of needlework that 'small findings' can speak to 'large histories and taken seriously, can close gaps in our knowledge of material culture from the Middle Ages to the Present'.[63] More recently, Clare Hunter's *Threads of Life* and Cassia St Claire's *The Golden Thread* expanded on Beaudry's critical framework by offering a series of case studies stressing the importance of textiles to human endeavours throughout history.[64] Viewed through these critical lenses, von Brauchitsch's embroideries should be understood as one historical woman's material engagement with design reform and modernity. Von Brauchitsch deployed her embroidery work to negotiate her identity as a modern woman within the patriarchal structures of the German Empire's conservative cultural–political landscape. But contrary to recent feminist interventions into dress and textile histories, this chapter does not read von Brauchitsch's motifs as a 'hidden' visual language that potentially reveals her experience as a gendered historical subject.[65]

In 1899 Irene Braun published a review of the recent exhibition 'Old and New Embroideries' at the Munich Applied Arts Association's headquarters in Munich's Pfandhaus Strasse. In it, she positioned Margarethe von Brauchitsch's embroidery work within a historical context that disclosed fascinating gender biases in late-nineteenth-century design historical debates over what a modern style should look like.[66] Braun opened her review with a short discussion of the exhibition poster, which showed a strong male hand reaching across circles of intertwined flower stems to clasp the delicate hand of a woman. According to Braun, this act symbolized a union of the fine arts and the applied arts, which was one of the Bavarian Applied Arts Association's key mandates. She went on to note that 'women play a significant role in the applied arts through their executive, interpretative and creative activities, as well as through their fostering of artistic taste in domestic life.'[67] This leaves no doubt that the strong male hand represented the fine arts, which is slightly disturbing given the Association's mission to promote the applied arts. The exhibition covered embroidery work from the Middle Ages to the present day, with most of the historical examples drawn from the Applied Arts Association's own teaching collection. Braun used the exhibition to present an authoritative discussion of the technical and iconographic developments of embroidery through the ages, and her essay was supported by copious illustrations. Her more conceptual argument suggested that embroidery had always played an important role within the textile arts, especially during the Middle Ages and the Renaissance, and therefore warranted closer attention within current design historical debates. Braun stated that the nineteenth century registered a shift whereby embroidery was primarily associated with vernacular traditions and local customs across southern Germany and central Europe (costume). But, according to Braun, embroidery came back into its own during the 1890s, when needlework became an important constituent of the aesthetically unified interior.

Braun argued that embroidery's key role in the re-conceptualization of the domestic interior as *Raumkunst* opened up important new spaces for experimentation, not so much in terms of technique but via the introduction of new motifs, the recalibration of the relationship between stitch-work and background, and the innovative choice of colour – or, in von Brauchitsch's case, the lack thereof as she tended to prefer a more monochromatic colour scheme in her mature work.[68] According to Braun, women embroiderers once again viewed themselves as artists (*Künstlerinnen*).[69] Braun offered Margarete von Brauchitsch and the sisters Hedwig and Elsa Lesker as powerful examples of the exciting reintegration of embroidery into progressive design discourses and practices taking place within contemporary needlework.[70] Despite Braun's enthusiastic celebration of modern embroidery as an important component of Jugendstil interiors, readers need to be reminded that needlework as a whole continued to be riddled by ambiguities and contradictions. Jugendstil needlework could never fully escape its feminine associations within the realms of production and consumption.[71] The spectre of a seemingly unresolvable dichotomy between conventional femininity and serious artistic ambition haunted progressive needlewomen throughout their careers. Margarethe von Brauchitsch forcefully pushed against these stereotypes by being fully in charge of the design, execution and dissemination of her embroidery work within the parameters of the United Workshops as well as her own embroidery studio – where she created economic and professional opportunities for other women. But despite the recognition of her exceptional talent and business accruements by her contemporaries, Margarethe von Brauchitsch suffered the fate of many other women designers and was gradually erased from twentieth-century Jugendstil historiography.

1.9 Machine embroidery

A photograph taken around 1910 shows Margarethe von Brauchitsch at work in her commercial embroidery studio (Plate 3). She was in the process of making one of her signature spherical cushions that were regularly showcased in exhibitions and in Germany's design press. Intriguingly, she is pictured using a machine rather than embroidering by hand. This photograph perfectly illustrates Brauchitsch's, and by extension the United Workshops', pioneering attitude towards the role of 'the machine' in the production of high-quality design objects. Von Brauchitsch is operating a Cornely Chain Stitch Machine Type K, which was an industrial chain-stitch machine also known in the textile industry as *couso-brodeur*. The technology was first developed by Antoine Bonnaz (1836–1915) in France during the 1860s. Bonnaz eventually sold his patent to the Parisian textile manufacturer Ercole Cornely, who fitted the machine with a hook-shaped needle that produced a precise line of continuous chain stitches and formed a type of braid that was difficult to distinguish from hand embroidery.[72] The aforementioned photograph shows von Brauchitsch feeding her Cornely K machine with silk thread from a distaff, which she holds in her left hand while operating the machine with a foot treadle. A rotary handle enabled her to guide the stitches produced by her Cornely K in any direction. The quote at the beginning of this book chapter comes from an essay by Otto Schulze, who observed in 1907 that for Margarethe von

Brauchitsch 'the machine has become the hand of the artist',[73] and this idea is perfectly illustrated in this photograph.

The unapologetic use of embroidery machines such as von Brauchitsch's Cornely K radically impacted the production of needlework on two closely interconnected levels. First, a once laborious production process (hand embroidery) became more time efficient and quality control (uniformity of stitches) was made much easier. Second, machine embroidery liberated needlewomen like Margarethe von Brauchitsch from the tedious and exhausting burdens of domestic femininity. Like the mechanized loom (1785) or the sewing machine (1830), the chain-stitch machine revolutionized an entire industry and moved a traditional hand-practice from the domestic sphere into the workshop that was often run and staffed by women.[74] Cornely machines are still employed by couture houses today, but their main use is with embroidery companies operating out of India. Unlike its close relatives, the sewing machine and the loom, embroidery machines have not attracted anywhere near as much critical attention from historians of technology, economists or, let alone, design historians.[75]

1.10 Embroidery and Jugendstil historiography

Hermann Obrist's iconic designs for hand-embroideries realized by Berthe Ruchet and exhibited at the 1896 *Kunstsalon* Littauer are firmly entrenched in Jugendstil histories. And yet, Margarethe von Brauchitsch's machine embroideries are virtually written out of these narratives. The designation of machine-produced embroideries as 'art embroidery' (*Kunststickerei*) might strike some readers as a contradiction of terms. But this did not seem to trouble contemporary observers. It can be argued that this anxiety over handicraft versus machine represents more of a preoccupation of twentieth-century design history than a historical reality. Design historian Glenn Adamson recently argued that hand skills, which are central to the definition of craft, need not be diametrically opposed to manufacture because the division of labour intrinsic to industrialization actually fostered individual skill through specialization.[76] In his view, craft should be conceived as 'the application of skill and material-based knowledge to relatively small-scale production'.[77] This implies that the distinction between industry and handicraft is one of scale rather than of production processes or materials. Adamson's reassessment of craft gives manufacture a space within heterogeneous craft practices that nicely tailors with early-twentieth-century German discourses at the centre of applied arts reform. Within Germany's progressive design circles, an appropriately deployed machine could become a powerful ally in the battle against cheap imitations of luxury objects that had propelled historicism for the past twenty years. In his essay on Margarethe von Brauchitsch, Otto Schulze explained that the 'machine can be a blessing' when operated by talented hands and in the service of a distinct style.[78] Von Brauchitsch perfectly embodied this observation because, according to Schulze, she transformed 'machine embroidery, the disciplined regime of an expedient mechanism, into a succinct expression of her effervescent formal language . . . She wrestled with the consequences of modernity and came out victorious'.[79]

Members of the United Workshops produced handmade furniture and decorative objects for special commissions or for important exhibitions. But they were keenly aware that mechanization and standardization kept prices (relatively) low and allowed makers to tap into rapidly expanding middle-class markets. Richard Riemerschmid developed his ideas for *Maschinenmöbel* (machine-made furniture) in 1903 and started producing these under the auspices of the German Workshops Hellerau in Dresden. He used standardized components that were, in principle, interchangeable. He first exhibited his machine-made furniture in 1906 at the 'Third German Applied Arts Exhibition' in Dresden and received a largely positive critical response.[80] Riemerschmid's *Maschinenmöbel* and Margarethe von Brauchitsch's machine embroideries marked an important difference to the British Arts and Crafts movement upon which the United Workshops had modelled itself. This also conjured up a different legacy of the United Workshops in relation to the German Empire's market dynamics and consumption patterns. Von Brauchitsch achieved great commercial success with her soft-furnishing lines (table linens, bedspreads, pillow covers, parasols, chair covers, screens) and sold her work through the United Workshops as well as department stores and interior design shops across Germany. Her career underlined the German Empire's unique affiliation between design and industry that was about to be cemented, albeit not without controversy, by the founding of the Werkbund in 1907. Indeed, Margarethe von Brauchitsch would become a member of the Werkbund and sit on its *Fachausschuss für Textil- und Bekleidungsgewerbe* (Committee for the Textile and Garment Industry).

1.11 Was Margarethe von Brauchitsch a Jugendstil woman?

Gender historians continue to grapple with the challenge of how to best write women back into history as active agents who participated in the articulation and formation of cultural, economic, social and sociopolitical relationships that constituted Wilhelmine society. Design historians and scholars of material culture are increasingly attentive to the importance of women makers and consumers in the flourishing of modern design. But it is not enough to re-inscribe 'forgotten' makers like Margarethe von Brauchitsch back into the history of Jugendstil design – although a lot of this type of excavation work is still needed before more critical analytical frameworks can be applied. Margarete von Brauchitsch's embrace of technology, her important contributions to the manufacture of quality embroideries for an upper-middle-class market and her pivotal role as a businesswoman and employer deserve our attention. Her progressive attitude towards 'the machine' combined with her artistic training and her entrepreneurship created socio-economic opportunities for herself and her studio employees. This makes Margarete von Brauchitsch a worthy subject of study in Jugendstil design history; full stop. Von Brauchitsch was actively connected to all of the networks and institutions that played a role in the generation of German Jugendstil. As discussed earlier, she regularly participated in important national and international exhibitions, and her embroideries and interiors were enthusiastically received by critics writing in some of Germany's premier design journals. In addition to her constitutive role within the United Workshops, she was an active contributor of the Bavarian Association for the Applied Arts and, later, the German Werkbund. She intermittently taught at the Debschitz School, discussed in Chapter 3. But von Brauchitsch was also a member of the Munich Association for Women's Interests, which put her into orbit with Anita Augspurg and Sophie Goudstikker discussed in the next chapter. Unfortunately, nothing is known (to date) about her political activities within the parameters of this powerful advocacy group.[81]

Margarete von Brauchitsch might not have called herself a feminist, but she was a Jugendstil woman in the truest sense of the word. She embarked on a design career during a time when women's artistic opportunities were severely curtailed by the German Empire's misogynist institutional landscape; a cultural context that not only made it prohibitively difficult for women to train as professional artists and designers, but that curtailed their careers by limiting access to Munich's official exhibition spaces and dealer-run gallery system. The United Workshops were, of course, in part set up to intervene into these deep hierarchies of art and design. But despite its founders' best intentions, the cooperative could not escape the German Empire's normative gender dynamics. Even though the United Workshops' programme mandated the dismantling of age-old hierarchies between designer and maker, the fine arts and the applied arts as well as handicraft and the machine, its members seemed blind to the deeply entrenched fault lines between female and male designers when it came to studio space and teaching curricula.

Design historians have long discussed the United Workshops as a progressive institution that radically transformed German design practices, hailed in a truly modern style and prepared the path for International Modernism (Werkbund; Bauhaus). But the United Workshops' positioning of women designers and makers remains largely unquestioned. As alluded to in this book's Introduction, a number of recent exhibitions commemorated the Bauhaus' 100th anniversary in 2019 by acknowledging the importance of women, the so-called Bauhäuslerinnen or Bauhausmädels (a catchy but problematic term that disparages women's contributions by labelling them 'girls'), in the history of Germany's most famous twentieth-century design school. But even the most well-intended books, documentary films and exhibitions did not venture beyond writing women back into Bauhaus histories, let alone queried the troubling gender politics and/or institutional structures that relegated Bauhaus women to the weaving shed or, worse, considered them bemusing *Bauhausmädels* in the first place.[82]

Ironically, this chapter could be accused of falling into the very trap critiqued above as it brings back into view a woman designer who was widely acknowledged by her contemporaries and yet has been nigh on absent from histories of Jugendstil design. On a most basic level, I am guilty as charged because this chapter 'writes' an innovative and prolific Jugendstil designer, who happened to be a woman, back into the canon. But this chapter also tried to show that despite Margarete von Brauchitsch's affiliation with one of Germany's most progressive design cooperatives, she had to battle her contemporaries' pernicious attitudes towards needlework as (inferior) women's work and tenaciously prove embroidery's merit as a constitutive element of the modern interior.

1.12 Relegated to the sidelines

The persistent gendering of needlework as domestic, repetitive and decorative by twentieth-century design historians wedded to the heroic (masculine) narrative of 'form follows function' continues to relegate progressive makers such as Margarete von Brauchitsch to modernism's sidelines.[83] This is, of course, particularly ironic in light of the fact that the decorative played such a constitutive role in the articulation of modernism both in the visual and applied arts. A stunning and extremely rare colour photograph of a selection of pillows featured in *Dekorative Kunst* in 1909 leaves no doubt that von Brauchitsch's embroideries communicated cultural values that questioned the ideological parameters of the very sociopolitical landscape inhabited by von Brauchitsch and her contemporaries (Plate 4). Jane Marcus argued, in her book on Virginia Woolf, that literary history is 'preserved not in the art object but in the tradition of making the art object'.[84] This holds true for Margarethe von Brauchitsch. Her needlework practice was multifaceted; she was a designer, a maker, a teacher and an entrepreneur who created professional opportunities for other women. And yet, her important contributions to modern design have been largely ignored.

Sadly, Margarete von Brauchitsch's flourishing career as one of Germany's premier Jugendstil embroiderers and designers came to an abrupt halt with the outbreak of the First World War in 1914. The economic and political realities of a nation at war forced her to close her Munich embroidery studio and dismiss her employees. As a divorced woman who could not count on the financial support from a husband, she had to find alternative employment and secured a position as housekeeper in Carl von Thieme's Tyrolian estate Castle Weissenstein. Carl von Thieme and his wife Else were avid patrons of the United Workshops and supporters of modern art and design.[85] Their Munich residence was completely refurbished by Richard Riemerschmid and included early examples of his 'machine' furniture (1902–3). [86] They would have provided another fascinating case study in this book but could not be brought in due to spatial constraints. However, one of their sons remembered von Brauchitsch as an eccentric presence in the house:

> Little Madame was a decidedly strong personality, with short hair, rather abrasive, but with great discipline. She got up at five in the morning, oversaw the large laundry operation of the house (…), engaged in a myriad of handicraft activities, and never went to bed before midnight. During her free time, she smoked a pipe and drank whiskey out of water glasses. She bathed like the Japanese in incomprehensibly hot water.[87]

This alludes to von Brauchitsch's strong character, but it also points to the harsh economic realities of a woman designer in imperial Germany whose fortunes could turn on a dime. A once-successful entrepreneur who produced cutting-edge designs for progressive patrons and who was intimately involved in the articulation of a modern design language was reduced to running the laundry and making 'handicrafts', which presumably included a great deal of mending, for an industrialist's household.

Notes

1. Otto Schulze, 'Neue Stickereien von Margarete von Brauchitsch', *Deutsche Kunst und Dekoration* 21 (1907): 31.
2. The *Riemerschmid Weinbrennerei und Likörfabrik* was founded by Anton Riemerschmid in 1835 and produces high-quality liquors and fruit syrups to this day. 'Praterinsel: Familie Geschichte der Familie Riemerschmid', accessed 4 June 2020, https://web.archive.org/web/20071008023106/http://www.praterinsel.org/index.htm?page=/afp/riemer.htm
3. Cornelia Oelwein, *Max Littmann (1862-1931): Architekt, Baukünstler, Unternehmer* (Petersberg: Michael Imhof Verlag, 2013).
4. The theatre now houses the *Kammerspiele*, a German-language theatre company established by Erich Ziegel (1876–1950) that stages experimental theatre as well as a more mainstream repertoire. It is one of only two Jugendstil theatres still in operation in Germany; the Cottbus State Theatre (Bernhard Sehring, 1906-8) being the other. Peter Jelavich, *Munich and Theatrical Modernism* (Cambridge, MA: Harvard University Press, 1985).
5. 'Das Neue Schauspielhaus in München', *Dekorative Kunst* 8 (1901): 366–71.

6   Henceforth referred to as the United Workshops.
7   Angelika Burger, 'Textile Kunstwerke einer unabhängigen Unternehmerin', in *Ab nach München: Künstlerinnen um 1900*, ed. Antonia Voit (Munich: Süddeutsche Zeitung GmbH, 2014), 320-3.
8   I purposely employ the term 'maker' to give these women the provenance they deserve and to acknowledge their agency.
9   Despina Stratigakos, 'Women and the Werkbund: Gender Politics and German Design Reform, 1907-14', *Journal of the Society of Architectural Historians* 62, no. 4 (December 2003): 490–511.
10 Jenny Anger, 'Forgotten Ties: The Suppression of the Decorative in German Art and Theory, 1900-1915', in *Not at Home: Suppression of Domesticity in Modern Art and Architecture,* ed. Christopher Reed (London: Thames & Hudson, 1996), 130-46; Rebecca Houze, *Textiles, Fashion, and Design Reform in Austria-Hungary before the First World War* (Farnham: Ashgate, 2015); Penny Sparke, *As Long as It's Pink: The Sexual Politics of Taste* (Halifax: Press of the Nova Scotia College of Art and Design, 1995) and *The Modern Interior* (London: Reaktion Books, 2008); Antonia Voit, *Ab Nach München*; Tulga Beyerle and Klára Nemecková, *Gegen die Unsichtbarkeit: Designerinnen der Deutschen Werkstätten Hellerau 1898–1938* (Munich: Hirmer, 2019).
11 Mary C. Beaudry, *Findings: The Material Culture of Needlework and Sewing* (New Haven: Yale University Press, 2006), 4. Beaudry takes her cue from Arjun Appadurai's important work on *The Social Life of Things: Commodities in Cultural Perspective* (Cambridge: Cambridge University Press, 1986).
12 Maureen Daly Goggin and Beth Fowkes Tobin, 'Introduction: Materializing Women', in *Women and Things, 1750-1950,* ed. Maureen Daly Goggin and Beth Fowkes Tobin (Aldershot: Ashgate, 2009), 4.
13 Her father Fredrik Vilhelm Carl Gustav von Boltenstern (1823-85) married into one of Prussia's old aristocratic families through his wife Anna Charlotte Louise von Baerenfels-Warnow (1834–1901). Burger, 'Textile Kunstwerke', 320.
14 Kathryn Bloom Hiesinger, *Art Nouveau in Munich* (Munich: Prestel Verlag, 1988), 42.
15 Miriam Paeslack, *Constructing Imperial Berlin: Photography and the Metropolis* (Minneapolis: University of Minnesota Press, 2019), 35–68.
16 Kerstin Stöver, 'Zwei Facetten engagierten Unternehmerinnengeistes – Charlotte Krause und Margarete von Brauchitsch', in *Gegen die Unsichtbarkeit: Designerinnen der Deutschen Werkstätten Hellerau 1898 bis 1938,* ed. Tulga Beyerle and Clara Nemeckova (Munich: Hirmer Verlag, 2018), 57-9.
17 'Erste Kunst- und Kunstgewerbe-Ausstellung in Darmstadt 1898: Abteilung B: Moderne Kleinkunst und Zimmer-Ausstattung', *Deutsche Kunst und Dekoration* 3 (1898/99): 105-14. Margarethe von Brauchitsch was featured in this discussion with three illustrated examples of her embroidery work.
18 Nikolaus Heiss, *Mathildenhöhe Darmstadt* (Regensburg: Schnell & Steiner, 2018); Wolfgant Pehnt, *Die Mathildenhöhe: Ein Jahrhundertwerk* (Darmstadt: Justus Liebig Verlag, 1999); Hans-Christoph Hoffmann, *Darmstadt und der Jugendstil* (Bremen: Mader, 1981).
19 Adolf Loos, *Ins Leere gesprochen 1897-1900* (Berlin: Der Sturm, 1921), 10.

20 Hiesinger, 'Statutes of the Board for Art in Handicraft', in *Art Nouveau in Munich*, 169.

21 Stefan George (1868–1933) was one of Germany's leading lyric poets and champion of Aestheticism. He had a wide following in Munich that is known as Schwabing's Bohème (named after the Munich district of the same name). Dirk Heisserer, *Wo die Geister Wandern: Eine Topographie der Schwabinger Bohème um 1900* (Munich: Diederichs, 1993).

22 Reinhard Wittmann, *Hundert Jahre Buchkultur in München* (Munich: Hugendubel, 1993), 48.

23 Achim Aurnhammer and Wolfgang Brungart et al., *Stefan George und sein Kreis: Ein Handbuch* (Berlin/Boston: de Gruyter, 2012), 424–6.

24 Wilhelm Bode, 'Hermann Obrist', *Pan* 5 (1896): 318–34.

25 For an excellent history of the Munich Secession see Maria Makela, *The Munich Secession: Art and Artists in Turn-of-the-Century Munich* (Princeton: Princeton University Press, 1990) and Robert Jensen, *Marketing Modernism in Fin-de-Siècle Europe* (Princeton: Princeton University Press, 1996).

26 The historicist interiors featured an 'Arabian Room' by Ferdinand Bredt and an 'Empire-Style Vestibule' by Martin Dülfer, *Illustrirter Katalog der VII. Internationalen Kunstausstellung im königlichen Glaspalaste* (Munich: Rudolf Mosse, 1897), n/p.

27 Christoph Hölz, '150 Jahre Kunsthandwerk: Ein Bilderbogen', in *Schön und Gut: Positionen des Gestaltens seit 1850*, ed. Christoph Hölz (Munich: Deutscher Kunstverlag, 2002), 46; Sonja Günter, *Interieurs um 1900* (Munich: Wilhelm Fink Verlag, 1971), 21.

28 Fischer was a founding member of the German Werkbund in 1907 and was an advocate of the German Garden City Society founded in 1902. See Ulrich Kerkhoff, *Theodor Fischer: Eine Abkehr vom Historismus oder ein Weg zur Moderne* (Stuttgart: Karl Krämer Verlag, 1987).

29 Hiesinger, *Art Nouveau in Munich*, 169.

30 Wilhelm von Bode, 'Künstler im Kunsthandwerk: Die Abteilung der Kleinkunst in den Internationalen Ausstellungen zu München und Dresden, 1897', *Pan* 3, no. 2 (1897): 113.

31 Stefan Muthesius has written extensively on the painterly interior in his book *The Poetic Home: Designing the Nineteenth-Century Domestic Interior* (London: Thames & Hudson, 2009).

32 Richard Wagner, *The Artwork of the Future and other Works*, trans. William Ashton Ellis (Lincoln: University of Nebraska Press, 1993).

33 This seminal exhibition is discussed at length in Wieber, *Designing the Nation: Neo-Northern Renaissance Interiors and the Politics of Identity in late Nineteenth-Century Germany, 1876–1888*' (PhD Dissertation, University of Chicago, 2004).

34 Friedrich Pecht, 'Aus dem Münchner Glaspalast', *Beilage zur Allgemeinen Zeitung* (15 June 1876): 2551.

35 Annette Carruthers, *The Arts and Crafts Movement in Scotland* (New Haven: Yale University Press, 2013); Elizabeth Cummins and Wendy Kaplan, *The Arts and Crafts*

Movement (London: Thames & Hudson, 1991); Mary Greensted, *The Arts and Crafts Movement in Britain* (Oxford: Shire, 2018).

36 Hermann Muthesius, 'Kunst und Maschine', *Dekorative Kunst* 10 (1902): 142.

37 Joseph Lux quoted in Hiesinger, *Art Nouveau in Munich*, 15.

38 Werner Sombart quoted in Hiesinger, *Art Nouveau in Munich*, 15.

39 The legal requirements for work and marriage in the German Empire were complex and their discussion exceeds the parameters of this study. However, it should be noted that the Empire's unified law code of 1900 (the *Bürgerliche Gesetzbuch* or, for short, BGB) upheld male authority within the family. Married women required their husband's permission to engage in employment and/or sign any kind of contract including the opening of a bank account. Any money women earned was legally their husband's property. The BGB also re-inscribed the legal principle of an indissoluble marriage and divorce was curtailed by a principle of guilt (*Schuldprinzip*). These regressive legal stipulations make von Brauchitsch's divorce and entrepreneurship all the more remarkable.

   For an in-depth discussion of the complex legal and social frameworks that impacted women's everyday life experiences in Wilhelmine Germany see Lynn Abrams, 'Martyrs or Matriarchs? Working-Class Women's Experience of Marriage in Germany before the First World War', *Women's History Review* 1, no. 3 (1992): 357–76.

40 John Hopper, 'The Embroidery of Margarete von Brauchitsch', *The Textile Blog*, accessed 23 January 2019, https://thetextileblog.blogspot.com/.

41 'Dekorative Stickereien', *Die Kunst* 1, no. 2 (1900): 347.

42 Ibid.

43 Otto N. Witt, *Weltausstellung in Paris 1900: Amtlicher Katalog der Ausstellung des deutschen Reichs* (Berlin: Reichskommissariat, 1900).

44 Bartesch served as the head of the Lette Verein's vocational department for dressmaking (*gewerbliche Berufsfachschule*) in Berlin. She co-published an extensive survey and manual for professional dressmaking in 1918. Hermine Bartesch, Mathilde Fiedler and Helene Wesley, *Die moderne Damenschneiderei in Wort und Bild* (Leipzig: Killinger, 1918). To my knowledge, Bartesch left virtually no archival trace beyond her published writings.

45 Hermine Bartesch, 'Die Kunststickerei auf der Pariser Weltausstellung', *Kunstgewerbeblatt,* 12, no. 6 (1901): 105. Bartesch was the head of the School for Dressmaking at the Lette Verein in Berlin, which was founded in 1866 as a technical school for girls by Wilhelm Adolf Lette. See Doris Obschernitzki, *Der Frau ihre Arbeit? Lette-Verein – zur Geschichte einer Berliner Institution 1866-1986* (Berlin: Ed. Hentrich, 1987).

46 Mary Pepchinski, *Feminist Space: Exhibitions and Discourses between Philadelphia and Berlin, 1865-1912* (Kromsdorf: VDG, 2007), 115.

47 Wilhelm Michel, 'Ein Frühstücksraum von Margarete von Brauchitsch', *Deutsche Kunst und Dekoration* 15 (1905): 255–61.

48 *The Studio* 42 (1908).

49 Irene Braun, 'Alte und Neue Stickereien', *Kunst und Handwerk* 50, no. 12 (1899/1900): 381–95; Marie Schuette and Sigrid Müller-Christenen, *The Art of Embroidery* (London: Thames & Hudson, 1964).

50 Jennifer Wearden, 'Stitches and Techniques', in *Samplers from the Victoria and Albert Museum*, ed. Clare Browne and Jennifer Wearden (London: V&A Publications, 1999), 129.

51 D.R., 'Moderne Stickereien von Margarethe von Brauchitsch', *Deutsche Kunst und Dekoration* 16 (1905): 498.

52 Michel, 'Frühstücksraum', 77.

53 Ibid.

54 Ibid.

55 Jeremy Aynsley and Charlotte Grant, *Imagined Interiors: Representing the Domestic Interior Since the Renaissance* (London: V&A Publishing, 2006).

56 Muthesius, *The Poetic Home*.

57 Wagner, *The Artwork of the Future and other Works*.

58 Robin Schuldenfrei, *Luxury and Modernism: Architecture and the Object in Germany 1900-1933* (Princeton: Princeton University Press, 2018), 157.

59 On the complicated and fascinating interplay of modern architecture, design and 'truth' see Leslie Topp, *Architecture and Truth in Fin-de-Siècle Vienna* (Cambridge: Cambridge University Press, 2004).

60 Wilhelm Michel, 'Margarete von Brauchitsch', *Deutsche Kunst und Dekoration* 15 (1904/05): 257.

61 Rozsika Parker, *The Subversive Stitch: Embroidery and the Making of the Feminine* (London: Women's Press, 1984), 11.

62 Ibid.

63 Beaudry, *Findings*, 4.

64 Clare Hunter, *Threads of Life: A History of the World through the Eye of a Needle* (London: Hodder & Stoughton, 2019); Cassia St Clair, *The Golden Thread: How Fabric changed History* (London: John Murray, 2019).

65 This approach is advocated, for example, by A. Mary Murphy, 'The Theory and Practice of Counting Stiches as Stories: Material Evidence of Autobiography in Needlework', *Women's Studies* 32, no. 5 (2003): 641–55 and Mara Witzling, 'Quilt Language: Towards a Poetics of Quilting', *Women's History Review* 18, no. 4 (2009): 619–37.

66 Braun, 'Alte und Neue Stickereien'.

67 Ibid., 381.

68 Ibid., 383.

69 Ibid., 386.

70 The Lesker sisters completely disappeared from design history's radar and no information on even their birth and death dates could be retrieved.

71 Anthea Cullen explored this dynamic in relation to needlewomen working within the British Arts and Crafts movement. They were regularly excluded from the design

process itself and channelled into gendered work patterns and social identities. Anthea Cullen, *The Angel in the Studio: Women in the Arts and Crafts Movement* (London: Astragal, 1979).

72 Val Holmes, *The Encyclopedia of Machine Embroidery* (London: Batsford), 27–39; Christine Risley, *Machine Embroidery* (London: Studio Vista, 1973), 102–3.

73 Schulze, 'Neue Stickereien', 31.

74 Allice Kettle and Jane McKeating, *Machine Stitch: Perspectives* (London: A&C Black, 2010), 146–7.

75 For a recent research project on the Singer Sewing Machine see 'Making and Selling Singer Sewing Machines: A Local History of a Global Commodity', *The University of Glasgow*, accessed 16 February 2021, https://www.gla.ac.uk/schools/humanities/research/historyresearch/researchprojects/makingandsellingsingersewingmachines/.

76 Glenn Adamson, *The Invention of Craft* (London: Bloomsbury Academic, 2013), 8–10.

77 Adamson, *The Invention of Craft*, 2.

78 Schulze, 'Neue Stickereien', 31–2.

79 Ibid.

80 Klaus Peter Arnold, *Vom Sofakissen zum Städtebau: Die Geschichte der Deutschen Werkstätten und der Gartenstadt Hellerau* (Dresden: Verlag der Kunst, 1993); Astrid Nielsen, *Jugendstil in Dresden: Aufbruch in die Moderne* (Dresden: Minerva, 1999).

81 A deep dive into the archives of the Association of Women's Interests might reveal some of this information, but this research exceeded the parameters of this study.

82 Penny Sparke wrote eloquently in her book *As long as It's Pink* (2010) about the insidious ways in which women designers and makers were obliterated by twentieth-century modernism and its subsequent reception in design history. Elizabeth Otto's excellent work on the women of the Bauhaus is an exception to this observation. See, for example, *Haunted Bauhaus: Occult Spirituality, Gender Fluidity, Queer Identities, and Radical Politics* (Cambridge: MIT Press, 2019).

83 See Allison Morehead, Review of 'The Nabis and Intimate Modernism: Painting and the Decorative at the Fin-de-Siècle' by Katherine M. Kuenzli, *CAA Reviews* (August 2012), accessed 13 February 2020, http://www.caareviews.org/reviews/1848#.XkVPXhP7QW8.

84 Jane Marcus, *Art and Anger: Reading like a Woman* (Columbus: Ohio University Press, 1988), 222.

85 Carl von Thieme founded the Munich insurance company Münchener Rückversicherungs-Gesellschaft in 1880, which became Allianz Versicherung and still represents one of Germany's most prominent insurance companies.

86 Beate Menke, *Die Riemerschmid-Innenausstattung des Hauses Thieme Georgenstrasse 7*, Schriften aus dem Institut für Kunstgeschichte der Universität München 37 (Munich, 1990).

87 Kay Thieme quoted in Burger, 'Textile Kunstwerke', 323.

2 ACTIVISTS

THE ELVIRA PHOTOGRAPHY STUDIO AND MUNICH FEMINIST POLITICS

What do we mean by women's rights? Nothing beyond basic human rights.
ANITA AUGSPURG (1897)[1]

In the summer of 1937, the Munich Building Authority (*Oberste Baubehörde*) ordered the removal of the 'ugly [and] disruptive façade of the former photography studio [. . .] in such a way that its decoration is replaced by smooth plaster work and a fresh coat of paint'.[2] The building in question was the Photo-Studio Elvira designed in 1898 by Oskar Dietrich with a façade and interiors by August Endell (1871–1925). The Photo-Studio Elvira was located on one of Munich's grand boulevards, the Von-der-Tann Strasse, that connected the city centre with the English Garden (Figure 14). Its ornate interior and exterior stucco work collided with the Nazi regime's austere Neoclassicism, and it was deemed an eyesore along the route of the Nazi regime's imminent pageant '*Der Tag der deutschen Kunst*' (The Day of German Art).[3] The Photo-Studio Elvira's current owner followed the Building Authority's order and promptly removed the offending façade (Figure 15).[4] This episode virtually erased one of Munich's most iconic Jugendstil buildings and foreshadowed its demise after the Second World War. This chapter explores the building's rich genesis in relation to ongoing debates over the role of ornament in Jugendstil design and August Endell's notion of 'experiential form'. But more importantly, it brings back into focus Endell's patrons, Anita Augspurg (1857–1943) and Sophia Goudstikker (1865–1924), who were key figures in Munich's women's movement and jointly founded the Photo-Studio Elvira in 1887.

FIGURE 14 Georg Pettendorfer, Von-der-Tann Strasse with view towards the English Garden, Photograph 1912. Pettendorfer Nachlass, Stadtarchiv Munich.

FIGURE 15 Georg Pettendorfer, Photo-Studio Elvira c. 1937 without the façade. Pettendorfer Nachlass, Stadtarchiv Munich.

The two women lived and worked in one of Munich's quintessential Jugendstil spaces, generated their own incomes by running a busy photography studio and actively participated in Germany's incipient feminist movement. This chapter untangles some of their multiple identities and complex relationships across Munich's artistic and political geographies. This offers new insights into the rich cultural–political entanglement between late-nineteenth-century gender politics and Jugendstil design

2.1 August Endell's first commission

During the late nineteenth century, Munich's Von-der-Tann Strasse was a predominantly residential area that had been designed under Ludwig I to provide housing for Munich's upper classes and members of the Bavarian aristocracy. The neighbourhood featured small shops and a few restaurants, but it was a curious location for a photography studio. Most of the Hof-Atelier Elvira's competitors had their premises in Munich's inner city along the Kaufinger Strasse and the Central Station (*Hauptbahnhof*). Anita Augspurg and Sophia Goudstikker originally purchased a narrow strip of land (13 metres in width) between two existing apartment buildings in 1887.[5] They bought the neighbouring plot ten years later (1897) and enlisted the architectural firm of Oskar Dietrich & Martin Heinrich Voigt to design a purpose-built studio and living space. They commissioned the young Jugendstil designer August Endell (1871–1925) to furnish the interior spaces and decorate the studio façade (Figure 16). Endell had just made his artistic debut with the critically acclaimed frieze and door-curtain in Cabinet 25 at the Glaspalast's 'Seventh International Art Exhibition'. He was also a founding member of the United Workshops. Augspurg and Goudstikker probably met him through their mutual friend Hermann Obrist, another key actor within Munich Jugendstil circles who is discussed in more detail in the next chapter. Endell and Obrist were both actively involved with Munich's *Verein für Fraueninteressen* (Association of Women's Interests) and supported Munich's bourgeoning women's rights movement. Endell had actually just delivered a lecture on the conceptualization of work within the sexes ('*Begriff der Arbeit bei beiden Geschlechtern*').[6]

Endell was born and raised in Berlin. He moved to Munich in 1892 to study philosophy under the philosopher and psychologist Theodor Lipps (1851–1914). Lipps founded the Academic Society for Psychology in 1895, and he is often regarded as one of Germany's founding fathers of phenomenology.[7] Endell was deeply impressed by his teacher, and he engaged with Lipps's notion of *Einfühlung* (empathy) throughout his artistic career. *Einfühlung* is a notoriously difficult concept to translate into English, but it is probably best described as a philosophical and psychological bid to understand the emotional impact of perception. Lipps famously declared that 'beauty is what we call the ability of the object to conjure

FIGURE 16 August Endell, Photo-Studio Elvira, Munich 1898, in *Dekorative Kunst* 6 (1900): 298. Bayerische Staatsbibliothek, München, 4 Art. 49 sk-11, urn:nbn:de:bvb:12-bsb00087576-3.

a particular effect in me. [. . .] *Einfühlung* is thus a complete absorption in that which is optically perceived.'[8] Endell used this idea to think about the beholder's subjective experience of art, architecture and design and their potential to generate profound emotions. This soon led Endell to reject naturalism because he believed that form and colour had to be divorced from their conventional associations before they could strike a deep emotional chord:

> Those who learned to separate their visual impressions from any associations, who refused to add any secondary thoughts (*Nebengedanken*), who once experienced the emotional impact of form and colour, will be able to always tap into a never-ceasing fountain of extraordinary and unexpected pleasure (*Genuss*). It is indeed a whole new world that opens up here.[9]

Martina Mims recently argued that Endell's interconnection of emotional experience and material form was grounded in his support of social reform.[10] For Endell, architecture and design represented vehicles for social change. Endell believed that what he called 'experiential form', that is, form as it was experienced by its beholder generated empathy that, in turn, prepared the ground for moral responsibility.[11]

Endell did not complete his university degree because he became more and more involved with Munich's progressive artistic circles. Endell was particularly drawn to the Symbolist poet Stefan George (1868–1933) and his avant-garde followers. George founded a literary circle known as the George-Kreis that attracted some of Munich's brightest young writers. He was a venerated fixture in Munich's *Schwabinger Bohème* and dabbled in esotericism, mysticism and Germany's Life Reform movement as potential response to an increasingly alienating modern world.[12] Augspurg and Goudstikker were not official members of the George Circle, but they regularly crossed paths with many of its disciples and embraced shared sociopolitical causes. Endell idolized George: 'the only Modern I really knew, and who nobody else knows, [is] Stefan George. He taught me form and sound (*Klang*). But my thoughts are my own and my sound is different from his.'[13] Endell experimented with literature, but he soon realized that architecture and design were his true calling and promptly abandoned his literary efforts. By all accounts, Endell was a difficult personality, but according to his friend and supporter Karl Scheffler, he was completely dedicated to his work.[14]

2.2 August Endell and Munich Jugendstil

Endell met Hermann Obrist in 1897 and the two became close friends. As previously mentioned, Obrist was one of Jugendstil's driving figures. He was a co-founder of the *Vereinigte Werkstätten für Kunst im Handwerk* (Chapter 1) and the so-called Debschitz School (Chapter 3). Art historians primarily engage with him as a sculptor, but he also designed textiles, ceramics, furniture and metalwork while acting as a shrewd networker, teacher and insightful art critic.[15] The two men met on the eve of Obrist's and Berthe Ruchet's groundbreaking exhibition of modern embroideries at the *Kunstsalon Littauer* (1896), which was a key moment in Jugendstil's inception. Endell was deeply affected by their embroideries and wrote to his cousin Kurt Breysig that

> These embroideries represent the most beautiful and mature art since the Rococo. No example of modern painting can even come close to their maturity, depth, perfection and beauty. [. . .] They are the new style that everybody is looking for but that so many doubted could even exist. Here, the grand puzzle is solved in a playful and self-evident manner. This is the entirely new, entirely independent, entirely mature, entirely grand art. This is the beginning of a new epoch.[16]

Endell closely studied Obrist's textile designs and concluded that 'it should be possible to achieve vivid effects in the applied arts and architecture through freely invented forms'.[17] He continued to compose programmatic writings on art but henceforth devoted most of his energies to designing furniture, decorative schemes, textiles and illustrations for Germany's various Jugendstil magazines. His big break came in 1897 when Obrist invited him to contribute to the *Kleinkunst* Cabinet at the afore-discussed Glaspalast exhibition. His spectacular plaster frieze and door-curtain generated much publicity for the young designers, and he was lauded for his progressive approach to the creation of a modern interior (Figure 11).[18] Endell had successfully catapulted himself right into the centre of Munich Jugendstil circles, and the 1897 exhibition undoubtedly paved his way for the Photo-Studio Elvira's design work the following year. Interestingly, no history of German Jugendstil is complete without discussing Endell as the originator of the iconic Photo-Studio Elvira façade, but his oeuvre at large, including his erudite design theories, remained conspicuously absent from Jugendstil historiography for most of the twentieth century. This changed only in 2012 when the Bröhan Museum in Berlin mounted a solo exhibition on Endell's multifaceted career.[19]

2.3 The building and its façade

In another letter to his cousin dated 23 November 1897, Endell enthusiastically described his first proper design commission, which was none other than the Photo-Studio Elvira:

> It looks like my first building works will already start next spring [1898]. Only small, but I oversee everything – the entire interior decoration, doors, windows, friezes, columns, painted ornaments, staircases and railings, wrought iron works, doors etc. And for each component, I am making several designs so that I can offer [my clients] variety and choice.[20]

It remains unclear if Augspurg and Goudstikker commissioned Endell directly, a likely scenario due to their shared sociocultural networks such as Munich's *Verein für Faueninteressen*, or if their architects subcontracted Endell. In any case, Dietrich & Voigt submitted plans to Munich's Building Authority in February of 1898 and after some back and forth over the proposed façade decoration, they were granted permission to proceed.[21] The civil servant issuing the permit on 16 April 1898 was reluctant to approve Endell's façade because it so radically departed from the kinds of historicist designs that had become the mainstay of Munich domestic and public architecture. He annotated the plans with the following statement:

> The undersigned emphatically states that he is against giving permission for the attached façade plans, because they deride the art of drawing. The assumption that its execution will be any better seems misplaced since this permission does not allow any deviation.[22]

His perplexity and outright refusal to consider Endell's modern design language would soon be repeated by the largely negative reception of the Photo-Studio Elvira's façade across Munich's conservative press. And it sadly foreshadowed its ultimate demise at the hands of Munich's National Socialist government in 1937.

Despite these initial harangues, the building commenced in the summer of 1898 and Endell was soon able to oversee the realization of his façade and the interiors' stucco work. He was in a bit of a bind over who would be willing and able to put his challenging design into material form. Munich was not short of highly skilled plasterers who had learned their metier by working on King Ludwig II's various castle projects. But who would be brave enough to venture into Endell's strange design territory inhabited by stylized dragons and cresting waves? Endell approached the Munich sculptor Simon Korn in August of 1898 to inquire about a plasterer for the Photo-Studio's façade. Korn called upon his young apprentice Josef Hartwig (1880–1956) and tasked the then-seventeen-year-old to work with Endell.[23] Hartwig later studied sculpture under Balthasar Schmidt at the Munich Academy of Fine Arts (1904–6) before he settled in Berlin. Walter Gropius invited him to the Bauhaus in 1921, where he acted as the head of the Wood and Stone Sculpture workshops. Hartwig collaborated with Oskar Schlemmer and is today probably best known for his iconic geometric chess set 'Model XVI'. He later recalled his experience of working on Endell's façade as follows:

> The next day I stood in front of the newly built premises of the elegant photography studio 'Elvira' in the von-der Tann-Strasse, drew a Jugendstil dragon, 13 metres wide and 7 metres tall, across three floors of scaffolding and asked for a mason to make the plaster. [. . .] Endell explained his forms and structures in relation to nature, to peach stones, to fluttering ribbons or ocean waves, which break at the beach etc. [. . .] I got along very well with him. [. . .] I also want to mention that it was not easy to get a design of this proportion plastered onto the façade, especially since I was unable to see the overall design due to the scaffolding. Endell was only able to show me the silhouette of the design that he had drawn in a pencil sketch, I had to come up with its three-dimensional form by myself.[24]

Hartwig's recollection reminds readers that this extraordinary building was the result of a joint effort between modern architects and craftsmen at the top of their game. Although Endell designed the Photo-Studio's exterior stucco work, doors, iron fittings, staircase, heating covers and railings, Munich's most skilled craftsmen translated his vision into material form. Their names have been largely expunged from the chronicles of design history and yet, they made important creative decisions during the process of turning a paper design into a material object. Reinhold Kirsch, for example, made the complicated ironwork featured at the entrance, across the front windows and on the door plates (Figure 17). J. Müller, on the other hand, created the spider-web like railings along the central staircase and the garden house's balcony as well as the heating covers (Figure 18). Their contributions are too often overshadowed by Endell's magnificent façade design and again signal design history's privileging of designer over maker.[25]

The iconography of Endell's façade has puzzled onlookers, contemporary critics, fellow designers and historians from the moment it was completed in 1898. It has most commonly been interpreted as a limbless dragon or a sea-creature with a speer-like nose and a scaled body (achieved through Hartwig's clever application of pebble dash). Is this creature riding a Japanese inspired wave with ocean vegetation streaming across its face?[26] The kelp-like stucco work to the left of the dragon and above the Photo-Studio's entrance supports an interpretation of the façade's visual programme as a possibly prehistoric underwater world. This elucidation tailors nicely with contemporary interest in submarine organisms and geographies that were spurred by new scientific discoveries and artistic interpretations of the natural world. The German biologist Friedrich August Haeckel's (1834–1919) beautiful lithographs of natural organisms collated in 1904

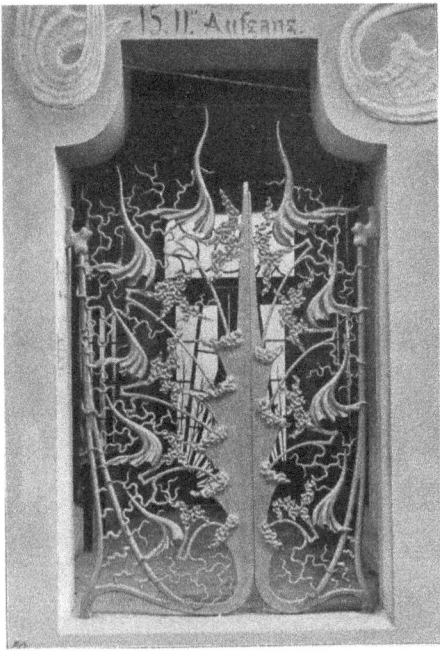

FIGURE 17 Reinhold Kirsch, ironwork at main entrance, Photo-Studio Elvira, 1898, in *Dekorative Kunst* 6 (1900): 299. Bayerische Staatsbibliothek, München, 4 Art. 49 sk-11, urn:nbn: de:bvb:12-bsb00087500-5.

HEIZKORPER IM ATELIER
ELVIRA ◆ SCHMIEDEARBEIT
VON J. MÜLLER, MÜNCHEN

FIGURE 18 Müller, Radiator Covers, Photo-Studio Elvira, 1898, in *Dekorative Kunst* 6 (1900): 304. Bayerische Staatsbibliothek, München, 4 Art. 49 sk-11, urn:nbn:de:bvb:12-bsb00087500-5.

as *Kunstformen der Natur* (*Art Forms of Nature*) as well as August Specht's (1849–1923) animal prints in popular journals like *Die Gartenlaube* are regularly cited by design historians as some of Jugendstil's most important source materials.[27] Endell never offered an explanation of his façade design and simply referred to it as 'the ornament'. This refusal kept in line with his belief that ornamental form should resemble, but not depict, nature because only then could it serve as a stimulus for its beholder's emotional response:

> Not a single ornament was derived from the study of nature; it is of course impossible to entirely avoid echoes of natural formations, given the rich source that nature represents; the depiction of nature (*Narturwiedergabe*) was never the goal. [. . .] The objective is aesthetic effect, not narration of nature or education about animals and plants.[28]

The final sentence entails a curious disjuncture because Endell's ornaments remained firmly anchored in nature when compared to his contemporary Wassily Kandinsky's (1866–1944) impeding experimentations with geometric abstraction. Art historian Peg Weiss convincingly argued that Kandinsky's abstraction came out of Jugendstil's recalibration of ornamentation. Although their visual language went into different directions, Endell and Kandinsky shared a deep commitment to the manipulation of form and light to induce emotional states in their beholders/viewer. On the Photo-Studio Elvira's façade, Endell projected fantastical shapes that were painted in vivid colours with little resemblance to the 'real' world so that its beholder could not be tempted to analyse, interpret or rationalize the façade's visual programme. This strategy offered radical new possibilities for the articulation of a modern design language that continued to allocate a meaningful role to ornament.[29] Here, Endell positioned himself against his Austrian contemporary Adolf Loos (1870–1933), who vehemently repudiated any kind of ornament in architecture or design in his proposition of a causal relationship between form and function.[30] Architectural historians like to argue that modernism was driven by the expulsion of ornament from building facades. This left Jugendstil at loose ends and, in his seminal book *The Pioneers of Modern Design* (1936), the eminent architectural historian Nicholas Pevsner, for example, declared Art Nouveau as a 'blind alley'.[31]

2.4 The interior

Upon passing through Kirsch's magnificent cast-iron gate, visitors of the Photo-Studio Elvira entered a spacious reception area that was capped by a large semi-circular arch decorated with extraordinary stucco work. This space opened onto a staircase that snaked around a 90° angle and led to the second floor, which housed the actual photography studio and darkrooms. The staircase showcased delicate ironwork and an undulating bannister with intertwining organic shapes reminiscent of Viktor Horta's work in Brussels (Figure 19). At the bottom, a spiky five-pronged light fixture projected into the space. A similar guard rail adorned the balcony of the adjacent living quarters in the so-called garden house located across the Photo-Studio's courtyard in the back (Figure 20). This building housed the two women's living quarters and bordered Königin Strasse. The main vestibule's ceiling was festooned with lichen-like stucco work that was anchored in a bulging Octopus-like shape, from which electric light fixtures that looked like bats shot out (Figure 21). This ornamental programme pushed Endell's 1897 stucco frieze at the Glaspalast exhibition towards new technical and visual possibilities. In the back of the entrance hall, a set of solid oak doors, embellished with custom-made escutcheon plates by Kirsch, opened into the aforementioned courtyard (Figure 22). Befitting for an utterly modern space, in terms of both its design language and its function as a photography studio, the whole interior was fitted with electric lighting, which began replacing gas lighting in homes across Germany from the early 1890s onwards.[32] The entrance hall's decorative programme kept in line with Jugendstil design principles, and each individual component, including soft furnishings and lighting, played a key role in the composition of an aesthetically

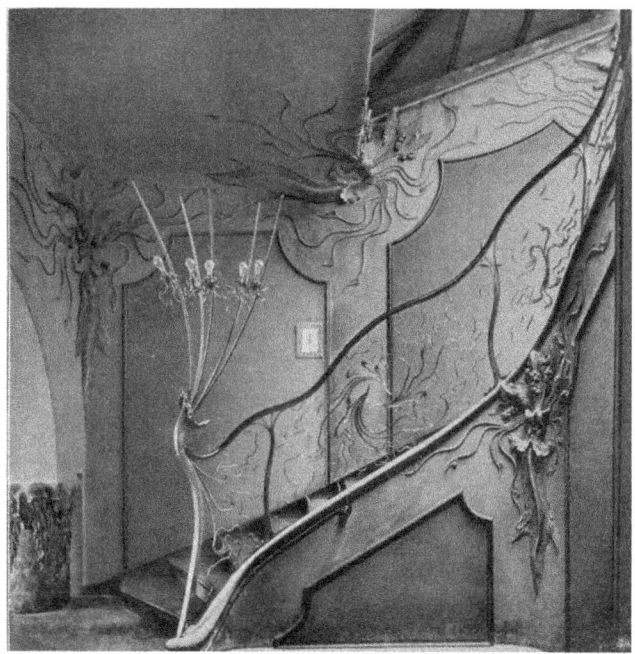

FIGURE 19 August Endell and J. Müller, Stairways, Photo-Studio Elvira, 1898, in *Dekorative Kunst* 6 (1900): 301. Bayerische Staatsbibliothek, München, 4 Art. 49 sk-11, urn:nbn:de:bvb:12-bsb00087500-5.

FIGURE 20 Photo-Studio Elvira, Garden House with Sophie Goudstikker on the lower balcony, Königin-Street 3a, *c.* 1900, in *Dekorative Kunst* 6 (1900): 305. Bayerische Staatsbibliothek, München, 4 Art. 49 sk-11, urn:nbn:de:bvb:12-bsb00087500-5.

FIGURE 21 August Endell, Entrance Hall, Photo-Studio Elvira, 1898, in *Dekorative Kunst* 6 (1900): 300. Bayerische Staatsbibliothek, München, 4 Art. 49 sk-11, urn:nbn:de:bvb:12-bsb00087500-5.

FIGURE 22 Reinhold Kirsch, oak doors with ironwork, Photo-Studio Elvira, 1898, in *Dekorative Kunst* 6 (1900): 302. Bayerische Staatsbibliothek, München, 4 Art. 49 sk-11, urn:nbn:de:bvb:12-bsb00087500-5.

unified and atmospheric (i.e. emotionally charged) interior. Contrary to his usual reluctance to say anything about his design scheme, Endell described the Photo-Studio Elvira's interior as striving to mobilize 'a varied distribution of ornament and a multifariousness (*Mannigfaltigkeit*) of form to prompt as many different spatial effects as possible'.[33]

Unsurprisingly, the Photo-Studio Elvira's exterior divided Munich opinion along familiar fault lines between supporters of a modern style, advocates of moderation and champions of a regressive status quo. Friedrich Ahlers-Hestermann, one of Germany's first art historians to seriously engage with Jugendstil, wrote in 1956 that Endell's façade 'agitated and appalled the peaceful, art- and beer-loving Munich, which was so well served by [the painter Franz] Lenbach's old-masters style'.[34] Endell's long-time supporter Karl Scheffel recalled that the Photo-Studio Elvira was no different to Olbrich's Vienna Secession building built the same year (1898), which caused Viennese locals to rant and rave about this modern aberration in the centre of their city.[35] Over the course of its lifespan, the Photo-Studio Elvira was referred to in the vernacular as the 'dragon castle', the 'Chinese embassy' or simply the 'seahorse house'. It even made an appearance in Thomas Mann's novella *Gladius Dei* (1902) when his protagonist Hieronymus encounters 'the work of a creative young architect that is wide and flat with bizarre decoration, full of esprit and style'.[36] More detrimentally, though, many of Munich's more progressive architects and designers also rejected Endell's decorative scheme because they were perturbed by his seemingly idiosyncratic vision and accused the young designer of over-egging the cake, arrogance and capriciousness.[37] These personal attacks combined with frail health – Endell suffered from chronic kidney disease – left a deep mark on Endell and cause him to question the integrity of his artistic programme. He complained that the interior stucco work was too heavy, the additional window on the façade superfluous and the façade's colour scheme wrong.[38] Endell moved to Berlin in 1901, and the Photo-Studio Elvira was his first and last major project in Munich.

2.5 The patrons: Anita Augspurg and Sophia Goudstikker

Who then were these two formidable women running a successful photography studio for over twenty years out of Endell's iconic, yet controversial, Jugendstil building? Even a cursory glance at their biographies quickly reveals that they broke with late-nineteenth-century conventions of proper behaviour for bourgeois women of their generation. They each chose female companionship over heteronormative marriage structures, and they each embarked on a professional career long before this was a respectable trajectory for German women. Anita

Augspurger (1857–1943) was Germany's first fully qualified female lawyer and Sophia N. J. Goudstikker (1865–1924) trained as a professional photographer. They were already running a successful photography studio for over ten years before they commissioned Endell to design their home/workspace in 1897. They were both active in Germany's burgeoning feminist movement and closely connected to Munich's progressive cultural and sociopolitical circles. They were card-carrying members of the Munich *Verein für Foueninteressen* (Union for Women's Interests), a women's rights group founded in 1894 to advocate for gender equality and universal suffrage. The Union represented one of Munich's most important reformist political organizations of the day and, as will be discussed shortly, was closely connected to Munich Jugendstil circles. As previously mentioned, Endell joined the Union in 1896 and might well have met Augspurg and Goudstikker even before Obrist brokered the introduction in 1897.

Anita Augspurg was born in 1857 as the fifth and youngest child of politically liberal parents in the Lower-Saxon town of Verden on the River Aller. Her father was a lawyer at the local court and spent time in prison during the 1848 Revolutions for his political views. Her mother came from Protestant clergy and encouraged her daughters' education. Augspurg moved to Berlin in 1878 to study for Prussia's teacher's examination, one of the few professions open to German women of the time. An inheritance from her grandmother gave Augspurg the financial freedom to follow her dream and become an actress. She was engaged at several stages across Europe (Amsterdam, Riga, Dresden, Altenburg), but decided in 1884 to leave behind the 'miming of long-passed historical events on stage'.[39] She moved to Dresden, where her sister Amalie ran a painting school for women and where she met a young Jewish woman from Hamburg by the name of Sophia Goudstikker. Goudstikker was born in Rotterdam in 1865, but her parents moved to Hamburg in 1867. The Goudstikkers were assimilated Jews, and Sophia was a first-cousin-once-removed of one of Holland's premier art dealers, Jacques Goudstikker (1897–1940).[40] Sophia's father was also an art and antiques dealer specializing in Dutch Masters but on a much smaller scale. Sophia's father left for Paris in 1886 after a failed business venture in Dresden and did not take his wife and ten children. Sophia subsequently enrolled in Amalie Augspurg's private painting school, where she met her future business partner and companion Anita Augspurg, who was seven years her senior.[41] Goudstikker was a committed feminist throughout her life, but she tends to be described as the artistic counterpart to Augspurg's political activism. This is too simplistic a characterization, and both women's personal and professional identities were much more complex.

When they first met in Dresden, Augspurg and Goudstikker liked each other right away. They soon embarked on the ambitious and, at the time, daring plan to open a shared photography studio.[42] Neither of the two had any educational or practical background in the profession, but photography offered late-nineteenth-century middle-class women certain artistic and economic opportunities that remained out of their reach in Germany's otherwise deeply gendered art world. Augspurg's later companion, the prominent German feminist and pacifist Lida Gustava Heymann (1868–1943), explained that the two young women chose Munich as their adopted home because 'out of all the major cities, Munich appeared as the most liberal, least judgemental city; it was in a beautiful location, artistically of highest significance and [they] already had some connections to local personalities, theatre people and painters'.[43] They wanted to live and work together, which seemed possible in Munich. They settled in the Bavarian capital in November of 1886 and secured two practical training places in a sadly unnamed photography studio that Goudstikker later described as the 'best photographic studios in terms of technical ability and professional management'.[44] Photography arrived in Munich relatively late in comparison to London or Paris, but by the 1880s, the city was renowned as a key production site for precision mechanical and optical instruments as well as cameras and lenses. On 13 July 1887, Augspurg drew funds from her aforementioned inheritance and the two women opened their first photography studio in rented premises right next to the site that eventually housed their Jugendstil building. They proudly named it Photo-Studio Elvira. Why they chose this name is not known, and it might have carried a personal meaning that has since been lost or it might simply have been a fashionable name at the time.[45] Their business venture was Munich's first incorporated company run by two unmarried women, and Goudstikker was the German Empire's first businesswoman to be granted a royal licence, which allowed them to name their studio *Hof-Atelier*. It was very difficult to obtain such a licence, even more so for two women, and their success speaks to the clever ways in which Augspurg and Goudstikker strategically deployed modern architecture and design to articulate and disseminate their professional identities as studio photographers with a royal licence.

2.6 Studio photography in Munich around 1900

As mentioned, the two women moved to Munich in 1886 with the intention of obtaining a practical education in studio photography. A discussion of the trajectory of late-nineteenth-century photography in Munich exceeds the parameters of this book but two things should be noted.[46] One, the practice of amateur and professional photography experienced a considerable upsurge in Munich from the 1860s onwards. And two, photography offered an attractive medium for women because they could acquire technical knowledge within the parameters of an apprenticeship rather than an academic education, which excluded women until 1919. This assumes that photography studios were willing to take on female apprentices, which was often not the case due to prejudices over women's presupposed inability to handle heavy equipment and/or chemical processes in the lab. But since photography was a relatively young artistic medium in relation to drawing, painting or print making, it was less entrenched in the kinds of institutional limitations that characterized the Germany Empire's educational system at large. Interestingly, the imperial government granted *Gewerbefreiheit* (freedom to trade) to professional women photographers, which made photography an appealing source of income in an otherwise very limited field of employment opportunities. One of Germany's first daguerreotype studios, for example, was opened in 1840 by Bertha Beckmann (1815–1901) in Dresden, and Antonia Correvont (1818–?) worked as a professional daguerreotypist alongside her father and brother as early as 1843.[47]

Some of Augspurg's and Goudstikker's contemporaries felt decidedly perturbed by the two women's foray into the field of photography. They were quick to dismiss photography as a fashionable occupation and worried that photography studios headed by women were 'sprouting out of the ground like mushrooms'.[48] This was linked into larger debates waged at the time over artistic skill and originality that came to a head when it was revealed that Munich's famed portraitist Franz von Lenbach (1836–1904) used photographs as aides-memoires in his studio.[49] Despite all of the noise over women practitioners, photography continued to be a male-dominated and deeply classed profession. Only women from Germany's upper classes could afford the expense involved in setting up their own studio. As previously mentioned, Augspurg and Goudstikker would have been unable to pursue their ambition had they not had access to Augspurg's inheritance. To make matters worse, female photographers were rarely taken seriously within the profession and their activities were regularly dismissed as self-indulgences. Most women working in German photography studios actually came from the lower middle classes and they worked as retouchers, copiers (responsible for developing photographs from negatives) or receptionists.[50] Rising numbers of women entering the workforce caused great anxiety among the German Empire's political classes. The Berlin photographer Fritz Hansen, for example, argued in 1898 that although photography was well suited for women because of their innate qualities like 'skilled hands, visual acuity, detail-orientation, and neatness', he quickly pointed out that once young women completed their apprenticeship and secured a 'poorly-paid position in a small studio, [their employer] soon realised that they were unable to do the job and could only be used for inferior tasks'.[51]

Women working in the German Empire's photography industry responded to this rhetoric by forming their own interest groups and associations such as the *Club der ehemaligen Schülerinnen des Lette-Vereins* (Club of former students of the Lette Association) in 1896. Wilhelm Adolf Lette had founded the *Lette Verein* in 1866 to offer girls and young women a technical education.[52] Needless to say,

Augspurg and Goudstikker faced considerable prejudices when they first opened their photo studio in 1887. But they did not allow themselves to be distracted and became pioneers in the truest sense of the word: they worked as professional photographers in a relatively hostile field, and they achieved financial independence. When they opened the doors of their original premise in the late 1880s, Munich was renowned for its portrait photography specializing in visiting cards and the cabinet photographs.[53] Augspurg and Goudstikker tapped into these lucrative markets and specialized in portraits of prominent members of Munich society with a particular focus on women and children (Plate 5). The two proprietors perfectly complemented one another; Goudstikker was hard-working with a keen business sense and a seemingly natural eye for photography, while Augspurg contributed the studio's starting capital and fostered invaluable contacts across Germany's cultural and social elites.[54] The Photo-Studio soon counted Bavarian royals and aristocrats, artists, actors, politicians, members of the educated upper-middle classes, bankers, lawyers and industrialists as well as military personnel among their regular clientele.[55] They were particularly well connected within the German Empire's theatre world on account of Augspurg's early career as a stage actress. Photographs of stage actors and actresses represented a lucrative offshoot of their business as celebrity culture was on rise across late-nineteenth-century Europe. These photographs were used as promotional material, collected by their sitters' admirers and published in newspaper and magazine articles.[56] Their studio became so successful that Goudstikker's younger sister Mathilde opened a branch in nearby Augsburg (1891–5).

A closer look at the actual portraits produced by the Photo-Studio Elvira reveals that these works were very much of their time and tailored to mainstream tastes. One is struck by the conservative nature of their visual language in terms of pose and setting as well as their technical conventionality in terms of lighting and cropping. Some of the photographs might be considered as offering a nod towards more progressive modes of representation that were gaining foothold at the time such as pictorialism. The studio's output as a whole, however, was far removed from the kind of avant-garde experimentation tackled, for example, by their fellow female photographer Madame d'Ora (1881–1963) in Vienna.[57] It is equally unexpected that the Photo-Studio Elvira did not participate in some of the high-profile exhibitions of women photographers that were regularly organized in conjunction with women's congresses and national fairs across Germany.[58] This comes as a bit of a surprise given Augspurg's and Goudstikker's support of Jugendstil design, their commitment to progressive social politics and their fight for women's rights. But this fact might attest to the stark historical reality that the Photo-Studio Elvira was a vehicle towards economic independence in the first instance. The two women founded this enterprise to break free from social conventions of their day and to finance their political activism. For Augspurg in particular, the Photo-Studio epitomized a means towards an end and, as discussed shortly, her interest in the private and professional relationship with Goudstikker waned once her politics became more radical.

2.7 The Photo-Studio Elvira and Munich's women's movement

As their photography business grew, Augspurg and Goudstikker planted firmer roots in Munich's cultural–political landscape. They gradually became more involved in the city's progressive politics and the women's movement in particular. An extraordinary photograph taken by the Photo-Studio Elvira in 1894 shows the two of them amidst a group of women who were all closely connected to Munich's *Verein für Fraueninteressen* that was founded that year and continues to advocate for women's interests to this day (Figure 23).[59] The photograph alludes to the women's sense of humour as they are parodying portraiture conventions of representing intellectuals and writers in deep thought and with their tools of the trade in hand. They each look directly at the viewer as if to let him or her in on the joke. Augspurger is on the left and Goudstikker on the right, with Marie Stritt (1855–1928), Lily von Gizycki (1865–1916) and Minna Cauer (1841–1922) positioned between them. This light-hearted photograph speaks to their comradery and wit. It also confirms that Augspurg and Goudstikker comfortably moved within the German Empire's more radical political fractions. As proprietors of a thriving business in the heart of the Bavarian capital that boasted clients from across the

FIGURE 23 Verein für Fraueninteressen Munich, photograph, 1896. https://commons.wikimedia.org/w/index.php?title=File:Anita_Augspurg_(1896).jpg&oldid=485311591

city's upper sociocultural strata, Augspurg and Goudstikker were ideally located to disseminate their progressive gender politics across their diverse networks and social circles. In 1902, Goudstikker published an essay on her fellow women's rights advocate Friedericke 'Ika' Freudenberg (1858–1912) in the journal *Die Frau: Monatsschrift für das gesamte Frauenleben unserer Zeit* (The Woman; 1893–1944), which had been founded by Helene Lange (1848–1930) as a middle-class organ for the support of the women's movement.[60] In this piece, she wrote that 'it has to be stressed that a special characteristic of the Munich women's movement was the fact that it succeeded in winning men, academics, artists and industrialists for its cause and work'.[61] Augspurg's and Goudstikker's relentless networking efforts and their public profiles thus made a crucial contribution to the women's movements high visibility and significant sociopolitical impact in the Bavarian capital.

2.8 The Association for Women's Interests (1894)

Germany's women's movement has a rich and diverse history. This chapter can only scratch the surface of this complex historical phenomenon by introducing some of Munich's key protagonists who were also vested in Jugendstil debates over the meaning of modernity. Art historians Marita Sturken and Lisa Cartwright defined the modernist period as being characterized 'by a sense of knowing that was forward-looking and positive, and believing one could know what was true and real as well as what was for the best in a given society'.[62] This assessment encapsulates the sense of hope and progress displayed by Munich Jugendstil's various progenitors. For some, like Obrist, Endell and the liberal patrons of the Photo-Studio Elvira, this 'forward-looking' included expectations for a Germany with more equal gender relations engendered by political action geared towards a more just society at large. Augspurg and Goudstikker joined the *Deutscher Frauenverein Reform* (German Women's Association Reform) in 1890, which had been founded in Weimar by Hedwig Kettler (1851–1937) two years prior to advocate for equal education and professional opportunities for women. Its goal was different from earlier pedagogical reform efforts that called for a better education for girls. Kettler demanded shared access (co-education) to secondary schools and universities as a precondition for equal employment across the German Empire's economic sectors.[63] Regrettably, the Munich chapter of the German Women's Association Reform could only exist on paper because of Bavaria's strict laws that policed the formation of non-governmental organizations since the 1848 Revolutions. Augspurg and Goudstikker circumvented these laws in 1894 when they set up the Society for the Promotion of Intellectual Interests of Women, which became the more commonly known *Verein für Fraueninteressen* in 1899. Augspurg served as the association's first president and was responsible for much of the political legwork that allowed this body to stay under the police radar.[64]

The *Verein für Fraueninteressen* wanted to achieve legal and social equality for German women. Its members called for the admission of girls into secondary education, which was a crucial precondition for enrolling at university. These basic measures were viewed by supporters as the fundamental building block for a more just society in which women could choose their profession, earn fair wages and were no longer subjected to the kinds of economic dependencies on fathers and/or husbands that characterized late-nineteenth-century society. Like their fellow campaigners for women's rights across Europe, the association fought for women's suffrage and its membership was not restricted by social status or religious confession, which was very progressive in the deeply Catholic Bavaria.[65] Augspurg and her fellow reformers were keenly aware that these goals could be achieved only if they won supporters – female and male – from across Munich society and the association's statutes stipulated that

> The Association will use its meetings as a venue to discuss the ideas of today's women's movement before as large an audience as possible. In this way, the interest from ever widening circles should be focused on the earnest strife of women to elevate the intellectual levels of their sex (*Geschlecht*) and enable [them] to fulfil their individual life-tasks as well as their social obligations in a more thorough manner than has thus far been the case and been possible.[66]

The association organized regular public lectures and discussions to realize these objectives. Many of their meetings took place in the Munich Applied Arts Association's clubhouse on Parcelli Strasse 7, which is a curious historical constellation given the Applied Arts Association's conventional gender politics. These evenings proved very popular and served as important opportunities to solicit new members and cement the association's ideological platform around the advocacy of women's rights.

Membership grew under the leadership of Augspurg and Freudenberg from 144 registered supporters in 1896 to 736 in 1912.[67] The association defied popular expectations and deliberately targeted male members to join the ranks in their fight for women's equality. The list of prominent supporters is too long to recite here, but a few notable names should be mentioned. Hermann Obrist and August Endell have already been flagged as some of the association's earliest male members. Obrist's interest in Germany's women's question was probably triggered by his business partner Berthe Ruchet (Chapter 3). The poets Rainer Maria Rilke and Max Haushofer as well as the author and founder of Germany's first cabaret 'Überbrettl' (Berlin 1901) Ernst Freiherr von Wolzogen mingled with literary figures formerly associated with Munich's *Gesellschaft für Modernes Leben* (Society for Modern Life), which had become defunct in 1893. Wolzogen was an intriguing individual because his iconic novel *The Third Sex* (1899) caricatured Munich's *Bohème* while immortalizing members of the association and their quest for more equally balanced gender relations.[68] Significant women members of the association were Gabriele Reuter (1859–1941), whose serialized novel *Mrs Bürgelin and her Sons* (1900) offered a thinly veiled fictional account of Herman Obrist's upbringing by his Scottish aristocratic mother Alice Jane Grant Duff; the writer Karoline 'Carry' Brachvogel (1864–1942); the historian Ricarda Huch (1864–1947) as well as the painter Gabriele Münter (1877–1962) and the sculptor/ceramicist Emmy von Egidy (1876–1913). One of Germany's leading feminists, Gertrud Bäumer described the association in her memoires as the 'most colourful, energetic and stimulating ring-of-life ever generated by the women's movement. [. . .] Strong temperaments, artistic talents, warm and passionate hearts, fiery souls – a lively animated atmosphere of departure full of power, humour, spirit and taste'.[69]

The association opened a legal aid office for women in 1898 that was managed by Goudstikker in a premise on Munich's Von-der-Tann Strasse 2 and only a stone's throw from the Photo-Studio Elvira. The following October, the association organized Bavaria's first Women's Congress (*Allgemeiner Bayerischer Frauentag*) in Munich and invited different regional women's rights organizations to discuss the legal, economic and social position of women in the kingdom of Bavaria. These topics were especially pressing since the German Empire's civil code was about to be passed in Berlin after many years of legal and political wrangling.[70] Marie Stritt's lecture on 'The Role of Woman in the New Civil Code' was a sell-out event in the City Hall's ballroom and generated a petition supported by 1,000 signatures.[71] Congress organizers closed the proceedings with an impressive tableau-vivant of twelve historical scenes exploring the cultural roles of women throughout history. The accompanying text was written by the painter and poet Marie Haushofer (1871–1940), and Goudstikker was in charge of stage direction and photography.[72] The Congress itself was a resounding success, but the fight for equal rights suffered a brutal blow when the Empire's new civil code was passed on 1 January 1900. None of the women's movements' central demands over political, legal and economic parity were taken into account, and German fathers, brothers and husbands retained their unabated authority over women. In this context, Paragraph 1354 of the German Civil Code stated that 'the man is entitled to make all decisions in relation to all affairs to do with their shared life' [*dem Manne steht die Entscheidung in allen das gemeinschaftliche Leben betreffenden Angelegenheiten zu*].[73] Women were not allowed to keep their name, were prohibited from conducting business without their husband's permission, had to transfer their financial/material wealth to their husband and, in case of a divorce, were not entitled to child custody. Shockingly, some of these paragraphs remained on legal books until the 1970s. The association's calls for women's right to vote and access to higher education also fell on deaf ears. German women had to wait until 1919 before they could enrol in universities and academies, vote and/or freely enter a profession of their choice. Augspurg's partner Lida Gustava Heymann rejoiced after Kurt Eisner's declared the *Freistaat Bayern* (Free State of Bavaria) on 8 November 1918: Now a new life begins? [...] The heavy burden of the war years is over, and we look towards the future! [...] Finally, women can be fully productive. Women's participation in the labour force is welcomed across all political and social arenas.[74]

2.9 Going their separate ways

Augspurg and Goudstikker were closely involved in the political actions of the association throughout the 1890s while running their successful photography studio. But their relentless battle for women's rights combined with a shared domestic life and professional career took a toll on their relationship. They went their separate ways in 1899, even though Augspurg remained as a silent partner in the Photo-Studio Elvira. Her politics had become increasingly radicalized since she attended the International Women's Congress in Berlin (19–26 September 1896), where she met Lida Heymann, who would become her life partner. Augspurg completed her law degree in Switzerland in 1893 and qualified as Germany's first lawyer. She continued her advocacy work and built an international reputation as a skilled political orator. This left very little time for her photographic practice. It has been suggested that her political commitment and strong personality served as inspiration for Wolzogen's character of Dr Babette Girl in *The Third Sex*, a woman who 'was a real man' and whose 'strong intelligence left no room for a man'.[75] Augspurg broke with the association in 1899 and joined the International Union of Progressive Women's Associations based in London. She then moved to Berlin to live with Heymann and to work as the legal correspondent for Minna Cauer's feminist newspaper *Die Frauenbewegung* (Women's Movement; 1895–1919). Cauer promoted radical left-wing causes like women's welfare and campaigned for abortion rights.[76] Augspurg produced witty political commentary under Cauer's tutelage and regularly spoke at conferences and meetings. Cauer, Heymann and Augspurg organized women's marches during the First Hague Peace Conferences (1899 and 1907), called for hunger strikes and closely aligned themselves with the international suffragette movement. Cauer later observed that 'the radical women's movement developed alongside the social-democratic, the bourgeois-moderate and the confessional women's movement. One should not view these different directions as a splintering of the women's movement because, in the end, we all had the same goals' (Figure 24).[77]

Sophia Goudstikker, on the other hand, stayed in Munich and kept running the Photo-Studio. She had also moved on in terms of her personal affairs and was living with Ika Freudenberg (1858–1912) until Freudenberg's death in 1912.

FIGURE 24 Martha von Kranz and Laura Lange (Debschitz School), three-part photo-frame with photographs of Anita Augspurg, 1911, in *Kunst und Handwerk* 62 (1911–12): 52. Universitätsbibliothek Heidelberg, urn:nbn:de:bsz:16-diglit-68434.

Contrary to Augspurg, who was committed to big political issues and women's rights, Goudstikker was more focused on improving Munich women's day-to-day realities. As previously mentioned, she was in charge of the association's legal clinic until her death. Even though she lacked Augspurg's legal qualifications, she represented clients at Munich's Youth Court, for which a formal legal licence was not required. Entirely self-taught, Goudstikker soon earned the respect of local judges who recognized her as a formidable adversary.[78] Goudstikker balanced this advocacy work with the practicalities of running of her photography studio, which continued to be an important meeting place for Munich's progressive cultural and political circles and a breeding ground for early-twentieth-century modernity. As previously explained, the Photo-Studio Elvira's output did not actively participate in modernist experimentation across the visual arts but it represented an important intellectual and political space for contemporary debates that strove to redefine gender roles in Wilhelmine Germany. The most 'radical' that the Photo-Studio Elvira ever got was in its production of several iconic portraits of key actors in the German Empire's women's movement. From a purely practical point of view, it made sense that contemporary feminists supported a photography studio run by a friend and political collaborator. But Goudstikker's photographs of the writers Lou Andreas-Salome (1861–1937) and Gabriele Reuter (1859–1941), for example, also offer a wonderful insight into their personalities (Figure 25). They are portrayed as strong intellectuals with active minds and an unwavering commitment to their chosen profession and/or political causes.

FIGURE 25 Photo-Studio Elvira, Lou Andreas-Salome, photograph, c. 1897. https://commons.wikimedia.org/w/index.php?title=Lou_Andreas-Salom%C3%A9&oldid=378732942.

2.10 Jugendstil experimentation and political advocacy

The Photo-Studio Elvira represented a complex site in which professional, private and political identities were formed, rearticulated and disseminated. Gender historians have long argued that women created alternative communities to escape the German Empire's heteronormative gender roles.[79] Gender identities blurred in interesting ways within the physical parameters of Endell's Jugendstil interior for the Photo-Studio Elvira: Augspurger and Goudstikker were business partners who both lived on the premises; they collaborated in their political lives as feminists and surrounded themselves with their feminist co-advocates; they were lesbians and, possibly, in an intimate relationship until Augspurg met Heymann in 1896 and Goudstikker became involved with Freudenberg the same year. Art historian Bibiana Obler recently explored the fascinating confluence of private and professional lives in relation to some of modernism's iconic artist couples like Gabriele Münter and Wassily Kandinsky as well as Sophie Taeuber and Hans Arp.[80] She coined the term 'intimate collaboration' to scrutinize the charged artistic and connubial relationships that drove aesthetic innovation in early-twentieth-century Germany with the purview of revaluing women's distinct contributions to the avant-garde project. These 'intimate collaborations' often blurred the lines between creative, personal and professional dynamics of these relationships.

Augspurg's and Goudstikker's intertwined private and professional lives should be viewed as another instantiation of this kind of an 'intimate collaboration'. But in this context, the distinct component of 'visionary feminism' must be added to the construct. This idea was first iterated by historian Harriet Anderson, who tried to untangle the problematic dichotomy between radical feminism and cultural feminism in early-twentieth-century Vienna. She coined the term 'visionary feminists' as a third possibility to describe historical agents who sought equal rights for women, a new social order and cultural modernity.[81] Augspurg's and Goudstikker's feminism was certainly visionary in Anderson's sense of the word even if they pursued different ideological and political directions in later years.

A recent exhibition in Munich explored the rich histories of the city's early-twentieth-century women's movement.[82] In this context, Christa Elferich, the Association for Women's Interests' current director, observed that in late-nineteenth-century Munich, 'modernity and pioneering spirit did not automatically lead to social stigmatisation'.[83] This certainly applied to the Photo-Studio Elvira, whose proprietors carefully intertwined modern aesthetics and progressive politics in their quest for an ultimately more just society. Their bravely modern building and daringly unconventional lifestyles declared their intention of breaking free from societal constraints bestowed upon women of their generation. In her autobiography, Lida Heymann described life at the Photo-Studio Elvira's as follows:

> That two women opened their own successful business and thus gained independence, had short hair – imagine in the Eighties of the past century – Titus-Heads that is, nourished stimulating, interesting soirées in their home, publicly fought for women's liberation, were physically active, rode horses and bikes, hiked, and had the audacity to live how they saw fit, of course raised all kinds of eyebrows in Munich. This provided plenty of ammunition for gossip amongst philistines and enviers, but this not only left the two women completely cold, it actually amused them to no end, which in turn did not help diminish the envy [of others].[84]

Augspurg's and Goudstikker's used their physical appearances as New Women riding bicycles, wearing Reform Dresses (Chapter 5) and sporting short haircuts ('Titus-Heads') to articulate a distinctly modern identity that signalled their progressive politics. Endell's innovative Jugendstil façade and interior played a crucial role in this narrative because it provided the physical and conceptual setting for their self-identification as independent modern women. They were well aware of the fact that their commissioning of one of Munich's most daring and committed Jugendstil architects would not go unnoticed.

But Augspurg and Goudstikker did not simply recruit Endell as a clever self-promotional act. They lived and worked in one of Germany's most iconic Jugendstil buildings. Its physical fabric played a crucial role in the production of Augspurg's and Goudstikker's private and professional identities as committed feminists and progressive New Women. While their political struggles were fought in the public eye, their personal relationship with one another and with members of Munich's artistic and literary avant-garde was formed in the privacy of their photography studio. And their most intimate relationships were nourished in their living quarters across the Photo-Studio's courtyard. Gertrud Bäumer beautifully evoked the interconnections between emotion, spirit, intellect and politics in her moving eulogy for Goudstikker, who died in 1924:

> I spoke of your social work elsewhere. Today I remember your small, lively house, with its sassy ironwork and railings, *with its enigmatic deep-sea monsters* in stucco on the walls, and all the beautiful [and] animated things . . . *Your* world! Developed on your own grounds, in your very own style, bearing witness to your independent strength and joy and most unique, enthusiastic being (*Formung*).[85]

Endell's Jugendstil façade and interior signposted a number of important identities embodied in the daily lives, professional practices and political activism of these two pioneering women. They were modern, unconventional, progressive, brave, confident, irreverent and entrepreneurial – in short, they were Jugendstil women in the truest sense of the word.

2.11 Postscript

After running the Photo-Studio for more than twenty years, Goudstikker leased the studio to the young photographer Emma Uibeleisen (1880–1928) in 1908. Uibeleisen trained at the Bavarian State Photography School (*Staatslehranstalt*) and ran the Photo-Studio Elvira until her death in 1928. By this point in time, Goudstikker had died (1924) and Augspurg was still living in Munich with her partner Heymann and still actively engaged in politics. After demanding Hitler's extradition from Bavaria in 1923, the two women were put on the Nazi Party's blacklist. When the National Socialists came to power in 1933, they went into exile in Switzerland but continued their political activism. Augspurg died in 1943 and was virtually forgotten until second-generation feminists rediscovered Heymann's autobiography in the early 1970s.[86]

Notes

1 Anita Augspurg quoted in Christiane Berneike, 'Nichts ist Unmöglich: Anita Augspurg, eine biographische Recherche', *FrauenMediaTurm*, accessed 8 June 2020,

https://frauenmediaturm.de/historische-frauenbewegung/nichts-ist-unmoeglich-anita-augspurg-eine-biographische-recherche/.

2   Letter to Nana Merbitz deposited in Bauakte 10, 240 Lokalbaukommission, Stadtarchiv Munich.

3   The pageant was organized on occasion of the grand opening of Munich's first 'Great German Art Exhibition' on 18 July 1937 in Paul Ludwig Troost's grandiose Haus der Kunst.

4   Rudolf Herz, 'Von-der-Tannstrasse 15: Zur Geschichte eines Hauses und einer Strasse', in *Hof-Atelier Elvira, 1887-1928: Ästheten, Emanzen, Aristokraten*, ed. Rudolf Herz and Brigitte Bruns (Munich: Stadtmuseum, 1985), 61.

5   Ibid.

6   Christine Salge, 'August Endell: Leben, Werk und Schriften', in *August Endell, 1871-1925: Architekt und Formenkünstler*, ed. Nicola Bröcker, Gisela Moeller and Christiane Salge (Petersberg: Michael Imhof Verlag, 2012), 42.

7   Theodor Lipps, *Ästhetik: Psychologie des Schönen und der Kunst* (Hamburg: L. Voss, 1903); Robin Curtis and Richard George Elliott, 'An Introduction to Einfühlung', *Art in Translation* 6, no. 4 (December 2014): 353-76; Alessandro Salice, 'The Phenomenology of the Munich and Göttingen Circles', in *Stanford Encyclopaedia of Philosophy*, accessed 26 August 2019, https://plato.stanford.edu/entries/phenomenology-mg/

8   Lipps quoted in Helge David, 'Ein fliessender Teppich: Zur Ästhetik von August Endell', in *August Endell, 1871-1925*, 71.

9   August Endell, *Um die Schönheit: Eine Paraphrase über die Münchener Kunstausstellung* (Munich: 1896), 11.

10 Martina Mims, 'August Endell's Construction of Feeling' (PhD Dissertation, Columbia University 2013), 3.

11 For an in-depth discussion of Endell's complex theories see Stacy Hand, 'Embodied Abstraction: Biomorphic Fantasy and Empathy Aesthetics in the Work of Hermann Obrist, August Endell and Their Followers' (PhD Dissertation, University of Chicago, 2008).

12 Robert Edward Norton, *Secret Germany: Stefan George and His Circle* (Ithaca: Cornell University Press, 2002).

13 David, 'Ein fliessender Teppich', 72.

14 Karl Scheffler, *Die fetten und die mageren Jahre: Ein Arbeits- und Lebensbericht* (Leipzig: Paul List 1924), 24 and 'August Endell', *Kunst und Künstler* 5 (1907): 314-24.

15 Eva Afuhs and Andreas Strobl, *Hermann Obrist: Sculpture, Space, Abstraction around 1900* (Zurich: Scheidegger & Spiess, 2009).

16 Letter August Endell to Kurt Brysig, late March 1896, fo. 95r-99r, reprinted in Bröcker et al., *August Endell, 1871-1925*, 446-7.

17 Endell quoted in Bernd Mollenhauer, *Jugendstil in München* (Munich: Hirschkäfer Verlag, 2014), 15.

18 Eduard von Berlepsch, 'Endlich ein Umschwung!', *Deutsche Kunst und Dekoration* 1 (1897): 1-12; Von Poellnitz, 'Betrachtungen über den modernen Stil', *Deutsche Kunst und Dekoration* 2 (1898): 301.

19 Bröcker et al., *August Endell, 1871-1925*.
20 Nachlass Kurt Breysig, DE-611-BF-981, Handschriftenabteilung, Staatsbibliothek zu Berlin: Preussischer Kulturbesitz.
21 Herz, 'Photo-Atelier Elvira', 35.
22 Ibid.
23 Rolf Bothe, *Das frühe Bauhaus und Johannes Itten* (Ostfildern-Ruit: Hatje, 1994).
24 Josef Hartwig, *Leben und Meinung des Bildhauers Josef Hartwig* (Frankfurt: Kunstgewerbeverain, 1955), 12.
25 For an innovative exception see Jesse Adams Stein, *Hot Metal: Material Culture and Tangible Labour* (Manchester: Manchester University Press, 2016).
26 Inga Ganzer. 'Spuren Ostasiens: August Endell im Kontext der Japanrezeption nach 1900', in *August Endell, 1871-1925*, 91-101.
27 Paul Greenhalgh, *Art Nouveau: 1890-1914* (London: Victoria and Albert Museum, 2000); Rainer Willmann and Julia Voss, *The Art and Science of Ernst Haeckel* (Cologne: Taschen, 2017). Walther May, *Goethe, Humboldt, Darwin, Haeckel* (Berlin: Steglitz, 1906); Eduard von Bodenhausen, 'Entwicklungslehre und Aesthetik', Pan 5, no. 4 (1900): 236–41.
28 August Endell, 'Architektonische Erstlinge', *Dekorative Kunst* 6 (1900): 304.
29 For an in-depth discussion of the viability of ornament in modern architecture and design see María Ocón Fernández, *Ornament und Moderne: Theoriebildung und Ornamentdebatte im deutschen Architekturdiskurs, 1850–1930* (Berlin: Reimer Verlag, 2004).
30 Adolf Loos, *Ornament and Crime: Selected Essays,* translated by Michael Mitchell (Riverside: Ariadne, 1998). Loos first delivered this as a lecture on 21 January 1910 at the *Akademischer Verband für Literatur und Musik,* Vienna. Christopher Long, 'The Origins and Context of Adolf Loos's "Ornament and Crime"', *The Journal of the Society of Architectural Historians* 68, no. 2 (June 2009): 200–23.
31 Nicholas Pevsner, *Pioneers of modern design: From William Morris to Walter Gropius* (Harmondsworth: Penguin Books, 1960), 89.
32 Carl Auer von Welsbach perfected his metal filament light bulb in 1898, which was brought to market as the Auer-Oslight in 1902 and replaced the arc light.
33 Endell, 'Architektonische Erstlinge', 300.
34 Ahlers-Hestermann quoted in Herz, 'Photo-Atelier Elvira', 36.
35 Scheffler, *Die fetten und die armen Jahre*, 24.
36 Thomas Mann, 'Gladius Dei', in *Tristan: Sechs Novellen* (Berlin: S. Fischer Verlag, 1903), accessed 28 August 2019, http://www.gutenberg.org/cache/epub/12053/pg12053.html.
37 Herz, 'Photo-Atelier Elvira', 38.
38 Endell, 'Architektonische Erstlinge', 300.
39 Berneike, 'Nichts ist unmöglich'.
40 Jacques Goudstikker's collection of old masters was looted by the National Socialists and only 200 of the 1,400 lost works were returned to the Dutch government after the

war. The Goudstikker heirs fought until 2006 before they finally won their restitution case. Peter T. Sutton, *Reclaimed: Paintings from the Collection of Jacques Goudstikker* (New Haven: Yale University Press, 2008).

41 Herz, 'Photo-Atelier Elvira', 64.
42 Ibid., 65.
43 Lida Gustava Heymann, *Erlebtes – Erschautes: Deutsche Frauen kämpfen für Freiheit, Recht und Frieden, 1850–1940* (Meisenheim: Anton Hain, 1972), 14.
44 Goudstikker quoted in Herz, 'Photo-Atelier Elvira', 65.
45 Herz, 'Photo-Atelier Elvira', 66.
46 For a brief discussion of photography in nineteenth-century Germany see Rolf Sachsse, 'German', in *Encyclopedia of Nineteenth-Century Photography*, ed. John Hannavy (London: Routledge, 2013), 581–6.
47 Heinz Gebhard, *Königlich Bayerische Hof-Photographie 1838–1918* (Munich: Verlag Richter, 1979), 79.
48 Hanni Schwarz, a woman photographer working in Berlin, quoted in Heike Foth, 'Fotografie als Frauenberuf (1840–1913)', in *Hof-Atelier Elvira*, 154. Foth's essay offers an excellent discussion of the educational and professional development of women photographers in the second half of the nineteenth century.
49 Anna Sachova, *Fotografie als Hilfsmittel in der Malerei von Franz Lenbach, Max Slevogt, Franz von Stuck, Alfons Mucha* (Munich: GRIN Verlag, 2014).
50 Foth, 'Fotografie als Frauenberuf', 155.
51 Fritz Hansen, 'Zur Frauenfrage in der Photographie', *Photographisches Wochenblatt Berlin* 1, (1898): 3.
52 Doris Obschernitzki, *Der Frau ihre Arbeit! Lette-Verein: Zur Geschichte einer Berliner Institution 1866–1986* (Berlin: Hentrich, 1987).
53 Sachsse, 'German', 582.
54 Herz, 'Photo-Atelier Elvira', 67.
55 Ibid., 79.
56 Timm Starl, 'Das "Starfoto" im 19. Jahrhundert', *Parnass* 2, no. 3 (März/April 1983): 60–4.
57 The fascinating link between avant-garde photography and Jugendstil warrants scholarly attention but exceeds the remit of this book. For a recent exhibition on Dora Kallmus/Madame d'Ora at the Neue Galerie, New York see Monika Faber, *Madame d'Ora* (New York: Prestel, 2020).
58 Foth, 'Fotografie als Frauenberuf', 165–8.
59 Fascinatingly, the association's current website prominently features a drawing of Endells's dragon from the Photo-Studio Elvira's façade; accessed 12 September 2019, https://www.fraueninteressen.de/.
60 Lange was a prominent member of Germany's moderate, middle-class wing of the women's movement. She also co-authored one of Germany's first accounts of the women's movement with her partner Gertrud Bäumers (1873–1954), the five-volume *Handbuch der Frauenbewegung* (Berlin: W. Moeser, 1901–6). James C. Albisetti, 'Could Separate be Equal? Helene Lange and Women's Education in Imperial Germany', *History of Education Quarterly* (Fall 1982): 301–17.

61 Sophie Goudstikker, 'Ika Freudenberg und die Frauenbewegung in München', *Die Frau* 9, no. 5 (February 1902): 292.

62 Marita Sturken and Lisa Cartwright, *Practices of Looking: An Introduction to Visual Culture* (Oxford: Oxford University Press, 2001), 251.

63 Kettler was instrumental in founding Germany's first secondary school for girls (*Mädchengymnasium*) in Karlsruhe in 1893, which exists to this day as the Lessing-Gymnasium. Marion Bock, 'Hedwig Kettler: Eine Wegbereiterin gymnasialer Mädchenbildung', *Hannoversche Geschichtsblätter* 44 (1990): 53–70.

64 Christa Elferich, 'Die Gründungsgeschichte (1894-1899) des Vereins für Fraueninteressen', in *Evas Töchter: Münchner Schriftstellerinnen und die modern Frauenbewegung 1894-1933*, ed. Ingvild Richardsen (Munich: Volk Verlag, 2018), 50.

65 For a history of the association see 'Vereinsgeschichte 1894 bis 2019', accessed 12 September 2019, https://www.fraueninteressen.de/der-verein/zur-geschichte-des-vereins/.

66 Statutes cited in Marita A. Panzer, 'Zwischen Küche und Katheder: Bürgerliche Frauen um die Jahrhundertwende 1890–1915', in *Frauenleben in Bayern*, ed. Sybille Krafft (Munich: Bayerische Landeszentrale für politische Bildungsarbeit, 1993), 109.

67 Ingvild Richardsen, 'Modern Sein 1894-1933', in *Evas Töchter*, 230–1.

68 Brigitte Bruns, 'Das dritte Geschlecht von Ernst von Wolzogen', *Hof-Atelier Elvira*, 171–90.

69 Bäumer quoted in Richardsen, 'Modern Sein', 230.

70 Harriet Anderson, *Utopian Feminism: Women's Movement in Fin-de-Siècle Vienna* (New Haven: Yale University Press, 1992).

71 'Vereinsgeschichte 1894 bis 2019'.

72 The play and photographs are reproduced in *Evas Töchter*, 158–87.

73 'Das Bürgerliches Gesetzbuch 1900 und die Rechte der Frauen', 01 January 1900, accessed 8 June 2020, https://www.zeitklicks.de/kaiserzeit/zeitklicks/zeit/alltag/frau-und-familie/das-buergerliche-gesetzbuch-1900-und-die-rechte-der-frauen/.

74 Heymann quoted in Zara S. Pfeiffer, 'Wir haben es gewagt', in *Ab nach München*, 21.

75 Ernst von Wolzogen, *Das Dritte Geschlecht* (Berlin: R. Eckstein, 1900), 157.

76 'Minna Cauer (1841-1922)', *Towards Emancipation: Women in Modern European History. A Digital Exhibition & Encyclopedia*, accessed 9 June 2020, http://hist259.web.unc.edu/minna-cauer-1841-1922/.

77 'Programm des Verbandes fortschrittlicher Frauenvereine', accessed 12 September 2019, https://www.digitales-deutsches-frauenarchiv.de/akteurinnen/verband-fortschrittlicher-frauenvereine#footnote3_lmd4by2.

78 Marti M. Lybeck, *Desiring Emancipation: New Women and Homosexuality in Germany, 1890–1933* (Albany: State University Press, 2014), 57.

79 Patricia Mazón, *Gender and the Modern Research University: The Admission of Women to German Higher Education, 1865-1914* (Stanford: Stanford University Press, 2003); Biddy Martin, *Women and Modernity: The (Life)Styles of Lou Andreas-Salomé* (Ithaca: Cornell University Press, 1991).

80 Bibiana Obler, *Intimate Collaborations: Kandinsky & Münter, Arp & Taeuber* (New Haven: Yale University Press, 2014).

81 Anderson, *Utopian Feminism*.

82 'Evas Töchter: Münchner Schriftstellerinnen und die modern Frauenbewegung 1894-1933', Monacensia im Hildebrandhaus, Munich 15 March–16 September 2018.

83 Elferich, 'Die Gründungsgeschichte', 52.

84 Pfeiffer, 'Wir haben es gewagt', 14.

85 Gertrud Bäumer, 'Das lebendige Haus', *Die Frau* 31, 7 (1924), reprinted in Herz, 'Photo-Atelier Elvira', 113.

86 Ursula Scheu and Anna Dünnebier, *Rebellion ist eine Frau: Anita Augspurg und Lida G. Heyman. Das schillernste Paar der Frauenbewegung* (Basel: Sphynx Verlag, 2002).

3 STUDENTS

EDUCATING WOMEN AT THE DEBSCHITZ SCHOOL

The argument that women did not produce geniuses is neither sound nor supportable.
Geniuses do not fall out of the sky, they must be given the opportunity to form and develop, [from which] women have thus far been excluded.

AUGUST BEBEL (1879)[1]

The third '*Bayerische Landes-Gewerbe-, Industrie- und Kunstausstellung*' (Bavarian Trade, Industry and Art Exhibition) took place in Nuremberg over the summer of 1906 (12 May to 15 October). This event is of interest to this study because its Applied Arts Pavilion allocated a sizeable space to student exhibits from a private art and applied arts school in Munich: the *Lehr- und Versuchs-Ateliers für angewandte und freie Kunst* (Studio for Teaching and Experimenting in Applied and Free Art), or Debschitz School for short. The exhibition as a whole was the final, and most comprehensive, effort in a series of events conceived to showcase the latest achievements in Bavarian manufacture ranging from industrial products to art objects (Figure 26).[2] Its organizers were keen to encourage a healthy sense of competition among contributors. By the late nineteenth century, the Franconian capital of Nuremberg was one of Bavaria's leading industrial centres and home to such prestigious firms as the pencil manufacturers Faber-Castell and Staedtler, the toy makers Issmeyer, Bub and Fleischmann, and the electronic companies Heller and Schuckert.[3] The exhibition format followed into the footsteps of the Universal Expositions but on a smaller and national scale. Nuremberg's city fathers created a new exhibition park for this event that covered 700,000 square metres

FIGURE 26 Main Boulevard, 'Bavarian Trade, Industry and Art Exhibition', Nuremberg 1906, in *Schweizerische Bauzeitung* 48, no. 11 (1906): 130. Eidgenönissische Technische Hochschule, Zurich.

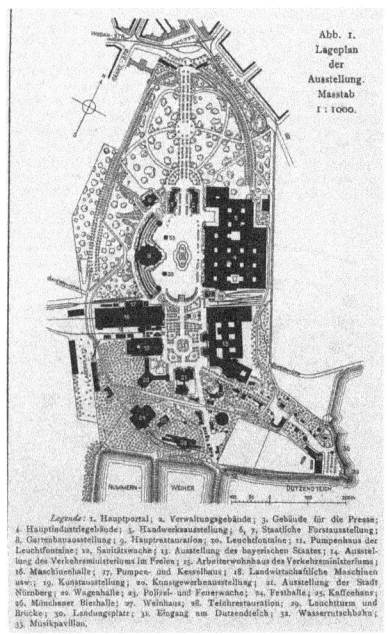

FIGURE 27 Map of the 'Bavarian Trade, Industry and Art Exhibition', Luitpoldhain, Nuremberg 1906, in *Schweizerische Bauzeitung* 48, no. 11 (1906): 129. Eidgenönissische Technische Hochschule, Zurich.

on the shores of the Dutzendteich, erected a series of pavilions with Jugendstil facades and christened the site Luitpoldhain in honour of Bavaria's prince Regent Luitpold (Figure 27).[4] The 1906 exhibition was a major critical success, and 2.5 million visitors came over the course of its five-month run.[5] The applied arts were allocated their own building right next to the Fine Arts Pavilion and surrounded by beautifully landscaped grounds that conveyed the impression of a country villa or pleasure palace (Plate 6). Bavarian craftsmen and manufacturers showcased their wares and tried to impress juries, visitors and potential clients with their skills. In terms of style, the exhibited objects ranged from historicism to Jugendstil, although historicism was definitely waning.

3.1 The Debschitz School at Dresden

The Debschitz School was an innovative educational institution founded in 1902 by Hermann Obrist and his collaborator from the United Workshops Wilhelm von Debschitz (1871–1948). Their space at the 1906 exhibition was once again curated as an aesthetically unified interior, which had become a signature design concept of the United Workshops, if not modern design in general (Chapter 1). The school's director Wilhelm von Debschitz oversaw the logistics, and the room itself was arranged by Friedrich Adler (1878–1942), who was one of the school's first students and by now one of its instructors. A short essay with seventy-two (!) illustrations celebrated the Debschitz School's varied contributions to the Nuremberg exhibition in one of Germany's premier design journals, *Dekorative Kunst*.[6] Staff and students from the school exhibited their work, and no distinction was made between the two. A photograph of the room curated by the Debschitz School shows Wilhelm von Debschitz' chandelier (his only contribution to the ensemble), Karl Schmoll von Eisenwerth's mythological painting cum mural above the doorway, Hermann Lochner's carpet and a beautiful glass vitrine filled with precious objects from the Debschitz School's highly accomplished silversmithing studio (Figures 28 and 29). The school was also given a section in the pavilion's adjacent mock 'cemetery', in which they displayed modern cast-iron and stonemason gravestones (Figure 30).

All of Munich's key Jugendstil designers participated in the Nuremberg exhibition because they recognized its potential to attract new clients and widen their production networks across crafts(wo)men and manufacturers beyond the geographical perimeters of Munich. Perhaps more importantly, the 1906 exhibition featured second-generation Jugendstil designers, most of whom had trained at the Debschitz School. This was significant for two reasons. First, it attested to the successful dissemination of applied arts reform and its embedded modern design language. And, second, it laid important groundwork for Jugendstil design's move towards a more restrained and less ornamental design language. The Nuremberg exhibition competed to a certain extent with the simultaneous 'Third Applied Arts Exhibition' in Dresden the same year (21 May to 31 October) that was organized as a national event but restricted to the applied arts. The Debschitz School did not send any design work to Dresden. This decision indicates that faculty members were keen to cultivate links with industry

FIGURE 28 Applied Arts Pavilion, Nuremberg 1906, Concept by Friedrich Adler, in *Dekorative Kunst* 14 (1906): 345. Museum für Kunst und Gewerbe, Hamburg, MKDH Z D.

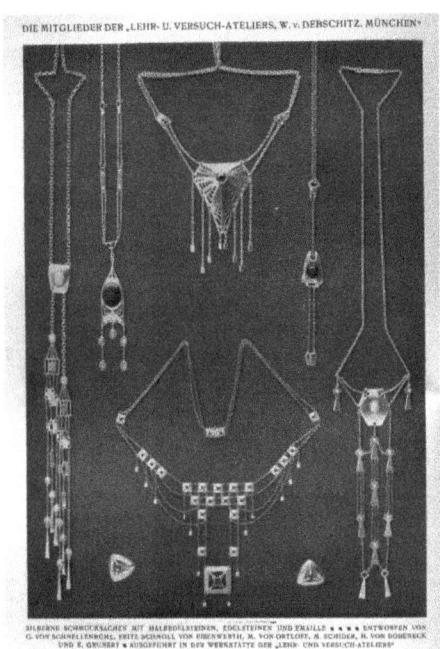

FIGURE 29 Debschitz School, Silver Work, Nuremberg 1906, in *Dekorative Kunst* 14 (1906): 362. Museum für Kunst und Gewerbe, Hamburg, MKDH Z D.

D. POLSTER GRABKREUZ FR. ADLER GRABSTEIN
AUSFÜHRUNG: E. HÄUSNER, MÜNCHEN   AUSFÜHRUNG: CONSTANTIN FRICK, MÜNCHEN

FIGURE 30 Dora Polster; Friedrich Adler, Gravestone, Nuremberg 1906, *Dekorative Kunst* 14 (1906): 351. Museum für Kunst und Gewerbe, Hamburg MKDH Z D.

that would generate future employment for their graduates' employment and reach a more diverse audience than the Dresden exhibition.

This chapter investigates the Debschitz School's pedagogy and curriculum in relation to Germany's hitherto limited educational and, consequently, professional opportunities for women. It discusses the Debschitz School's important contributions to ongoing debates over *Kunsterziehung* (art education) that engaged with applied arts reform and offered a rare opportunity for German women to become professional artists and designers. But first, a brief look at the Debschitz School's two founders to set the scene.

3.2 Hermann Obrist (1862–1927)

Hermann Obrist was born in 1862 as one of four children to the Swiss physician Carl Kaspar Obrist (1828–1901) and the Scottish aristocrat Alice Jane Grant Duff of Eden (1834–1891).[7] The family lived in Switzerland, and the children were raised in a typical upper-middle-class household that encouraged the pursuit of high culture but, in this instance, with a particular focus on music and literature.[8] Obrist initially followed in his father's footsteps and studied medicine at the Universities of Heidelberg (1884–6) and Berlin (1886–7). But he soon abandoned his academic studies and enrolled at the School of Applied Arts in Karlsruhe, which was then under the directorship of the historicist mural-painter Hermann Götz (1848–1901).[9] According to his autobiography, Obrist was a self-avowed loner and he quickly grew discontent with his formal education in Karlsruhe.[10] He embarked on a short apprenticeship in ceramics in Bürgel, Thuringia (1888) and then studied sculpture at the Académie Julian in Paris (1889–90). He also cut his time in Paris short but not before he had fallen in love with Auguste Rodin's work.[11] Obrist launched his career as a sculptor in Goethe's hometown of Weimar and subsidized his income by producing ceramics and metalwork. After inheriting his mother's wealth in 1891, Obrist relocated to Florence and set up a sculpture studio, where he taught himself to work in marble, terracotta and bronze.[12]

The following year, Obrist founded a Studio for *Kunststickerei* (art embroidery) with his mother's former companion, Berthe Ruchet (1855–1932). In his autobiography, Obrist noted that embroidery was best suited to translate 'his love of colour, of shiny materials and of a free [and] playful decorative fantasy'[13] into material form. As discussed in Chapter 1, Ruchet and Obrist's collaboration produced some of Jugendstil's most iconic embroideries that were first exhibited at the *Kunstsalon* Littauer in 1896. Obrist moved among Florence's artistic circles and became close friends with the American art historian Bernard Berenson (1865–1950) and his soon-to-be wife, the British art critic Mary Smith Costelloe aka Mary Logan (1864–1944). Logan was responsible for bringing German Jugendstil to the attention of readers of *The Studio*, and Berenson soon praised Obrist as the most important Munich artist of his day.[14]

Ruchet returned to Munich in 1894 and temporarily lived with Anita Augspurg and Sophia Goudstikker in the Photo-Studio Elvira. Obrist followed Ruchet to the Bavarian capital and married Marie-Louise Lampe (1867–1952) in 1898. Obrist and Ruchet mingled among Munich's progressive sociopolitical circles and became members of the *Verein für Foraueninteressen* that is examined in the previous chapter. Obrist built a marital villa in Schwabing's Carl-Theodor-Strasse 24 (architect: Alfred Pinagel; interiors: Obrist, Bernhard Pankok and Richard Riemerschmid) and commissioned August Endell to design a space for Ruchet's Munich embroidery workshop that also housed his own studio.[15] Once settled in Munich, Obrist became closely involved with early Jugendstil initiatives such as the cabinets at the 1897 Glaspalast exhibition and the 1898 founding of the *Vereinigte Werkstätten für Kunst im Handwerk*. Already during his lifetime, Obrist was considered to be Munich's most important pioneer of a modern German style that liberated the applied arts from its perceived enslavement to historicism.[16] Looking back in 1910, the influential art critic Karl Scheffler called him 'the first leader of the modern German decorative [movement] ... a facilitator, a workshop-founder, an author, and an artist'.[17]

This label continues to stick and few Jugendstil exhibitions or publications are complete without including his designs for Ruchet's embroideries 'Whiplash' or 'Fire Lilies' as progenitors of German Jugendstil (Figure 31). But this chapter

FIGURE 31 Hermann Obrist and Berthe Ruchet, Whiplash, silk embroidery on linen, 1896, in *Pan* 5 (1896): 325. Universitätsbibliothek Heidelberg, urn:nbn:de:bsz:16-diglit-35346.

will show that Obrist played an equally important role in late-nineteenth-century applied arts reform and was deeply committed to replacing staid historicist design practices with a modern style. With hindsight, he declared in 1907 that 'there is only one God. This God is called reaction. Our new applied arts were such a reaction. One has to nourish and protect them [applied arts], because they are the beginning, the seed of a new and free art of the future.'[18] Obrist pushed for art education and reshaped Munich's institutional landscape as one of the co-founders of the Debschitz School. This innovative teaching facility trialled an unconventional curriculum, admitted women when official educational institutions shut their doors to them and thus gave them access to a serious art education that paved their way for professional careers as artists, designers, photographers and/or educators.

3.3 Wilhelm von Debschitz (1871–1948)

Very few biographical details about Debschitz have survived, and his oeuvre has not yet been adequately assessed by design historians. This might be in part due to the fact that he was eclipsed by Obrist's importance in design history coupled with a lack of surviving work– even though photographs of his designs regularly featured in Germany's leading applied arts journals. His work ranged from graphic design to ceramics, decorative figurines and sculptural ornaments, metalwork including jewellery and furniture design. Debschitz was born into an old aristocratic family in

FIGURE 32 Wilhelm von Debschitz, Bedroom Furniture, 1898, in *Kunst und Handwerk* 49 (1898–9): 177. Universitätsbibliothek Heidelberg, urn:nbn:de:bsz:16-diglit-68434.

Görlitz (Silesia, today Saxony) in 1871. He was the third child of Lieutenant General Kolmar von Debschitz (1809–1878) and Pauline von dem Borne (1830–1912). As befitted a young man of his social rank, Debschitz entered the Prussian Cadets Corps Lichterfelde to train as an officer, but he dropped out in 1891 and moved to Munich.[19] Debschitz was rejected by the Academy of Fine Arts and enrolled in Heinrich Knorr's (1862–1944) private art school instead.[20] He started his career as a painter but soon embraced the applied arts instead. He first exhibited a suite of bedroom furniture at the annual exhibition of the Bavarian Applied Arts Association in 1898 (Figure 32). He became a member of the United Workshops the same year and married the renowned Munich portrait photographer Wanda von Kunowski (1870–1935), who would be in charge of the Debschitz School's photography studio from 1905 onwards.[21] In 1900, the then director of the United Workshops F. A. O. Krüger (1868–1939) tried to convince Debschitz to take over his directorship, but Debschitz politely declined because he wanted to stay focused on his school.[22]

3.4 The *Lehr- und Versuchs-Ateliers für angewandte und freie Kunst*

On 3 January 1902, the *Lehr- und Versuchs-Ateliers für angewandte und freie Kunst*, or Debschitz School for short, opened its doors in a former carpentry workshop in Schwabing (Hohenzollern Strasse 7a).[23] Obrist had long been thinking about ways in which to tackle Germany's outdated educational systems in art and design. He had recently delivered a carefully crafted lecture at the 1901 *'Kunsterziehungstag'* (Conference on Art Education) in Dresden, and he was eager to push ahead with concrete measures. The 1901 event brought together academics, schoolteachers and museum officials to discuss how art education could be delivered more effectively within the institutional parameters of Germany's secondary school system.[24] Art education and applied arts reform, as discussed in the previous chapter, were closely intertwined in late-nineteenth-century Germany. Their respective advocates challenged traditional hierarchies between the fine arts and the applied arts – and by extension the German Empire's entrenched institutional landscape with its rigid curricula (fine arts academies, applied arts schools, polytechnical institutes, etc.).[25] Participants of the Dresden conference argued that German education was too focused on the written word (intellect) and pedagogues needed to put more emphasis on manual skills. The buzz word of the day was *Anschauung*, which harkened back to Immanuel Kant's eighteenth-century idea of an unmediated grasp, by which he meant an understanding of the external world through sensory experience in time and space.[26] The German word *Anschauung* connotes both literally seeing/viewing and understanding/conceiving.

Obrist was well versed in philosophical debates and, newly energized by the 1901 Conference, proposed a workshop system modelled on medieval guilds as a way out of Germany's pedagogical impasse. His close involvement in the United Workshops over the past three years provided Obrist with a road map for his new enterprise. Workshops, in his view, were ideally suited for his educational goals because they prioritized manual instruction over intellectual pursuit. For Obrist, practice always outweighed theory, be that in the learning of a language or the acquisition of artistic skills.[27] Based on this conviction, he advocated an 'artistic art education [that] should mean teaching the essential and varied elements of every category and not indiscriminately teaching a convention, even if it is a good one'.[28] It should, therefore, come as no surprise that Obrist and Debschitz turned to a workshop model as the basis of their joint educational venture. Obrist was not alone in his reform efforts and the Debschitz School represented one of a series of private art and design schools that emerged during the first decade of the twentieth century. Other privately funded schools established around this time were: Bernhard Pankok's Teaching Workshop for Applied Arts in Stuttgart (1902), Henry van de Velde's Applied Arts Seminar in Weimar (1902), August Endell's Form-School in Berlin (1904), Lothar von Kunowski's School in Munich (1902) as well as Wassily Kandinsky's Phalanx-Schule (1901), which was located right across the street from the Debschitz School. Despite this impressive range of initiatives, the Debschitz School was one of the first and most successful endeavours of its kind.[29] Each of these private institutions competed for the same student populations that were drawn from the *Bildungsbürgertum* (educated middle classes) and the upper echelons of

German society. The Debschitz School started very small, and its first intake in 1902 was made up of only four students: Friedrich Adler (1878–1942), Dora Polster (1884–1958), Hans Schmithals (1878–1964) and Wolfgang von Wersin (1882–1976). But within four years, the Debschitz School had established itself as the German Empire's largest private art and design school with 249 paying students.[30]

Obrist's idea for opening a private teaching facility was rooted in the United Workshops' original remit to include a teaching arm. In June of 1901, a short news bulletin in the Bavarian Applied Arts' Association's monthly journal *Kunst und Handwerk* informed readers that a *Lehrwerkstätte* (workshop-school) was finally about to open its doors under the auspices of the United Workshops. The notice promised that 'contrary to conventional applied arts schools, which offer artistic instruction to craftsmen, [the teaching-workshop] offered professional male and female artists instruction in the applied arts'.[31] This represented a radical volte-face of conventional art education, where women were largely excluded and applied artists were predominantly tasked with studying museum collections and drawing. This approach directly emerged from historicism's *Vorbilder* system (learning by example).[32] In the end, the United Workshops failed to realize their teaching-workshop, most likely due to strained finances. Instead, the Debschitz School was set up by two of the United Workshops' founding members. In addition to its important pedagogical mission, the school had to also be financially viable and the timing seemed just right. The idea of a workshop school had been floated among applied arts reformers since the early 1890s. On a more personal level, Obrist's collaboration with Berthe Ruchet had just come to an end (1900) and, as previously mentioned, Obrist's art educational fervour had been stoked by his recent participation at the Dresden conference. Debschitz might already have been teaching at the Munich branch of the famous Skærbæk weaving workshops and was looking for further teaching opportunities.[33] Be that as it may, Obrist and Debschitz made perfect business partners: Obrist had the philosophical and pedagogical vision, while Debschitz contributed his artistic talent and business acumen.

3.5 The curriculum

A detailed discussion of the Debschitz School's curriculum and pedagogy has already been offered by Zeynep Çelik Alexander, Dagmar Rinker and Beate Ziegert.[34] Hence, what follows is a focused spotlight on some of the school's key initiatives as they impacted women's educational opportunities in Wilhelmine Germany. The United Workshops had carved out space for women makers that enabled them to have a professional career, but it failed to overcome some of the deeply seated ideological and institutional limitations that curtailed the blossoming of women designers during the time period in question – and that, it might be argued, continue to haunt the design world well into the present. Obrist and Debschitz were regularly reminded by their feminist friends like Augspurg and Goudstikker of the gender imbalances inherent in art education across central Europe. Through their exposure to Munich's women's movement and their membership in the *Vereinigung für Fraueninteressen*, they became increasingly committed to providing middle-class women with better educational opportunities that would eventually enable them to secure viable careers as professional artists and designers. Obrist and Debschitz were undoubtedly driven by their progressive views on the role of women in German art and society, but they were also pragmatists. Ultimately, the Debschitz School was a private institution and needed to attract fee-paying students. What better way to increase student numbers than by opening their doors to a segment of German society that was virtually excluded from official art institutions?

The Debschitz School's formal name *Das Lehr- und Versuchs-Ateliers für angewandte und freie Kunst* indicated two of its core principles. One, Debschitz and Obrist avoided the use of the word 'school' and called their institution a studio (*Atelier*) instead. This allowed its founders to present a more fluid and experimental site than state art schools like Munich's Academy of Fine Arts and their rigid curricula and hierarchies of media. Emphasis was put on a more equal relationship between teacher and student as well as the applied and the fine arts. Debschitz and Obrist purposely listed *Angewandte Kunst* (applied arts) before the *Freie Kunst* (fine arts) in their school's name. They avoided the term *Kunstgewerbe* because of its persistent associations with historicism, and they were keen to stress that students would acquire transferable skills and technical expertise. At the Debschitz School, knowledge was garnered through practical instruction, working with diverse materials, critical dialogue and experimentation. True to their word, Debschitz and Obrist demanded from their staff that they teach across the fine and applied arts. Students were enrolled without specializing in a particular medium form the outset.[35] Today, foundation courses taught at art and design colleges across the world follow this model, but at the time, this set-up signified a radical departure from traditional curricula.

The Debschitz School's pedagogy was organized around the concept of *Gestaltung*, a notoriously difficult term to translate but, in this context, probably best described as 'design'.[36] The term *Gestaltung* also evokes processes of subject-formation and would soon be formalized through Gestalt-Psychology (1912) and its ongoing endeavours to understand the organization and processes of cognition.[37] Another important influence on their pedagogy was Great Britain's South Kensington System, which Obrist had encountered during his travels to England and Scotland in 1887.[38] It is not known if Obrist visited the Glasgow School of Art (GSA) during his time in Scotland, but he might well have done so given his interests in pedagogy, the applied arts and his close links to Scotland through his mother's family. At the time, it was under the directorship of the visionary Francis Henry Newbery (1855–1946; director of GSA 1885–1918), who drastically modernized the school's curriculum and is often credited with nourishing the Glasgow Style (Chapter 4).[39]

Students enrolled in the Debschitz School for a total of four years. Until the Bavarian State began to subsidize the school in 1912, tuition was considerably higher than at the Munich Academy of Fine Arts or the Applied Arts School.[40] The so-called *Einführungskurs*, or preliminary course, was mandatory for all students regardless of their eventual specialization in the applied or fine arts. This preliminary course served as the model for the Bauhaus' famous *Vorkurs* run by the Swiss painter Johannes Itten (1888–1967) in 1919. As mentioned earlier, the Debschitz School represented an important, albeit under-acknowledged, early experiment in the curricular integration of a fine arts and design education that later became the hallmark of the Bauhaus. This is not to suggest a simplistic teleology between the two but to draw attention to important earlier pedagogical experiments with important repercussions. Debschitz and Obrist offered, what today might be called, an interdisciplinary approach that grounded students in drawing (*zeichnerisches Entwerfen*), model making (*Modellieren*) and design (*Darstellungstechnik*). Students were only allowed to move into medium-specific workshops after three to twelve months, depending on their unique abilities and work ethic. An advertisement in Berlin's *National Zeitung* explains that 'students should have the opportunity to unhurriedly orient themselves across the whole spectrum of the arts so that they are able to determine what best suits their talent before committing to a specialisation'.[41]

Debschitz and Obrist originally delivered all the teaching but soon hired experts to lead specific workshops as their enrolment numbers increased. Else Hartmann-Sapatka (1878–1962), for example, was in charge of the workshops for ceramics and metalwork (1902), and Hans Schmithals took over textile and wallpaper design the following year.[42] Where possible, Obrist and Debschitz hired graduates from their school. The Debschitz School offered workshops in ceramics, graphic arts, metalwork, textiles and wood (Plate 7). This photograph shows the Metal Workshop in the early twentieth century and attests to the unmistakable presence of female students. After the school's move to larger premises in 1903, Eugen Meyer's sculpture school was integrated and Debschitz's wife Wanda Kunowski (1870–1935) opened one of Germany's first photography studios housed within the institutional parameters of a design school.[43] Beate Ziegert observed in one of the first critical analyses of the Debschitz School that its workshop system offered instruction across a range of disciplines that were 'otherwise available only at differentiated and specialised professional institutions' and fostered a close interaction between teachers and students that was impossible in oversubscribed government schools.[44] Instructors at the Debschitz School were to nourish their students' artistic potential, not impose a fixed curriculum.

In 1904, Debschitz described the school's teaching method and pedagogical impetus in a lengthy article published in *Dekorative Kunst*.[45] He emphasized the importance of tapping into his students' emotional, intellectual and technical abilities so that they could apprehend, process and eventually consolidate the external world within their design process. Students were tasked with drawing exercises that encouraged them to understand and extrapolate nature's inherent rhythms, lines, harmonies, movements and structures. Debschitz illustrated this principle with his now-famous drawing of 'An Oak Husk with Eight Different Effects' that shows aforesaid oak husk in different stages ranging from weightlessness to rise and fall (Figure 33).[46] Debschitz postulated that 'a flower, a seashell, a scraggy branch, a root, a skeleton were organised structures full of laws, full of structures, full of expressed forces, linear, plastic, constructive movements of unheard-of wealth and astonishing diversity'.[47] He wanted his students to capture this diversity through an act of *nacherleben* (experience) rather than *nachzeichnen* (copying).[48] Obrist used a sketch by one of his promising female students, Laura Lange, to illustrate his point (Figure 34). This image can be read in numerous ways. It might be a grasshopper with organic matter on its legs and wings, or it might be a grid with leaves draping over it, or it might be neither. Debschitz believed that the value of art and design depended on the 'value of the sensation that it evokes'.[49] The Debschitz School thus instigated a curriculum that was driven by what art historian Zeynep Çelik Alexander aptly characterized as

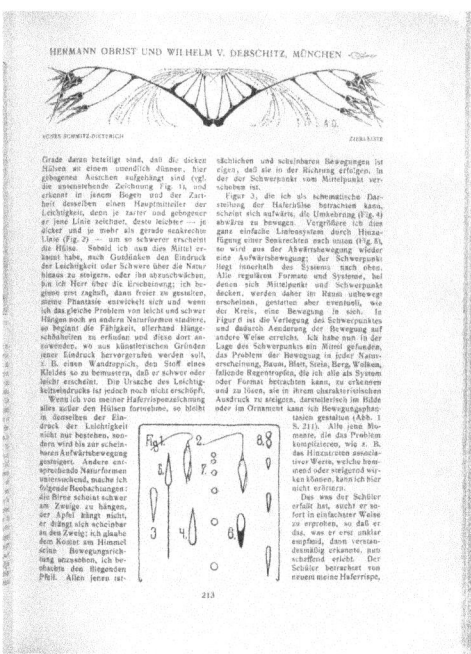

FIGURE 33 Wilhelm von Debschitz, oak husk, 'Eine Methode des Kunstunterrichts', in *Dekorative Kunst* 12 (1904): 213. Museum für Kunst und Gewerbe, Hamburg, MKDH Z D.

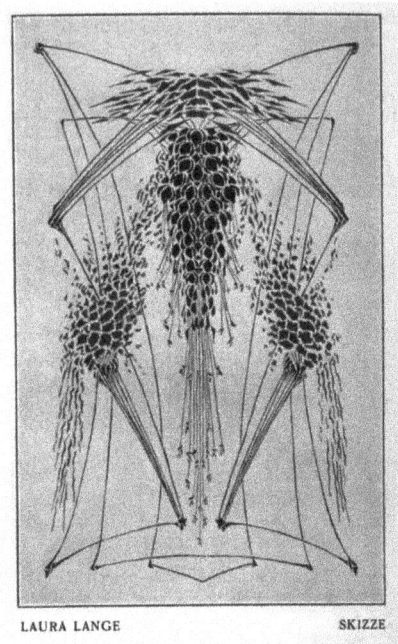

FIGURE 34 Laura Lange, Debschitz School, sketch, in *Dekorative Kunst* 12 (1904): 212. Museum für Kunst und Gewerbe, Hamburg, MKDH Z D.

'kinaesthetic learning' by which she meant that 'students at the Debschitz School were to develop a feeling for the rhythm of their hand movements and for an instinctual *Augenmass* (visual measure).'[50] In short, haptic experience trumped visual instruction. The Debschitz School was also keen on extracurricular activities such as excursions to manufacturers and factories, evening lectures open to any interested party and lavish parties (especially during Munich's carnival season). Similarities with the later Bauhaus are again plain to see. Georg Jacob Wolf fondly remembered the Debschitz School's cultural activities in his obituary for Hermann Obrist: 'All of Schwabing's Bohème was present. But so were serious "individuals from the city", art theoreticians, art historians, and other successful members of the field.'[51]

3.6 Women at the Debschitz School

Women made up a large proportion of the Debschitz School's student and staff bodies. Some of the school's most famous graduates were Dadaist and textile designer Sophie Taeuber-Arp (1889–1943); ceramicists Clara von Ruckteschell-Trueb (1882–1969) and Gertrud Kraut (1883–1980); graphic designer Dora Polster (1884–1958); lace makers Margarethe Bardt and

Hedwig von Dobeneck; painter and graphic designer Laura Lange (1868–?), and interior designer Olga Reynier(1874–1971). But it is important to not get distracted by a cursory nod towards a few women who made it into design history's deeply gendered canons. The Debschitz School produced so many more female designers, who had rich professional careers, actively exhibited, were discussed by contemporary critics and became progressive teachers. But as Julie Johnson so evocatively investigates in her book on forgotten Viennese women artists, their careers, institutional affiliations and critical successes have been practically eradicated from historical records.[52] Every single surviving photograph of the Debschitz School's workshops features spaces that were populated by women students, including the drawing studio, which, at the time, was very controversial because of ongoing debates over the unseemliness of life drawing classes for the 'fairer sex' that served as one of the rationales for excluding women from fine art academies across central Europe for most of the nineteenth century.[53] Even as sceptical a critic as Georg Fuchs had conceded in his 1927 obituary to Obrist that

> Obrist appeared as a liberator of our women. How many women are possibly out there who simply do not think of inventing ingenious motives for embroidery, who do not deploy their innate good taste as a source of their elevated artistic endeavours, because they have never heard that one can embroidery something else beyond mechanical copying of examples (*Vorlagen*).[54]

Fuchs's concluding observation of women mechanically copying motifs rather than designing these from scratch alluded to ongoing debates over the issue of dilettantism that were central to German Applied Arts Reform from the 1860s onwards. The term was deployed by reformers (who decried the lack of educational opportunities for women) as well as cultural conservatives (who considered women to be incapable of original thought). On a most basic level, dilettantism referred to the dabbling in the arts and sciences for pleasure rather than professional pursuit. Johann Wolfgang von Goethe and Friedrich Schiller famously distinguished between artists, art lovers and connoisseurs in their 1799 essay 'On Dilettantism'.[55] It soon became a deeply gendered term that singled out middle-class women but refused to acknowledge the lack of educational opportunities for young women as one of its root causes.[56] August Bebel's compelling impeachment cited at the opening of this chapter that 'geniuses do not fall from the sky but must be given the opportunity to be educated and develop'[57] drew attention to this very conundrum. The Debschitz was a private initiative that offered early-twentieth-century women from across central Europe new educational and professional opportunities that were so desperately lacking in the German Empire's official, that is state-funded, education system.

3.7 Art and design education in Munich around 1900

By 1900, Munich was home to two of central Europe's most important art educational institutions: the Academy of Fine Arts founded by Bavaria's king Max Joseph in 1808 and the *Königliche Kunstgewerbeschule* (Royal Applied Arts School) established by Max Joseph's great-grandson Ludwig II in 1868. A miniscule number of women were initially allowed to enrol in the academy, but its doors closed again to women from 1854 to 1919, at which point the Weimar Republic's Constitution mandated 'equality between men and women'.[58] The academy lagged behind German universities, which, after more than forty years of pressure from women's groups (Chapter 2), finally allowed German women to matriculate in 1909.[59] Ernst Heilemann's caricature of a group of female students in the Munich satirical magazine *Simplicissimus* reveals the disparaging attitudes of many contemporaries – male and female – towards women at universities (Plate 8). Its masculinized protagonists flaunt all bourgeois conventions of 'proper' female behaviour, including calling one of their members a piglet for getting engaged and pleading her removal from their association.

Common reasons cited for the persistent exclusion of women were a lack of appropriate facilities and moral anxieties over lecture content. These arguments were made in addition to the age-old promulgations of women's ostensibly inferior intellectual abilities caused by smaller brains, which had most recently been rehashed by the prominent Berlin neurologist Paul Julius Möbius in his offensively titled essay 'On the Physiological Imbecility of Women' (1900).[60] Möbius railed against feminist demands to allow female students into anatomy theatres and medical lectures. His work supplied ample ammunition to deem women physically, mentally and intellectually unsuited for the pursuit of a serious career in any field, including art and design. Möbius's anxieties were obviously in part driven by a fear of competition from capable women. These discourses bolstered German bourgeois ideologies that destined proper middle-class women as wives, mothers and heads of households – even as late-nineteenth-century economic and demographic realities increasingly challenged these gender roles.[61] Ferdinand von Rezniček's caricature titled 'Mother's Woes' aptly encapsulates these severely limiting bourgeois gender norms in its caption: 'What I wanted to tell you a long time ago, my Child; don't overdo it with your painting studies. One could actually be led to believe that you want to make a profession of it.'

3.8 The Royal Applied Arts School (1868)

If entry into the Academy of Fine Arts was essentially foreclosed to women, then where could they turn in search of a professional education? The Royal Applied Arts School (RAAS) offered a promising alternative because it allowed women to enrol in some of its courses. Art historian Claudia Schmalhofer published a detailed analysis of this important public institution from which this chapter draws a few key points that impacted the private Debschitz School.[62] The RAAS was founded on 1 October 1868 as a state-supported educational facility that was directly geared towards the professionalization of the applied arts.[63] The school was located in Schwabing's Louisen Strasse 37 and moved to a purpose-designed building by the prominent Munich architect Leonhard Romeis (1854–1904) on Richard Wagner Strasse 10 in 1902. Protracted discussions going back to the First Universal Exhibition in 1851 had long decried the state of affairs within Germany's applied arts, which was seen to be lagging behind English and French production in terms of economic heft and aesthetic value.[64] The Bavarian *Kunstgewerbeverein* (Applied Arts Association) was in part founded in 1851 as a response to the London fiasco and tasked to advance the quality of handicraft (*Handwerk*) through education, training, publications and exhibitions.[65] The association had an associated *Zeichnungs- und Modellierschule* (Drawing and Modelling School) that instructed emerging designers via the study of *Vorbilder,* that is, aesthetically valuable art and design objects from the past.[66]

Despite the fact that drawing represented one of the few artistic realms within which nineteenth-century women had some agency, the Applied Arts Association's School admitted male students only. This exclusion motivated a group of progressive advocates for better educational opportunities for middle-class girls and women to open a privately funded school, the *Kunstschule für Mädchen* (Art School for Girls), in 1868. In a funding application to the Bavarian State, its supporters explained that they intended to offer 'the female gender further educational opportunities in art and the applied arts to create a basis for autonomous earnings'.[67] Prospective students had to be at least fifteen years of age and make their case for admission before a panel. The curriculum was divided into classes for beginners and advanced students, who could be instructed in oil painting. These classes were supported by weekly lectures in art history.[68] The Art School for Girls attracted students from across Germany and abroad (by 1870, twenty-two out of fifty-five students were international).[69] The school's success was used by its supporters as leverage to petition the Bavarian Parliament for better funding based on the argument that Munich's reputation as one of central Europe's leading art centres was at stake. How could Munich afford to not tackle 'one of the large social questions within the arts, and open an educational institution for women that is worthy of a city of such repute?'[70] An unforeseen, albeit welcome, consequence of these lobbying efforts was the school's incorporation into the RAAS on 1 October 1872 under the jurisdiction of a *weibliche Abteilung* (women's department).[71]

3.9 The *weibliche Abteilung* at the Royal School of Applied Arts (1872)

The RAAS's *weibliche Abteilung* in essence offered the same syllabus as its predecessor, the Art School for Girls, but within the context of a more prestigious state institution. Under the long and effective directorship of the historicist architect Emil Lange (1875–1913), the RAAS earned an international reputation as one of Germany's leading training institutions for male and female students alike.[72] Clementine von Braunmühl (1833–1918) was hired in 1872 as Germany's first drawing instructor employed at a state institution.[73] This appointment was an extraordinary act on the part of the RAAS's first director Hermann Mey. Braunmühl was in charge of technical drawing classes and ornamental drawing while being taxed with the job of enforcing appropriate behaviour among the women in her charge. Female students at the RAAS underwent a somewhat comparable education to their male counterparts but they received one less year of tuition – three years for women versus four for men.[74] As well, the school curtailed some of the course choices open to women and, for example, steered female students away from the pursuit of a career in painting by prohibiting access to anatomical studies and life drawing. Women who were committed to become professional painters or sculptors were, therefore, forced to enrol in fee-charging private art schools or teaching-studios run by academic artists. Upon graduation from RAAS, employment opportunities also engendered a considerable difference between female and male graduates. Women had only two options: they could either work as a *Zeichenlehrerin* (drawing teacher) or find employment in the drawing department of a manufacture where they operated under a male designer. In this context, it should be noted that drawing represented a crucial aspect of the Enlightenment notion of *Bildung* (education in, or attainment of, culture), which played a key role in the constructions of class and gender norms in the German Empire.[75] Some graduates were subsequently hired back into the RAAS to deliver components of its curriculum or became drawing instructors at primary and secondary school levels. For the most part, female drawing instructors were relegated to teach at private institutions rather than following into their male counterpart's footsteps of entering well-paid and secure positions as public servants. The textile designer Else Jaskolla (1881–1957) became Germany's first female professor at a State Applied Arts School as late as 1920.[76]

3.10 The Munich Women Artists' Association

Advocates of women's education around 1900 faced a quintessential conundrum that continues to haunt gender equality activists to this day: Should women be admitted into existing institutions or should they create their own pedagogical sites? The *Frauenabteilung* at the RAAS offered a hybrid solution that proved increasingly unsatisfactory for Munich's more progressive women artists and students. Its head instructor, Clementine von Braunmühl, recalled in her memoires that 'since the incorporation of our private Art School into the State Applied Arts

School, women artists had depended on private tuition and lacked the motivation, the support of communal working'.[77] This led her to band together with a group of fellow women artists and launch the Munich *Künstlerinnen-Verein* (Women Artists Association) in 1882.[78] The association's primary aim was to support women's art and design practice, to create a community of like-minded professionals and to set professional standards.[79] To achieve these goals, the association offered members practical support (health insurance, loans and scholarships, funded competitions) and, from 1899 onwards, the sanctum of a clubhouse. The latter served as an important social space within an urban fabric that limited women's physical movement via strictly policed conventions and etiquette. Its carnival parties, for example, were legendary, which says a lot because the competition in Munich during *Fasching* was very stiff. As any other association of this kind, the *Künstlerinnen-Verein* organized regular lectures across a wide range of topics and formed mock juries to critique members' work before it was submitted to an exhibition.[80] To become a member, potential candidates had to submit a portfolio and attend an interview. Two types of membership were offered: an ordinary one that was extended to practicing artists and an extraordinary one by invitation to prominent members of Munich society and 'friends of the arts'.[81] Typically, networking constituted a crucial aspect of the *Künstlerinnen-Verein*'s remit and culminated in the 1908 founding of the *Bund deutscher und österreichischer Künstlerinnen-Vereine* (Association of German and Austrian Women Artists).[82]

The association's arguably most significant contribution to Munich's late-nineteenth-century art world was its campaign for a *Damenakademie* (Ladies' Academy), which came to fruition in 1884. Yvette Deyseve offers an exhaustive analysis of this important institution.[83] The Ladies' Academy essentially replicated the Munich Academy of Fine Arts' curriculum and provided instruction in anatomy and life drawing, painting technique and materials, perspective and art history. Its raison d'être was the provision of professional education on a par with what was on offer at the Academy of Fine Arts. Progressive male artists who supported women's access to education taught at the Ladies' Academy. Its most famous and sought-after instructor was undoubtedly the beguiling painter Maximilian Dasio (1865–1954), who also held a professorship at the RAAS. Initially, the virtually exclusive male teaching body was borne out of necessity because of a lack of female instructors but as time progressed, more women graduates filled the academy's ranks. The academy was subsidized by the Bavarian State Government from 1894 onwards, which made it possible to expand its physical location and its curriculum. Despite this subsidy, tuition fees were considerably more expensive than those at the Fine Arts Academy. During the 1890s, for example, tuition at the *Damenakademie* was 400 marks per annum compared to 70 marks at the Academy of Fine Arts.[84] Student numbers fell when women were given conditional university access in 1903 and the Ladies' Academy closed in 1920 after the Academy of Fine Arts opened its studios and lecture halls to women. It seems that in bringing to fruition the *Künstlerinnen-Verein*'s objective of granting women equal access to a professional training in the arts, the Ladies' Academy had manoeuvred itself out of existence. The *Künstlerinnen-Verein* remained active until 1967.[85]

3.11 Women at the Debschitz School

How then did Debschitz's and Obrist's school fit into this increasingly complex network of educational opportunities for women artists at the turn of the last century? The Munich institutions offering women an education in art and/or design can essentially be divided into two types. They either attempted to integrate female students into existing curricula and structures such as the *Frauenabteilung* at the RAAS, or they created new institutional frameworks that were specifically geared towards women such as the *Damen-Akademie* (Ladies' Academy). Art historian Megan M. Brandow-Faller formulated the productive concept of 'institutional equality of difference' to describe how and why Viennese women around 1900 set up their own separate yet equal institutions in an art world that continued to be dominated by male privilege.[86] The Debschitz School falls somewhere in between what Joan Wallach Scott identified as one of feminism's most divisive debates over difference versus equality: 'should women be entitled to equal treatment [...] because of or in spite of their difference?'[87] On the one hand, the Debschitz School was privately funded and required students to pay annual tuition fees, even after the Bavarian government conceded some state funding in 1912. On the other hand, it implemented a progressive and strict curriculum that could easily compete with the Academy of Fine Arts and the Royal School of Applied Arts. Indeed, its preliminary course was ahead of its time and, as previously discussed, offered a combination of applied arts and fine arts practices, techniques and material knowledge. In addition, the Debschitz School employed some of Munich's most progressive artists and designers, including its own female graduates who were well familiar with the school's reformist curriculum. The waters in the 'difference versus equality dilemma' were thus muddied in the institutional set-up and curriculum delivery of the Debschitz School. Design historians might be better served to look at its achievements and agenda from within the school's own historical context.

Women were given hitherto unimaginable educational access as well as professional prospects at the Debschitz School. As previously mentioned, Obrist had close personal ties to Germany's women's movement. His politically progressive views envisioned a fairer and more equal world. His school offered a space where female and male students were educated by the same teachers, worked side by side in workshops and were granted access to the same exhibition opportunities – as evidenced by the Debschitz School's entries into the 1906 Nuremberg exhibition. The school employed female and male instructors as far as possible because, despite the Debschitz School's progressive curriculum, women obviously continued to be disadvantaged in the German Empire's schooling system as a whole. Nonetheless, the Debschitz School represented an extraordinary intervention into Germany's strictly patrolled art world that, at most, allowed women to work as drawing teachers. Female students were exposed to opportunities in manufacture through fieldtrips to Bavaria's key applied arts industries. Women showcased their art and design alongside men in exhibitions organized either by the Debschitz School faculty or by any of the German Empire's applied arts associations. All students were encouraged to submit work to Germany's numerous design competitions. In 1903, for example, Bruckmann's journal *Dekorative Kunst* specifically invited the Debschitz School to send in designs for the journal's cover and the best entries were published in the journal.[88] Women formed an integral part of the school's many social activities, which allowed them to network and establish key connections with patrons and fellow artists in Munich's thriving art world. Lastly, Debschitz and Obrist believed that economic security provided the foundation stone for women's independence. Obrist observed that 'as women grow tired of their subjugation to parents, husbands, relatives and society as a whole, [they] are looking for their own income, their own life, and they are no longer willing to live an echo-life'.[89]

These convictions motivated Obrist and Debschitz to cultivate relationships with local and national workshops and manufacturers to encourage them to take on student designs into their production. Students kept the profit from any designs that went into production – after Obrist and/or Debschitz took a commission and the manufacturing cost was covered.[90] Obrist left the school in 1904 because he was growing increasingly deaf and struggled with the day-to-day responsibilities of teaching and tutoring. Debschitz opened the *Ateliers und Werkstätten für Angewandte Kunst* (Studios and Workshops for Applied Arts) in 1906, which functioned as a commercial arm of the school and produced designs by staff and students directly rather than selling them through manufacturers.[91] This initiative was followed in 1908–9 by the founding of the *Keramische Werkstätten München-Herrsching* (Ceramic Workshops Munich-Herrsching).[92] An analysis of the commercial arms of the Debschitz School exceeds the parameters of this chapter but warrants design history's attention. Without a doubt, the Debschitz School offered its students hitherto untapped commercial opportunities that enabled them to build an economic foundation for a viable professional career. It has been suggested that this 'commercialization' of the Debschitz School might have led to a widening rift between Debschitz and Obrist that had been brewing over workload allocation. Debschitz recalled in his unpublished memoires that 'Obrist had time for the school only after his own work, whereas I found time for my own work only after the school. The result was that I naturally received a predominance which Obrist seemingly could not tolerate.'[93] Be that as it may, the Debschitz School's commercial orientation was, of course, pivotal to its female student cohort and attracted women who were no longer content with being sidelined in the German Empire's design world.

3.12 Emilie Butters (1879–1961)

The ceramicist Emilie Butters offers an interesting case study to illustrate some of the dynamics outlined previously. Butters enrolled in the Debschitz School in 1905 and embarked on a successful career at the *Keramischen Werkstätten* Munich-Herrsching, located on Lake Ammersee, approximately forty-five minutes south-west of Munich. The *Keramischen Werkstätten* were founded by the young entrepreneur Otto Koebke (1882–?), who was a keen believer in the workshop system and wanted to start a business that produced *Nutz-Keramik* (functional ceramics) with artistic value but affordable prices. He had no known design background and turned to the Debschitz School for help. He hired Emilie Butters, who had just completed her studies and was keen to help Koebke to get his enterprise off the ground. Butters was born in 1879 in Neustadt on the River Haardt as one of seven daughters of the local schoolteacher Gerold Butters and his wife Lina. Her family supported her education, and she studied to become a French teacher. In 1896, she moved to Munich to matriculate in the *Frauen-Abteilung* of the RAAS. After graduation, she taught drawing for several years as a private tutor and a schoolteacher (1898–1905). She enrolled in the Debschitz School in 1905 to fulfil her ambitions of a serious artistic career. In a letter to a friend, she wrote, 'I finally realised my plan and work, by which I mean study, at the *Lehr- und Versuchsanstalt* and I think I found what I was looking for over such a long time.'[94] Butters already possessed drawing skills from her previous time at the Royal Academy but, keeping in line with the Debschitz School's pedagogy, she had to complete the foundational course before being granted permission to turn her hand to different applied arts techniques. This underscores the Debschitz School's emphasis on unlearning conventional approaches and methods to art making.

Obrist had retired from the Debschitz School by the time Butters enrolled, but she immediately found her footing and enjoyed her education as much as the expansion of her social horizon. She commented on the conducive, creative atmosphere at the Debschitz School, where female and male students freely exchanged ideas with one another as well as with their instructors. In a letter to her parents written in 1905, Butters described a typical day at the school as follows:

> I started to work, that is to say that I drew a leaf, while the hall filled with young men and women (*Männlein und Weiblein*), all of whom immediately set about drawing all the available dried leaves, just like me. [...] Around 10:30 Herr v. D. [Debschitz] arrived and talked to us. [...] I cannot tell you everything he was telling us but rest assured that I love how he converses with us. We are all very

studious and Herr v. D. puts great emphasis on the study of nature. We had to draw each leaf in all of its details of contours and veins.[95]

Butters treasured her time at the Debschitz School but due to her disadvantaged social background, money was always in short supply. Wilhelm Debschitz must have recognized her potential because he first waived Butter's student fees and then allowed her to offer private tuition to her fellow students in modelling (*Modellieren*).[96] This actually went against the Debschitz School's statutes that forbade students to teach at the school, but it points to Debschitz's compassionate nature. In 1907, Debschitz opened a ceramics workshop at the school and put his recent graduate Clara Rueckteschell-Truëb (1882–1969) in charge. Emilie Butters was one of the workshop's first students and found her calling in the designing and making of everyday objects – plates, butter dishes, cookie jars, vases, beer mugs (*Stein*). Before long, some of the vessels produced by the ceramics workshop were offered for sale. This germinated the idea in Debschitz to establish a commercial enterprise that was not linked to the school. The *Keramische Werkstätten W. v. Debschitz* were born. Curiously, Butters did not work for Debschitz but, for reasons unbeknownst to us, found employment with Koebke instead. She continued to design and make *Nutz-Keramiken* at Koebke's workshops, and soon became known for her technical expertise in glazing. She designed ceramics that, not unlike Richard Riemerschmid, combined a traditional colour palette and design language with modern shapes. This is evidenced by a vase that recently came up for sale at auction (Plate 9). Butters regularly showed her work at exhibitions and participated in the 1912 Bavarian Trade Show in Munich as well as the 1914 Werkbund Exhibition in Cologne.[97] She married the sculptor Wilhelm Krieger (1877–1945) in 1912 and continued working at the *Keramischen Werkstätten* as a freelance designer. Sadly, she shared the fate of so many of her contemporary Jugendstil women designers and makers in that she had to return to her profession as a drawing instructor when the *Keramischen Werkstätten* closed amidst the socio-economic cataclysm of the First World War.

3.13 Modernism's paradox

Throughout the nineteenth century, women's access to education was much more limited than that of their male counterparts. Government initiatives such as the *Damen-Abteilung* at Bavaria's RAAS, the Women Artists Association and Ladies' Academy tried to address some of these inequities, but they did not go far enough. The institutional and ideological landscapes within which they operated continued to relegate women to the sidelines. Women's curricular choices, for example, were considerably more limited than those of male students, and their career perspectives suffered as a result. They were tolerated but not accepted. Their 'maternal instincts' and supposedly biologically determined female disposition in regard to intellectual capacities and physical abilities made them ideal schoolteachers (*Zeichenlehrerinnen*) but foreclosed professional opportunities. Time and again, women were asked to translate or materialize their male counterparts' creative outputs, even within the context of progressive reform initiatives such as the United Workshops. And even today, the problematic historical hierarchy between Hermann Obrist (designer) and Berthe Ruchet (embroiderer), for example, still haunts the disciplines of art history and design history. Although design historians are ideally placed to interrogate the material properties of Jugendstil objects, it has taken a long time to overcome disciplinary habits of prioritizing aesthetics over materiality – although the so-called material turn has rekindled interest in embodied experience and materiality across the humanities.[98]

Jugendstil women were ultimately caught in a vicious circle. Historical attitudes and ideologies limited their educational opportunities, determined what medium they could work in, dictated their career choices and, ultimately, curtailed their agency. The Debschitz School's curriculum tried to push against some of these prejudices by way of a series of innovative and seemingly egalitarian interventions into the training process and eventual professional opportunities for Jugendstil women. But even within the parameters of a progressive pedagogical experiment that embraced the radical idea of co-education, emerging women artists and designer ran the risk of being relegated to the margins. Although Obrist and Debschitz were committed to women's equality, their vision was curtailed by the socio-historical parameters of their time. Zeynep C. Alexander aptly observed that Obrist was 'both exhilarated by the emancipation of hitherto marginalized subjects and anxious about the consequences of such liberation'.[99] This underscored one of modernism's quintessential paradoxes that pivoted around the precarious balancing act between liberation and discipline. Just as the Debschitz School's female students were given the tools to forge artistic careers for themselves, they were put back into their place by the very forces that encouraged this liberation in the first place.[100] Despite the Debschitz School's visionary intervention into Munich's gendered institutional landscape that opened up new educational opportunities for female students, Jugendstil women had to work twice as hard to overcome deeply entrenched gender biases that considered their work as either derivative or commercial. They had to continually prove themselves as worthy designers whose work was based on innovative concepts and executed to high technical standards. The notion of the 'decorative' became a pitfall for Jugendstil women.

Notes

1 August Bebel, 'Die Frau und der Sozialismus', cited in Anke Mariny, *Die Bildende Künstlerin-Ein Kopfarbeiter besonderer Art*, in *Profession ohne Tradition: 125 Jahre Verein Bildender Künstlerinnen* (Berlin: Berlinische Galerie: 1992), 369.

2   The two previous exhibitions took also took place in Nuremberg, in 1882 and 1896.

3   See 'Nürnbergs Industriekultur', accessed 30 July 2019, http://www.nuernberginfos.de/industriekultur-nuernberg.html.

4   The Luitpoldhain later housed the notorious Nazi Party rallies and is today the site of the Documentation Centre Nazi Party Rally Grounds, accessed 30 July 2019, https://museums.nuernberg.de/documentation-center/.

5   'Landesausstellungen in Nürnberg', accessed 30 July 2019, http://www.nuernberginfos.de/nuernberg-mix/landesausstellungen.html.

6   D.R. 'Die Mitglieder der 'Lehr- und Versuchs-Ateliers für Angewandte und Freie Kunst, Wilhelm von Debschitz, München' auf der Bayerischen Jubiläums-Landesausstellung Nünrberg 1906', *Dekorative Kunst* 14 (1906): 345–64.

7   Gabriele Reuter wrote a semi-fictional novel called *Frau Bürgelin und ihre Söhne* about the Obrist family in 1898 (published 1900). Alice Jane Grant Duff of Eden eventually settled in Weimar with her surviving sons, Hermann and Aloys.

8   Both of Obrist's brothers were highly talented musicians. His older brother Maximilian died young (1874) but his younger brother Aloys embarked on a career as a professional conductor, which came to a violent end when he shot his lover, the opera singer Anna Sutter (1871–1910), in a scandalous murder-suicide plot in Stuttgart in 1910. Georg Günther, 'Es liegt Mord und Selbstmord vor: Die Stuttgarter Künstlertragödie Obrist-Sutter von 1910', in *Musik in Baden-Württemberg*, ed. Georg Günther and Reiner Nägele (Stuttgart: J. B. Metzler, 2000): 79–130.

9   Hermann Götz, *Kunstschöpfungen von Hermann Götz: Ausgeführte Arbeiten und Entwürfe*, 3 vols. (Dresden: Gerhard Kühtmann, 1903).

10 Hermann Obrist, *Ein glückliches Leben: Eine Biographie des Künstlers, Forschers und Alleingängers Hermann Obrist* (1926). Obrist Nachlass, Staatliche Graphische Sammlung (SGS) Munich. See also Eva Afuhs and Andreas Strobls, *Herman Obrist: Skulptur, Raum, Abstraktion um 1900* (Zurich: Scheidegger & Spiess, 2009).

11 Afuhs and Strobls, *Hermann* Obrist, 127.

12 Sabine Gebhardt Fink and Matthias Vogel, *Hermann Obrist: Im Netzwerk der Künste und Medien um 1900* (Berlin: Kunstverlag Kadmos, 2013), 71.

13 Obrist cited in Afuhs and Strobls, *Hermann Obrist,* 129.

14 Logan, for example, wrote an enthusiastic essay on occasion of Obrist's submission of some of his key embroidery designs such as 'Whiplash' to the annual exhibition of the Arts & Crafts Exhibition Society in London. This represented one of the earliest international discussions of Obrist's work. Mary Logan, 'Hermann Obrist's Embroidered Decorations', *The Studio* 12, no. 56 (1897): 96–105.

15 The studio spaces were destroyed during the Second World War, and the Villa Obrist was heavily damaged during the Allied bombings of Munich in 1944.

16 Two essays published in Otto Julius Bierbaum's and Julius Maier Graefe's foundational Jugendstil journal *Pan* paved the ground for Obrist's reception as Jugendstil's father figure: Georg Fuchs, 'Hermann Obrist', *Pan* 1, no. 5 (1895–96): 318–25 and Wilhelm Bode, 'Hermann Obrist', *Pan* 1, no. 5 (1895–96): 326–8.

17 Karl Scheffler, 'Hermann Obrist', *Kunst und Kunsthandwerk* 8 (1910): 556.

18 Hermann Obrist, 'Stellungnahme zum Thema Kunstschulen', *Kunst und Künstler* 5 (1907): 209.

19 Ulrich Thieme, ed., 'Wilhelm von Debschitz', in *Allgemeines Lexikon der bildenden Künstler von der Antike bis zur Gegenwart* 8 (Leipzig: E. A. Seemann, 1913), 510.

20 Dagmar Rinker, *Die Lehr- und Versuchs-Ateliers für angewandte und freie Kunst (Debschitz-Schule): München 1902–1914* (Munich: Tuduv Verlag, 1993), 15.

21 Karl Eric Toepfer, *Empire of Ecstasy: Nudity and Movement in German Body Culture, 1910–1935* (Berkeley: University of California Press, 1997).

22 Beate Ziegert, 'The Debschitz School, Munich: 1902–1914', *Design Issues* 3, no. 1 (Spring 1986): 29. Sadly, Beate Ziegert died in 2016 age 85; she was Wilhelm von Debschitz granddaughter (maternal side).

23 Rainer Metzger, *Munich: Its Golden Age or Art and Culture 1890-1920* (London: Thames & Hudson, 2009).

24 Carl Götze, *Kunsterziehung: Ergebnisse und Anregungen des Kunsterziehungstages in Dresden am 28. und 29. September 1901* (Leipzig: R. Voigtländer, 1902).

25 For an excellent discussion of German reform movements across the cultural spectrum see Diethart Kerbs and Jürgen Reulecke, *Handbuch der deutschen Reformbewegung, 1880–1933* (Wuppertal: Peter Hammer Verlag, 1998). For more a specific analysis of art educational reform see John V. Maciuika, *Before the Bauhaus: Architecture, Politics, and the German State, 1880–1920* (Cambridge: Cambridge University Press, 2005).

26 Rudolf Eisler, 'Anschauung', in *Nachschlagwerk zu Immanuel Kant* (1930), accessed 2 February 2020, https://www.textlog.de/31941.html

For an astute analysis of Obrist's philosophical leanings see Zeynep Çelik Alexander, 'Jugendstil Vision: Occultism, Gender and Modern Design Pedagogy', *Journal of Design History* 22, no. 3 (2009): 203–26, esp. 205–8. Alexander published an expanded version of this essay in her more recent book *Kinaesthetic Knowing: Aesthetics, Epistemology, Modern Design* (Chicago: Chicago University Press, 2017).

27 Obrist in T. Götze, *Kunsterziehung*, 168.

28 Hermann Obrist, 'Ein künstlerischer Kunstunterricht', *Der Lotse: Hamburgische Wochenschrift für deutsche Kultur* 1, no. 23 (23 February 1901): 682–6.

29 See 'Kunstschulen', *Kunst und Künstler* 5 (1906–7): 206–10.

30 Ziegert, 'Debschitz School, Munich', 32.

31 'Lehrwerkstätte der Vereinigten Werkstätten für Kunst im Handwerk', *Kunst und Handwerk* 51, no. 6 (1901): 188.

32 Sabine Wieber, 'Designing the Nation: Neo-Northern Renaissance Interiors and the Politics of Identity in late Nineteenth-Century Germany, 1876–1888' (PhD Dissertation, University of Chicago, 2004).

33 Ziegert makes this observation but she does not offer archival evidence. Ziegert, 'The Debschitz School, Munich', 29. See also Sabine Wieber, 'The Warp & the Weft: Tradition and Innovation in Skærbæk Tapestries, 1896–1903', *Journal of Design History* 28, no. 4 (2015): 331–47.

34 Ziegert, 'The Debschitz School'; Alexander 'Jugendstil Visions'; Rinker, *Die Lehr- und Versuchs-Ateliers*.

35 Rinker, *Die Lehr- und Versuchs-Ateliers*, 35.

36 Haruhiko Fujita, *Words for Design: Comparative Etymology and Terminology of Design and its Equivalents*, vols. 1–3 (Osaka: Japan Society for the Promotion of Science, 2007–9).

37 Max Wertheimer, *Experimentelle Studien über das Sehen von Bewegung* (Leipzig: Johann A. Berth Verlag, 1912); Mitchell G. Ash, *Gestalt Psychology in German Culture, 1890-1967* (Cambridge: Cambridge University Press, 1995).

38 Fink and Vogel, 'Textchronik', 69.

39 George Rawson, 'Francis Henry Newbery and the Glasgow School of Art' (PhD Dissertation, The Glasgow School of Art, 1996).

40 Carl Malcomes, *Deutschlands Fachschulwesen* quoted in Alexander, 'Jugendstil Vision', 223. No precise figures exist because no archival material for the Debschitz School, such as curricula, student registers and annual reports, survived. Information thus needs to be extrapolated from contemporary journals and writings. Rinker attempted to locate primary material by sifting through the archives of former students, but her efforts did not yield any new evidence.

41 *National Zeitung Berlin* (13.9.1902) quoted in Rinker, *Die Lehr- und Versuchs-Ateliers*, 37.

42 Rinker, *Die Lehr- und Versuchs-Ateliers*, 39.

43 The Debschitz School remained in Schwabing and simply moved a few doors down to Hohenzollern Strasse 21–3. *Kunst und Handwerk*, 54 (1903–4): 25.

44 Ziegert, 'The Debschitz School', 34.

45 Wilhelm von Debschitz, 'Eine Methode des Kunstunterrichts', *Dekorative Kunst*, 12 (1904): 207–27.

46 This drawing has been cited as influencing Wassily Kandinsky's *Punkt und Linie zur Fläche* (1914). Kandinsky attended Obrist's Thursday Evening lectures, and the Debschitz School was located in very close proximity to the rooms housing Kandinsky's Phalanx Group. Peg Weiss, *Kandinsky in Munich: The formative Jugendstil Years* (Princeton: Princeton University Press, 1978), 122. Wassily Kandinsky, *Punkt und Linie zur Fläche* (Leipzig: Bauhaus Press/Hesse und Becker, 1926).

47 Obrist, 'Die Lehr-und Versuch-Ateliers für angewandte und freie Kunst', *Dekorative Kunst* 7 (March 1904): 230.

48 Obrist, 'Ein künstlerischer Kunstunterricht', 679.

49 Debschitz, 'Eine Methode des Kunstunterrichts', 210.

50 Alexander, 'Jugendstil Visions', 209.

51 Georg Jacob Wolf, 'Erinnerungen an Hermann Obrist', *Deutsche Kunst* 31 (1927/28): 166. Ziegert singles out the Debschitz School's Carnival Party in 1912, which was attended by Karl and Hanna Wolfskehl, Clara Rilke-Westhoff, Gabriele Münter, Wassily Kandinsky, Sophie Taeuber-Arp and possibly Franz Mark. Ziegert, 'The Debschitz School', 35.

52 Many public and private archives and libraries were destroyed during the Second World War. Although this fate also impacted their male counterparts, much less effort was made by twentieth-century art and design historians to reconstitute this

lost information. Johnson's carefully researched analysis of the multiple layers of this gender-specific erasure in Vienna 1900 opens up interesting possibilities for Munich. Julie Johnson, *The Memory Factory* (West Lafayette: Purdue University Press, 2012).

53 Linda Nochlin, *Women, Art and Power and other Essays* (New York: Harper & Row, 1988), 145–78; Whitney Chatwick, *Women, Art and Society,* 3rd ed. (London: Thames & Hudson, 2002).

54 Georg Fuchs, 'Hermann Obrist 1862–1927', *Dekorative Kunst* 35, no. 30 (1926/27): 323.

55 Safia Azzouni and Uwe Wirth, *Dilettantismus als Beruf* (Berlin: Kulturverlag Kadmos, 2010).

56 Renate Berger, *Malerinnen auf dem Weg ins 20. Jahrhundert* (Cologne: Dumont, 1986), 58–78.

57 Bebel, 'Die Frau und der Sozialismus', 369.

58 Marie Ellenrieder (1791–1863) was the first woman to enter the Academy in 1813 and studied portraiture and history painting. For an institutional history of Munich's Academy see Thomas Zacharias, *Tradition und Widerspruch: 175 Jahre Kunstakademie München* (Munich: Prestel Verlag, 1985). Astonishingly, the role of women/female students is not once discussed in this foundational publication.

59 Switzerland was central Europe's first country to allow women to enrol at university (1870, University of Bern). In Bavaria, women attended selected lectures from the 1890s onwards and they were allowed to matriculate as of 1903. See Patricia M. Mazón, *Gender and the Modern Research University: The Admission of Women to German Higher Education, 1865–1914* (Stanford: Stanford University Press, 2003).

60 Paul Julius Möbius, 'Über den physiologischen Schwachsinn des Weibes' was specifically targeted at bolstering arguments against allowing women to study medicine at universities. Max (aka Maxie) Freimann published a satirical rebuke in 1905 under the title 'On the Physiological Stupidity (*Stumpfsinn*) of Men', accessed 28 July 2019, https://archive.org/details/berdenphysiolog00freigoog/page/n8.

61 Reinhard Spree, *Geschlechterverhältnis und bürgerliche Familie im 19. Jahrhundert* (2011), accessed 28 July 2019, https://rspree.wordpress.com/2011/02/21/geschlechterverhaltnis-und-burgerliche-familie-im-19-jh/. See also Katharina Rowold, *The Educated Woman: Minds, Bodies, and Women's Higher Education in Britain, Germany and Spain, 1865–1914* (London: Routledge, 2010).

62 Claudia Schmalhofer, *Die Kgl. Kunstgewerbeschule München (1868–1918): Ihr Einfluss auf die Ausbildung der Zeichenlehrerin* (Munich: Herbert Utz Verlag, 2005).

63 This site is today owned by the Ludwig Maximilian University and houses Bavarian State Collection for Palaeontology and Historical Geology.

64 For a detailed discussion of these debates see Wieber, 'Designing the Nation' and 'Between Tradition and Innovation: In Search of a Modern Style, 1850–1914', in *Atlas of Furniture Design,* ed. Mateo Kries (Weil am Rhein: Vitra Design Museum, 2019), 125–39.

65 Christoph Hölz, *Schön und Gut: Positionen des Gestaltens seit 1850* (Munich: Zentralinstitut für Kunstgeschichte, 2002).

66 Schmalhofer, *Die Kgl. Kunstgewerbeschule*, 28.
67 Ibid., 32–3.
68 Ibid.
69 Ibid.
70 Petition for financial support submitted to the Bavarian Parliament on 13 February 1870. Quoted in Schmalhofer, *Die Kgl. Kunstgewerbeschule*, 34.
71 It is curious, but seemingly without reason, why these institutional changes all took place on 1 October.
72 The RAAS's first director was the Salon painter Herman Dyck (1868–74), followed by the painter Eugen Napoleon Neureuther (1874) – brother of the famous architect Gottfried Neureuther (1811–1887), Emil Lange (1874–1913) and Richard Riemerschmid (1913–18).
73 Braunmühl was employed at the RAAS for twenty-three years and, although sympathetic to the women's movement, she was not an open supporter because she feared the termination of her job should her political leanings become public knowledge. Schmalhofer, *Die Kgl. Kunstgewerbeschule*, 106.
74 Female students were excluded from anatomical studies and architectural drawing. As well, women were limited to choosing specialist options in design drawing geared towards textiles and jewellery; decorative painting geared towards porcelain; drawing instruction (*Zeichen-Lehramt*); lithography and xylography. Schmalhofer, *Die Kgl. Kunstgewerbeschule*, 83 and 116.
75 Matthew Jefferies, *Imperial Culture in Germany, 1871–1918* (Basingstoke: Palgrave, 2003); Catherine Dollard, *The Surplus Woman: Unmarried in Imperial Germany, 1871–1918* (New York: Berghahn, 2009).
76 Schmalhofer, *Die Kgl. Kunstgewerbeschule*, 106.
77 Braunmühl quoted in Antonia Voit, 'Ab nach München: Allgemeine Einführung', in *Ab nach München*, 15.
78 Additional founding members were the painters Sophie Dahn-Fries (1835–1898), Freiin Ilka von Fabrice (1846–1907), Johanna Tecklenborg (1851–1933) and Braunmühl's teaching colleague Olga Weiss (1853–1903).
79 Statutes of the Künstlerinnen Verein, 1888: §1. Deposited at the Munich City Archive and quoted in Yvette Deyseve, *Der Künstlerinnen-Verein München e.V. und seine Damen Akademie* (Munich: Herbert Utz Verlag, 2005), 50.
80 Voit, 'Ab nach München', 25.
81 Deyseve, *Der Künstlerinnen-Verein*, 52.
82 Maria Derenda, *Kunst als Beruf: Käthe Kollwitz und Elena Luksch-Makowskaja* (Frankfurt: Campus Verlag, 2018).
83 Statutes of the Künstlerinnen Verein.
84 Deyseve, *Der Künstlerinnen-Verein*, 76.
85 Ibid., 109.
86 Megan Marie Brandow-Faller, 'An Art of their Own: Reinventing *Frauenkunst* in the Female Academies and Artist Leagues of Late-Imperial and First Republic Austria, 1900–1930' (PhD Dissertation, Georgetown University, Washington, DC, 2010)

as well as *The Female Secession: Art and the Decorative at the Viennese Women's Academy* (University Park: Pennsylvania State University Press, 2020).

87 Joan Wallach Scott, 'Deconstructing Equality-versus-Difference, or the Uses of Post-Structuralist Theory in Feminism', *Feminist Studies* 14 (Spring 1988): 33–50.
88 'Unser Preisausschreiben', *Dekorative Kunst* 6, no. 12 (September 1903): 477–80.
89 Obrist quoted in Voit, 'Ab nach München', 15.
90 Rinker, *Die Lehr- und Versuchs-Ateliers*, 47.
91 Ziegert, 'The Debschitz School', 39.
92 Rinker, *Die Lehr- und Versuchs-Ateliers*, 47–50.
93 Debschitz quoted in Ziegert, 'The Debschitz School', 33. Debschitz sold the School in 1914 to Emil Preetorius, Paul Renner and philosopher Hans Cornelius to take up the directorship of Hannover's City Manufacturers and Applied Arts School (*Städtische Handwerker- und Kunstgewerbeschule*), which he held until 1921.
94 Butters quoted in *Ab nach München*, 268.
95 Ibid.
96 *Ab nach München*, 270.
97 Ibid., 271.
98 Tony Bennet and Patrick Joyce, *Material Powers: Cultural Studies, History and the Material Turn* (London: Routledge, 2010).
99 Alexander, 'Jugendstil Visions', 219.
100 Ibid., 220.

4 PATRON

FASHIONABLE TASTE AT ELSA BRUCKMANN'S SALON

We arrive home. Through the small garden gate we go, where the acacia stands, then past the old lime tree with the thick branches and the bench underneath.
Peaceful, lost in a dream our house sleeps.

H. ELGO AKA ELSA BRUCKMANN CANTACUZÈNES (1896)[1]

One of Germany's leading interior design journals, *Dekorative Kunst*, featured three separate articles in 1899 that introduced readers to a group of young designers from Glasgow, Scotland.[2] Their names were Charles Rennie Mackintosh (1868–1928), Frances (1873–1921) Margaret Macdonald (1864–1933), and Herbert McNair (1868–1955). Today, the group is famously known as the Glasgow Four, and its members are widely celebrated for their pioneering contributions to modern architecture and design. But at the time, they were virtually unheard of outside their hometown, and German critics were excited about the prospects of such a dynamic design culture emerging from the far reaches of Scotland. Two of the essays in *Dekorative Kunst* were illustrated with photographs of the group's recent work. One set of photographs stood out because it showcased a fully furbished interior by Charles Mackintosh and Margaret Macdonald rather than presenting individual design objects (Figures 35 and 36). Readers must have been astonished to find out that this thoroughly modern interior was in the Munich home of Hugo and Elsa Bruckmann rather than somewhere in Scotland. This chapter explores the compelling cross-cultural context for the Glasgow Four's Munich commission and draws attention to Elsa Bruckmann's pivotal role as a

FIGURE 35 Charles Rennie Mackintosh, dining room, Bruckmann Villa Munich, 1899, in *Dekorative Kunst* 4 (1899): 78. Bayerische Staatsbibliothek, München, 4 Art. 49 sk-11, urn:nbn:de:bvb:12-bsb00087595-4

FIGURE 36 Charles Rennie Mackintosh, dining room, Bruckmann Villa Munich, 1899, in *Dekorative Kunst* 4 (1899): 79. Bayerische Staatsbibliothek, München, 4 Art. 49 sk-11, urn:nbn:de:bvb:12-bsb00087595-4.

prominent supporter of modern design whose regular soirées provided a fertile seedbed for Jugendstil and the formation of upper-middle-class taste.

Late-nineteenth-century salons played a crucial part in the dissemination of Jugendstil design. They provide vital insights into the dynamic networks and connections between Jugendstil artists and designers, their patrons and members of central Europe's cultural elites. Salons are notoriously difficult to reconstitute since they were ephemeral events. But design historians are at an advantage over their colleagues in other disciplines because they have recourse to surviving material objects that once constituted the physical parameters of a salon. The anthropologist Arjun Appadurai asked historians to pay attention to the 'social life of things' because he argues that throughout history, objects were implicated in the articulation and recalibration of sociopolitical relationship.[3] This chapter takes its cue from Appadurai and proposes that anchoring Elsa Bruckmann's Munich salon practice in its man-made environment offers new insights into the compelling interconnections between Jugendstil design, identity formation and late-nineteenth-century imperial politics. Why did the Bruckmanns commission two young Scottish designers to decorate their dining room? And what role did the room's furniture and design objects play in the Bruckmanns' strategic acquisition of 'cultural capital' as taste makers of their day?[4] But first, a brief biography of Elsa Bruckmann because not only has this once prominent Munich salonnière been virtually forgotten but her biography fundamentally impacted her cultural politics.

4.1 Elsa Bruckmann (1865–1946)

Elsa Bruckmann (née Cantacuzènes) was born on 23 February 1865 as the oldest of three sisters. The Cantacuzènes originally came from Romania and traced their dynastic roots to the Byzantine emperor John VI Kantakouzenos (1293–1383).[5] Elsa Cantacuzènes's father, Prince Theodor, served as an army officer, and Elsa spent an idyllic childhood growing up in rural Bavaria before the family moved to Munich to send their daughters to school.[6] Elsa Cantacuzènes went to Munich's private School for Young Ladies, which had been founded in 1822 for upper-middle-class and aristocratic girls.[7] She completed her Munich education in 1880 and attended upper-secondary school in Geneva for the next two years. In the late nineteenth century, Switzerland offered better educational opportunities for girls and young women than many other European countries.[8] Here, Elsa Cantacuzènes discovered her passion for literature and her archive brims with mostly unpublished stories and poems she wrote throughout her life. Later in life, Elsa Bruckmann was especially drawn to fairy tales, an interest that was rooted in a cross-European revival of folklore and vernacular culture that now falls under the rubric of National Romanticism.[9] She published a short prose piece called 'Happiness' (1896) in the progressive German art journal *Pan* under her pseudonym H. Elgo and a fairy tale entitled 'The Four-Leaved

Clover' (1897) in the *Illustrirte Frauen-Zeitung* (Illustrated Ladies' Journal; 1897).[10] But Elsa Cantacuzènes could not turn her writing into a professional career because she was subjected to the strict social etiquette imposed on young aristocratic women of her time. This prompted Elsa Cantacuzènes's future husband Hugo Bruckmann to caution her that 'to earn a living with embroidery, painting, writing is difficult and volatile! Don't be cross with me but I have to repeat that marriage is the one and only means through which you and your relatives can be helped.'[11]

Hugo Bruckmann's undoubtedly well-intentioned advice reveals predominant late-nineteenth-century attitudes that carefully patrolled the lives and opportunities for young women of Elsa Cantacuzènes' social class. Despite her well-grounded education and unmistakable intellectual potential, Elsa Cantacuzènes was locked into a typical holding pattern that compelled her to while away the days until an appropriate marriage could be brokered. Until such time, Elsa Cantacuzènes became Baroness Sophie von Todesco's (1825–1895) lady's companion and moved to Vienna in 1893. The Todescos were one of Vienna's most prominent and wealthy Jewish families.[12] At the Todesco Palace, Elsa Cantacuzènes entered an elite sociocultural world that could not be further removed from her provincial home life in Bavaria. Despite Elsa Cantacuzènes's aristocratic status, her family lacked the financial resources to introduce their daughters into the refined social habitus of the Todesco household. Here, Elsa Cantacuzènes acquired the social ambition and cultural capital that she would bring in her marriage to one of Munich's most eligible bachelors, Hugo Bruckmann, in 1898.

4.2 Munich–Vienna: The Todesco Palais

Sophie von Todesco was a renowned patron of the arts and famous salonnière. She was born into the wealthy and highly educated Gomperz family from Moravia.[13] She married the Viennese entrepreneur, financier and philanthropist Eduard von Todesco (1814–1887) in 1845 and entered the city's so-called second society, which was inhabited by members of the Habsburg Empire's moneyed elite (banking, commerce, industry). Eduard von Todesco was an assimilated Jew and deployed culture to gain entry into Vienna's carefully patrolled haute monde. The prominent historian Carl Schorske argued that Jewish acculturation and Viennese modernism were inextricably connected in 'Vienna 1900'.[14] The Todescos represented a perfect example of this symbiosis and their patronage encompassed the *Ringstrasse*'s (Ring Street) historicism as well as the Secession's reaction to it. A discussion of Vienna's fascinating cultural landscape during this time exceeds the remit of this chapter, but a brief look at Sophie Todesco's famed salon grounds Elsa Bruckmann's later engagement with salon culture in *fin-de-siècle* Munich.

The Todescos lived in one of Vienna's most prestigious residential buildings on the city's famous *Ringstrasse*. The *Ringstrasse* was the centrepiece of Emperor

Franz Joseph's ambitious urban rejuvenation project (1857–1918) and replaced old city walls and military exercise grounds with a grand circular boulevard lined with apartment blocks, green spaces and representative civic buildings.[15] Eduard Todesco bought one of the first available plots located right across from the future site of the State Opera as soon as Jews were allowed by royal decree in 1860 to purchase land on Ring Street.[16] He commissioned the acclaimed historicist architects Ludwig Christian Friedrich Förster (1797–1863) and Theophil Hansen (1813–1891) to design a typically Viennese apartment block known as a *Zinspalast*.[17] A *Zinspalast* usually accommodated its owners on the opulent Bel-Étage, and the remaining apartments were rented out for income (*Zins*). But Todesco's entire Neo-Renaissance palace was occupied by his extended family and the building featured grand interiors: a dining room with a ceiling painting by Carl Rahl (1812–1865), a gilded ballroom decorated by Gustav Gaul (1836–1888), a study designed by the Munich architect Lorenz Gedon (1843–1883) and a lavish salon decked out in Neo-Rococo and Neo-Renaissance furniture (Figure 37). Eduard and Sophie Todesco were passionate art collectors and owned old masters (Tintoretto, Veronese, Pieter Brueghel the Younger) as well as moderate contemporary art by the likes of Hans von Makart (1840–1884) and Olga Wisinger-Florians (1844–1926).[18]

FIGURE 37 Salon at the Palais Tedesco, photograph, Vienna, c. 1900. https://commons.wikimedia.org/w/index .php?title=File:Parlour_in_the_Palais_Todesco,_Vienna,_ ca._1870_(detail).jpg&oldid=305160717.

These luxurious interiors provided the physical setting for the Todescos' legendary entertainment such as Sophie's extravagant costume balls and tableaux vivants.[19] When Elsa Cantacuzènes entered Sophie Todesco's household in 1893, she was introduced to an eclectic mix of individuals who socialized at Sophie's weekly salons. Multiple generations of liberal Jews and their gentile friends from Vienna's high society conversed with composers (Johannes Brahms and Franz Liszt), writers (Ludwig Ganghofer, Franz von Dingelstedt and Heinrich Laube), artists (Franz von Lenbach, Moritz von Schwind, Viktor O. Tilgener and Theodor Billroth) and prominent politicians (Alexander von Bach, Anton von Doblhoff-Dier and Anton von Schmerling).[20] On one such occasion, Elsa Bruckmann met the young poet Hugo von Hofmannsthal (1874–1929), and the two formed an intense, albeit short-lived, friendship, during which Hofmannsthal encouraged Elsa Bruckmann's literary endeavours.[21]

4.3 Marrying into a publishing empire

Elsa Cantacuzènes returned to Munich in 1894 as an educated, socially savvy, well connected and, by all accounts, beautiful young woman. She re-acquainted herself with Hugo Bruckmann (1863–1941), who was the wealthy heir to one of Germany's most respected art publishing houses, a successful entrepreneur in his own right and a member of central Europe's cultural elite (Plates 10a and 10b). The two first met shortly before Elsa Bruckmann departed for Vienna, but Hugo broke off their budding romance soon after Elsa Bruckmann's return to Munich.[22] The reasons for Hugo's retreat remain unclear, but they were probably rooted in their divergent social positions and parental pressures on both sides. This left Elsa Bruckmann heartbroken, but given Munich's relatively small social circles, their paths kept crossing and they eventually married on 24 November 1898.[23] From this point onwards, Hugo and Elsa Bruckmann built their reputation as a modern 'power couple'. Their marriage imbued Hugo with social prominence and Elsa Bruckmann's family received a much-needed injection of financial capital.[24]

At the time of their marriage, Hugo Bruckmann (1863–1941) was at the helm of one of Germany's premier art publishing houses that had been founded by his father Fritz in 1858.[25] The Bruckmann's 'Publishing House for Art and Science' offered a wide selection of publications that ranged from luxury monographs for elite collectors to museum guides for general audiences. Its in-house photography studio employed pioneering reproduction technologies such as multiple-plate photogravure (1890) that drastically reduced the cost of colour illustrations and increased the speed of production.[26] In this context, Hugo's older brother Alphons (1855–1945) developed a lucrative side business for colour postcards.[27] Hugo Bruckmann, on the other hand, expanded his father's magazine portfolio that already included one of central Europe's leading art journals *Kunst für Alle* (Art for All; 1886–1919). The journal was edited by the esteemed, albeit staunchly anti-French, critic Friedrich Pecht (1814–1903) and featured articles on the decorative arts.[28] But Hugo Bruckmann was keen to produce a publication that was exclusively dedicated to German and international design culture and thus founded *Dekorative Kunst* (Decorative Arts) in 1897. He convinced one of Germany's most perceptive commentators of modern art, Julius Meier-Graefe (1867–1935), to become his co-editor.[29] *Dekorative Kunst* was printed in German and French and included more illustrations than *Kunst für Alle*. Bruckmann's new journal offered a decidedly international outlook and introduced readers to up-and-coming architects and designers such as the Glasgow Four, whom it promoted in 1899. Financial pressures forced Bruckmann to amalgamate *Dekorative Kunst* and *Kunst für Alle* in late 1899, but his revamped journal *Die Kunst* (Fine Arts) continued to feature the decorative arts and design.[30]

According to his brother Alphons, Hugo dreamed of being an artist, but, when tasked with running the family business in 1897, he channelled his artistic talent into publishing instead. Hugo Bruckmann fostered professional and private contacts with progressive artists, architects, designers and critics across Europe and became a powerful supporter of modern art and design. This advocacy gained further traction when he married Elsa Cantacuzène and entered the carefully guarded social circles of central Europe's old aristocracy. The Bruckmanns deployed their joint social and cultural capitals to secure a reputation as one of Munich's, if not Wilhelmine Germany's, most eminent tastemakers. Elsa Bruckmann used her salons to introduce members of central Europe's artistic and intellectual elites to German industrialists, political powerbrokers and socialites. Hugo, on the other hand, promoted progressive artists, architects and designers on the pages of his journals. Together they nourished Munich's fertile cultural landscape and propagated the flowering of German Jugendstil.

4.4 The Bruckmanns' new headquarters

Elsa and Hugo Bruckmann's first marital home was an apartment in a Jugendstil building designed by Martin Dülfer (1859–1942). It was located on the grounds of the Bruckmann Publishers' new premises on Nymphenburg Strasse 86 (Plate 11). The Bruckmann brothers were aware of the area's rising property values and bought a series of adjacent lots in the late 1880s. Dülfer's building housed the publisher's administrative headquarters and a modest apartment for residential use on the top floor. Elsa and Hugo Bruckmann's first domestic arrangement might appear as slightly unusual for a couple of their socio-economic standing but reading between the lines of their premarital correspondence indicates that Hugo was reluctant to give up his bachelor ways.[31]

Dülfer was a prominent Jugendstil architect, but he has been somewhat ignored by architectural historians. This comes as a surprise because Dülfer not only designed some of Munich's most iconic Jugendstil buildings but also moved in the same artistic circles as his acclaimed Jugendstil contemporaries Richard Riemerschmid, August Endell, Bruno Paul and Peter Behrens. Dülfer studied under historicist architects in Hanover and Stuttgart before moving to Munich in 1885 to enrol in Friedrich von Thiersch's (1852–1921) architectural classes at the Technical University.[32] Thiersch introduced Dülfer to some of Munich's influential players in the city's art world like the painters Franz von Lenbach (1836–1904) and Franz von Stuck (1863–1928). Their acquaintance opened up important new contacts for the emerging young architect. Dülfer soon specialized in plaster design for façades known in German as *Putz-Architektur*. He started his own practice in 1893 and became one of Munich Jugendstil's most skilled and innovative designers of façades. His work was only rivalled by August Endell's extraordinary façade at the Photo-Studio Elvira, discussed in Chapter 2. By 1904, Dülfer was widely considered as a 'pioneer of modern architecture' and as 'one of Germany's most distinguished building-artists (*Baukünstler*)'[33] – the latter represents an interesting term and alludes to a desire to elevate architecture to the status of art, which dovetailed with German design reformers' desire to level age-old artistic hierarchies that put the visual arts at the apex and the 'manual' arts at the bottom.

Martin Dülfer's contributions to a distinctly German modern style were not limited to architecture. He also participated in key exhibitions that have since been hailed by art and design historians as the birthplaces of Munich Jugendstil such as the 'Seventh International Art Exhibition' in 1897 and 'Annual Art Exhibition' in 1898.[34] Dülfer thus moved among Munich's most progressive architects and designers. Consequently, Hugo Bruckmann deliberately aligned himself, and by extension his publishing house, with these champions of modern art, architecture and design when commissioning Dülfer to design his publishing house's new headquarters. This was not without risk in 1898 because Jugendstil was in its infancy and, as previously discussed, garnered a mixed reception in the contemporary press. In addition, Dülfer was still a relatively inexperienced architect and Bruckmann took a bit of a chance on him.[35] But Bruckmann's gamble paid off and Dülfer delivered a Jugendstil building of the finest order. Its façade showcases some of Jugendstil's key decorative elements, such as the frequently used motif of small scattered flowers, acanthus leaves, rosettes and a wide range of geometrical shapes. Some of these shapes were cast from commercial forms, but others were applied free hand by specialist plasterers.[36]

4.5 Munich–Glasgow: The dining room

Historical realities bear out the cliché that Hugo Bruckmann dealt with the architect and his wife was in charge of the domestic interiors. A letter written by

Elsa Bruckmann to her soon-to-be husband on 29 July 1898 encapsulated this dynamic:

> My dear Hugo, in case you have not visited Bernheimer yet to look at the fauteuil, I am [hereby] giving you its number: 1338. <u>Old</u> but upholstered with new leather [it] costs 85 Marks. – But Bernheimer said that it could be copied for 40-45 Marks and for another 32-36 Marks, we could get a matching chair. This does not sound too expensive. I am no longer sure if my first impression holds and the fauteuil is indeed as pretty and practical to sit on and to use but I think so. – Bernheimer can get the leather dyed in any colour. – How is the new building coming along?[37]

Elsa Bruckmann worked with Charles Rennie Mackintosh and his soon-to-be wife Margaret Macdonald to put together one of their apartment's most representative spaces, the dining-room-cum-salon. Mackintosh designed most of the room's key elements, such as the large-fitted sideboard. It was made up of two cabinets that were connected by a serving shelf (Figure 35). The two units were probably conceived as individual cabinets rather than having been conceived as a unit. Small artefacts were displayed on the connecting shelf. Mackintosh also designed a free-standing cabinet placed to the left of the entrance doors (Figure 38). This was most likely a smoker's cabinet because it closely looks like a similar piece Mackintosh

FIGURE 38 Charles Rennie Mackintosh, smoker's cabinet, 1899, in *Dekorative Kunst* 4 (1899): 79. Bayerische Staatsbibliothek, München, 4 Art. 49 sk-11, urn:nbn:de:bvb:12-bsb00087595-4.

made for his own use and is now in the collection of the Hunterian Art Gallery at the University of Glasgow.[38] Its repoussé panels were made by Margaret Macdonald and presented two stylized young women facing one another. The cabinet went up for sale at Sotheby's on 31 October 1997 (lot 44), but the University of Glasgow's Hunterian Museum owns two of its preparatory drawings (Plate 12).[39] These drawings would have been sent to the Bruckmanns for final approval before the cabinet was manufactured in Glasgow by one of the city's prominent cabinet makers, such as Robert Blair & Sons from Greenock. At the time, Glasgow was renowned for its high-quality cabinet makers, many of whom had links to the city's shipbuilding industry along the River Clyde.[40] Macdonald made a second repoussé panel that was displayed as an independent object d'art between the two sideboard cabinets (Figure 39). It depicted an ethereal female nude standing in a fertile landscape and flanked by two babies. The panel's iconography was connected to Macdonald's illuminated manuscript *Christmas Story*, which she created with her sister Frances around 1895.[41] Macdonald admired Belgian symbolism and this panel paid homage to the subjective idealism of Jan Toorop (1858–1928) or Fernand Khnopff (1858–1921).[42] A dining table and chairs, designed and made by the Munich furniture maker Karl Bertsch (1873–1933), completed the ensemble.[43]

FIGURE 39 Margaret Macdonald, Repoussé Panel for the Bruckmann dining room, 1899. *Dekorative Kunst* 4 (1899): 79. Bayerische Staatsbibliothek, München, 4 Art. 49 sk-11, urn:nbn:de:bvb:12-bsb00087595-4.

The room was decorated with small paintings (so-called cabinet pieces), Chinese ceramics, *Westerwald* stoneware ceramics, miniature bronzes of classical figures, a collection of antique and modern sculpture heads (two of them flanking the stained-glass doors on polychrome marble columns) and a selection of textiles. Elsa Bruckmann combined antiques from her husband's collection with nineteenth-century historicist objects and the Mackintosh/Macdonald modern pieces to achieve an overall effect of sophisticated taste that signalled the Bruckmanns' discerning collecting practices. The space was lit by a two-pronged light with delicate porcelain mantles. A small curtained alcove opened onto a low dais that housed two Neo-Renaissance chairs surrounded by mounted hunting trophies of mostly chamois antlers. One of the chairs resembled a medieval Scottish throne complete with a velvet state cloth and a targe, the latter describing a medieval shield used by Scottish Highland warriors. The curtain was mentioned in Elsa Bruckmann's diary because she sewed it herself as well as a tablecloth for the dining table.[44] Elsa Bruckmann was an accomplished seamstress and apparently derived great pleasure from choosing exclusive fabrics such as the alcove's Arts and Crafts–inspired floral design to make unique pieces.

Dark wallpaper covered the walls up to a high picture rail, at which point a custom-designed stencil frieze by Mackintosh marked the transition into a light-coloured ceiling. The stencil work showcased several motifs that were regularly employed by the Glasgow Four: the heart, the tulip bulb and the rose.[45] Variations of these motifs can be found right across Mackintosh and Macdonald's work, and they became a signature of their work. In the Bruckmann commission, the Glaswegian rose appeared on the leaded glass inserted into the entrance doors as well as the lower glass panels of one of the sideboard's cabinets and acted as a wonderful leitmotif for the room's overall decorative scheme. Mackintosh and Macdonald had perfected their usage of these symbols while working on Miss Cranston's tea rooms in Glasgow – the Buchanan Street Tearooms (1896) and the Argyle Street Tea Rooms (1897).[46] In the Bruckmann interior, they combined these recurring motifs with the harmonizing tones of the dark wood in the furniture, picture rails and door frames, the diffused lighting and the curtains. This manifested one of Jugendstil's core design principles: the aesthetically unified interior discussed in Chapter 1.

The Bruckmanns' dining room was Mackintosh's first-documented commission in continental Europe and predated the Glasgow Four's much celebrated *Scottish Room* at the Vienna Secession's Eighth Exhibition in 1900 (3 November to 27 December). Design historians often herald the *Scottish Room* as Mackintosh's first engagement with progressive design practice on the European continent.[47] This assertion not only ignores the significant input by the other three members of the Glasgow Four, but it also wrongly dates the creative exchange between Scotland and the Continent.[48] It is interesting to note that the Bruckmanns supported the Glasgow designers when they were effectively unknown beyond the British Isles.

But what impelled the Munich couple to commission a group of young Glaswegian architects and designers in the first place? And how did Mackintosh and Macdonald enter their radar this early in their careers? Mackintosh scholars regularly cite Gleeson White's 1897 essay on the Glasgow Four in *The Studio* as their critical debut.[49] White's support was crucial because he was one of *The Studio's* editors and his opinions carried a lot of weight. *The Studio* had international subscribers across Europe, and one might legitimately deduce that the Bruckmanns contacted Mackintosh and Macdonald after reading White's essay.[50] But a more complex story emerges when consulting the Bruckmann estate deposited at the Bavarian State Library in Munich.

4.6 Munich–London: Hermann and Anna Muthesius

Hugo Bruckmann had a distinctly international outlook as a publisher and as a patron. He was a self-declared Anglophile and a keen follower of artistic developments in Britain. Bruckmann regularly travelled to trade fairs in England and kept tabs on the country's rapidly evolving publishing industry.[51] He was in London during the Arts and Crafts Exhibition Society's fifth exhibition at the New Gallery in 1896. He did not specifically mention a visit of this exhibition in his regular correspondence to Elsa Bruckmann, but it is unlikely that he would have missed this well-publicized event. William Morris died on the day the exhibition was scheduled to open, and his death sent shockwaves through Europe's progressive cultural circles. The 1896 exhibition was therefore on everyone's horizon because it commemorated one of the Arts and Crafts movement's founding fathers. But it also introduced a dynamic group of young designers from Glasgow to an international audience. Here, the Glasgow Four first showed their watercolours, furniture and metalwork, and Bruckmann most likely encountered the Glaswegians on this occasion.[52]

Another link between Bruckmann and Scotland's progressive artistic circles existed through Hugo's friendship with Hermann Muthesius (1861–1927). Muthesius played a key role in channelling Britain's 'modern movement' into Germany's progressive design circles.[53] Muthesius was a Prussian architect who served as the German Embassy's cultural attaché in London (1896–1903). He was tasked with reporting on cultural developments in Britain and produced a series of reports for the German Empire's government whose members were deeply concerned about Britain's threat to the German economy. While in Britain, Muthesius pursued his own interest in domestic architecture. He admired English country houses as dwellings that invited hospitality and sociability – qualities that he considered to be sorely lacking in German homes. He was a loyal supporter of the Arts and Crafts movement and his three-volume book *The English House*

(1904) stood the test of time as it continues to serve as an indispensable resource for architectural and cultural historians alike.[54]

Muthesius was married to the dress-reform advocate Anna Trippenbach (1870–1961), discussed in the next chapter under her married name Anna Muthesius. Their London home at The Priory in Hammersmith was a lively hub for progressive designers, thinkers and crafts(wo)men of the day. Eminent Arts and Crafts proponents like Walter Crane (1845–1915) and Emery Walker (1851–1933) were regular visitors and the Muthesiuses forged a close friendship with Mackintosh and Margaret Macdonald after the 1896 exhibition.[55] Mackintosh became their son Friedrich Eckart's (1904–1989) godfather and designed a cutlery set for his christening.[56] Muthesius travelled to Glasgow on several occasions and actively promoted not only the Mackintoshes but the city's rich cultural fabric as a whole. In a letter dated 11 November 1898, for example, Mackintosh wrote that 'the pleasure of seeing you in Glasgow was ours and we hope when you come to Glasgow again it shall be our privilege to see you again'.[57] Muthesius's support for Mackintosh culminated in a long feature essay on the Glasgow architect/designer and his wife Margaret Macdonald in *Deutsche Kunst und Dekoration* in 1902.[58]

In May of 1899, Elsa and Hugo Bruckmann went on a joint trip to Britain. Their visit came several months after the Bruckmanns' dining room was completed, but it reveals the close personal and professional links between Munich, London and Glasgow. Elsa Bruckmann noted in her diary that they stopped in Ukkel (Belgium) to visit Henry van de Velde's (1863–1957) new home Bloemenwerf. She wrote that she thoroughly enjoyed meeting the van de Veldes and that 'they were both very charming. We had a great debate about artistic reform of women's dress',[59] a topic that is at the heart of Chapter 5. The Bruckmanns then travelled to London, where they called on Anna and Hermann Muthesius on several occasions (Plate 13). Elsa Bruckmann remarked that The Priory was furnished 'in the school of Arts and Crafts Oxford Street . . . disappointed in the lack of reform'.[60] Although she acknowledged the importance of the Arts and Crafts movement in relation to Munich Jugendstil, she felt that its design language had run its course by the late 1890s and she was looking for a more modern style. She also mentioned Arthur Lasenby's Liberty department store, but her statement was rather sanctimonious in relation to the aesthetic of her own dining room. Elsa Bruckmann did not like London and was happy to escape the city to visit a friend in Eastbourne while Hugo travelled to Glasgow. She recorded in her diary that Hugo was very satisfied with his visit to Glasgow where he was 'warmly received; spent stimulating, entertaining days (among other things, an excursion along the Clyde) with Mackintosh, the Macdonalds, Morris, Stevenson etc. And the artistic impressions were <u>so</u> much better than in London.'[61]

Elsa Bruckmann's diary entries offer readers a sense of the lived experiences of this eminent group of supporters of modern design. But Elsa Bruckmann's observations also unveil fascinating international networks and confluences between advocates of a modern movement in architecture and design. The couple's visits to Belgium and Britain attest to their deeply seated interest in dialogue with like-minded supporters of modern design. In this instance, Muthesius acted as an important cultural broker between Glasgow and Munich. Bruckmann took his cue from Muthesius and promoted the Glasgow Four in his journal *Dekorative Kunst*, which, as previously mentioned, was the first continental publication to feature the young Glaswegian designers. Elsa Bruckmann also supported their cause in an essay for the *Illustrirte Frauen-Zeitung* in which she devoted half of her discussion to the 'young Scots'.[62] For the Bruckmanns, and other like-minded supporters of modern design in Germany, the Glasgow Style offered a viable alternative to the English Arts and Crafts movement that was more in line with the United Workshops' design principles and philosophies.

4.7 Elsa Bruckmann's debut as salonnière

Elsa Bruckmann was able to dedicate her energies to her highly anticipated entry into Munich society once their apartment was furnished. After much planning, her first salon took place on Thursday, 26 January 1899, in her brand-new space furnished by Mackintosh and Macdonald. Elsa Bruckmann's diaries stay silent on why she chose that particular day to launch her career as a salonnière, but Thursdays at the Bruckmanns soon became a *jour fixe* on Munich's social calendar. Elsa Bruckmann noted that she received several apologies from invitees to her inaugural salon, but she was still pleased with the overall turnout.[63] The evening opened with an intimate meal for the British-German philosopher Houston Stewart Chamberlain (1855–1927) and his wife Eva von Bülow (1867–1942), the composer Richard Wagner's daughter.[64] This was followed by 'tea and a cold supper' for Elsa Bruckmann's other invited guests, namely, members of the Bruckmann family such as Elsa's younger sister Marie von Hellingrath and Hugo's brother Alphons; the sculptor Adolf von Hildebrand and his wife Irene Schäuffelen (1846–1921); the painter Eugen Kirchner; the conductor Hermann Levi and his wife Mary Fiedler (1854–1919), who was the art historian Julius Meyer's daughter and Konrad Fiedler's widow; as well as Julius Knorr, the prominent Bavarian politician and publisher of Munich's liberal newspaper *Munich's Latest News*, in addition to several other members of Munich's cultural elite.[65]

The highlight of the evening was a reading by Chamberlain from his recent book *The Foundations of the Nineteenth Century* that was about to be published by Hugo Bruckmann that year.[66] Chamberlain's anti-Semitic text tapped into familiar nineteenth-century concepts of race that cast Jews as Christianity's 'other', but Chamberlain added the troubling caveat that a respective *Rassengeist* (racial mentality) was generated by biology and culture alike.[67] According to Chamberlain, the process of acculturation posed a great threat to German civilization because it potentially masked biological race. He wrote that 'for all intents and purposes, the Jew is an artificial product. [. . .] One can be a Jew without being a Jew, and one does not have to be a Jew because one is a Jew'.[68] Several attendees of Elsa Bruckmann's salon strongly disagreed with Chamberlain's incendiary rhetoric and a lively debate ensued.[69] But Elsa Bruckmann proved her worth as an emerging salonnière of great skill and successfully diffused any impending conflict. Polite sociability was maintained, and Elsa Bruckmann lived up to the historian Benedeta Craveri's observation that 'the salonière's [sic] supreme talent lay in knowing how to create a harmonious gathering of people who differed not only in temperament and intelligence but also in their social backgrounds'.[70] Elsa Bruckmann's salon was quite homogeneous in terms of its social composition, but the described incident revealed troubling fissures over race and ethnicity. Elsa Bruckmann's guests held quite disparate views on Chamberlain's anti-Semitism. Adolf von Hildebrand, for example, quickly rushed to his Jewish friend Hermann Levi's defence, who, ironically, did not feel addressed by Chamberlain's argument because he did not view himself a 'racial' Jew.[71]

Chamberlain's book was widely discussed in Germany's contemporary press and received a positive response in Munich. Although late-nineteenth-century Munich was keen to cast itself as Germany's artistic capital, the city also nourished deeply conservative political currents. This dynamic gave rise to a vexing sociocultural landscape that was inhabited by individuals such as Elsa and Hugo Bruckmann, who actively supported progressive art and design on an international stage while, simultaneously, embracing regressive nationalist politics. Elsa Bruckmann's biography evinces these paradoxes in fascinating ways: she was born into a Catholic aristocratic family with strong German-national views and links to the military, she was culturally educated by a Jewish doyenne of Viennese society (Todesco), she married a member of Germany's liberal upper-middle classes with increasingly anti-Semitic leanings, and yet, she readily opened her early salons to Jewish artists and intellectuals.

Despite this kerfuffle, Elsa Bruckmann pronounced her inaugural salon as a resounding success and set aside Thursday evenings for these kinds of gatherings, albeit not on a weekly basis.[72] She regularly invited prominent artists, architects and designers as well as writers, philosophers, scientists and political figures until Hugo's death in 1941.[73] On a most basic level, the architectural setting, complete with furniture and lighting, facilitated the social interaction between a carefully chosen community of like-minded individuals. The salon's material properties shaped the very dialogues and knowledge transfers that took place within the space and thus manifested social relationships on a spatial as well as a conceptual level. How then did the physical setting of a dining room become a salon? Undoubtedly, Elsa Bruckmann's first post-marital domicile could never compete with Vienna's Todesco Palais and its lavish salon. As a married woman of her socio-economic status, Elsa Bruckmann was determined to hold a salon even within the confined setting of their Nymphenburg Street apartment. The Mackintoshes came up with an ingenious design scheme that engendered a dining room in the first instance but could easily be transformed into a more fluid and informal space conducive to the dynamics of salon culture.[74]

The Mackintoshes used soft furnishings, wallpaper, stencilling, wood, lighting and stained glass to create a room that could be used for dining as well as entertaining. For example, Mackintosh provided different light sources – gas, candle and natural – that allowed Elsa Bruckmann to change the room's atmosphere according to its required function. But the Mackintoshes' stroke of genius was the previously mentioned curtain that separated a small alcove from the rest of the room. This space housed two Neo-Renaissance chairs. The Mackintoshes further distinguished this element from the rest of the room by replacing the stencilled frieze with a group of antlers mounted on wooden supports. These constituted a typical feature in many Munich homes and attested to the popularity of hunting as a leisure activity, but they also signalled a distinctly regional identity because hunting was engrained in the Bavarian psyche. Even though space was tight, the Mackintoshes offered a series of ingenious design solutions that transformed an intimate dining room into a lively salon. The curtain was presumably drawn during the meal and opened for the evening's more performative aspects after dinner. At this point in time, the smoker's cabinet revealed its tempting content to the Bruckmanns' male guests while their female companions were served a glass of liqueur. In larger homes, these activities would have taken place in separate rooms, but the Mackintoshes' spatial organization squashed these gendered spaces and conventions.[75] Mackintosh again used a curtain (this time, with appliqué work by Margaret Macdonald) in his 1902–3 décor for Fritz Waerndorfer's music room in Vienna to separate the latter from Josef Hoffmann's adjacent dining room.[76]

Charles Rennie Mackintosh and Margaret Macdonald, therefore, created a physical environment for the Bruckmanns with multiple functions. For most days of the week, the room offered an intimate setting for informal family meals. But the dining room could also accommodate the more rigidly prescribed protocol of Elsa Bruckmann's Thursday evenings. Although limited space might have been the most immediate motivation behind the Mackintoshes' flexible dining-room-cum-salon concept, his design also materialized a distinctly German adaptation of French salon culture, namely, the kind of sociability produced by consuming a shared meal. Elsa Bruckmann's Thursday evenings had a complex genealogy that was rooted in French salon culture as well as early-nineteenth-century German table societies (*Tischgesellschaften*).

4.8 A brief history of salon culture

Salon culture originated in Renaissance Italy but is most commonly associated with the French Enlightenment (1685–1815). Historians use the term 'salon' to describe a physical setting (the original Italian *salone* being a large reception room in a palazzo) as well as a kind of sociability generated by conversation among educated individuals. Salon culture, therefore, has spatial and social dimensions that are anchored in communication and knowledge transfer. Salons were commonly hosted by elite women and provided opportunities for social interaction and political debate outside the court, academies, lodges, clubs and cafés. [77] Historians tend to view eighteenth-century salons as breeding grounds for proto-democratic politics, while nineteenth-century salons are seen to consolidate the bourgeoisie's social aspirations.[78] The historiography of salon culture is too wide-ranging to discuss here, but Jürgen Habermas's paradigm-shifting book *The Structural Transformation of the Public Sphere* (1962) must be briefly mentioned.[79]

Habermas argued that eighteenth-century salons (France) and coffeehouses (Britain) provided a 'realm of our social life in which something approaching public opinion can be formed'.[80] Away from the surveillant eyes of the authorities, educated individuals engaged in free rational debate and formulated opinions that were subsequently circulated in newspapers, periodical articles and other written formats. Historians following in his intellectual footsteps contend that salons imbued women with agency and generated 'women's culture'.[81] Others use actor-network theory to present early-nineteenth-century Prussian salons as fertile progenitors of modernity and drew attention to salons as a literary genre.[82] These scholars share the view that salons were semi-private sites that offered women unique opportunities to contribute to first, the Enlightenment project and, then, nineteenth-century modernity. These retrievals of a female-driven sphere of influence formed the building blocks for a seminal exhibition curated in 2005 by Emily Bilski and Emily Braun that explored the complex relationship between Jewish assimilation, female emancipation and modern secular culture from early-nineteenth-century Berlin to 1930s Los Angeles. [83] Even though the exhibition focused on Jewish salons, it presented new insights into identity construction that exceed these parameters.

A number of scholars remain unconvinced that salon culture offered an alternative to elite court etiquette or that it represented a 'femino-centric institution' at all.[84] They argue that salonnières were actually tasked with enforcing social rules and hierarchies rather than creating alternative spheres of conduct.[85] For others, the Enlightenment salon represents an anachronistic *lieu de mémoire* (memory site) that allows historians to project their own ideologies ranging from French exceptionalism to feminist agendas.[86] Gender historians levelled an even more serious critique at Habermas by questioning his rigid division of bourgeois subjectivity into private and public spheres, which failed to accurately describe modernity's complex social dynamics.[87] These are important interventions to consider when dealing with historically specific salons such as Elsa Bruckmann's Thursday evenings. But feminist historians should not outright dismiss Habermas. Despite his limited attention to the nuanced workings of gender, he assembled a theoretical framework that allows historians to examine the sociopolitical structures of modern life and their emancipatory potential along class and maybe even gender lines.[88]

4.9 The Mackintosh dining-room-cum-salon

In relation to Elsa Bruckmann's Munich salon, it is appropriate to take into account a distinctly German genealogy of salon culture, namely, early-nineteenth-century *Tischgesellschaften* (table societies). These bourgeois clubs were committed to defending German culture and language against foreign invasions (in this instance, Napoleon's military campaigns). Germany's first table societies were founded in Berlin in 1810 and advertised the kinds of patriotic Christian values that formed the core of German Romanticism.[89] Key literary figures such as Achim von Arnim, Adam Müller, Clemens Brentano, Heinrich von Kleist and Johann Gottlieb Fichte regularly discussed cultural–political issues over a shared meal.[90] These societies largely operated in secrecy because their Enlightenment values were perceived as a threat to established power structures and 'its public, even as a public, remained internal'.[91] Members endorsed Immanuel Kant's contention that a meal should not only satisfy one's bodily needs but nourish sociability among cultivated individuals.[92] Jews, women and French citizens were categorically excluded.

Food historians have long argued that sharing a meal manifests a complex set of social constellations and is closely tied to identity formation.[93] The German concept of *Tischkultur* (table culture), therefore, not only encompasses the material implements used to consume food and drink but also regulates the behavioural norms and conventions around the table. In other words, table culture defines the physical and symbolic parameters of its constitutive interactions.[94] Viewed from this perspective, the Mackintoshes' interior for the Bruckmanns provided the physical setting for a hybrid set of practices that combined elements from table society (gendered as masculine) with conventions from salon culture (gendered as feminine). Elsa Bruckmann's Thursday evenings usually started with a meal that could range from intimate gatherings to formal suppers.[95] Elsa Bruckmann's physical and symbolic enactment of late-nineteenth-century table culture underlined her ambition to become one of Munich's premier hostesses because she fed not only her invitees' bodies but also their minds.[96]

Elsa Bruckmann's salon functioned as a semi-private space that facilitated specific cultural activities and performances – readings, discussions, entertainment – and re-inscribed a distinctly upper-middle-class identity into Munich's increasingly fractured sociopolitical fabric.[97] Elsa Bruckmann's clever intermixing of elements from German table culture with French salon practices was anchored by the room's unmissable ambience of Bavarian *Gemütlichkeit*. The term *Gemütlichkeit* is difficult to translate, but it alludes to a sense of conviviality and congeniality, if not cosiness.⁹⁸ It is gendered as masculine because it was seen to distinguish late-nineteenth-century Bavarian sociability from its more formalized, feminized and, possibly, racialized (Jewish) Prussian counterpart. It is a well-known historical fact that Germany's unification in 1871 under the Hohenzollern emperor Wilhelm I (1797–1888) failed to alleviate age-old regional alliances that continuously undermined the German Empire's tenuous national unity.⁹⁹ Elsa Bruckmann carefully declared her, and by extension her guests', Bavarian allegiances through her dining room décor and its incumbent social practices.

4.10 Salon culture and gender

Gender played an equally important role in these negotiations. Elsa Bruckmann deployed her Mackintosh-designed interior to enact her own identity as an advocate of Jugendstil design, a taste maker and a member of Munich's intellectual as well as socio-economic elite. But she inadvertently reinforced late-nineteenth-century gender norms that cast women of her social class into the subservient roles of wives, mothers and companions.¹⁰⁰ Ironically, Elsa Bruckmann aligned herself with members of the educated upper-middle classes who had acquired their wealth through enterprise and industry rather than her own peers from the old aristocracy. Elsa Bruckmann never relinquished her title of 'Princess of Cantacuzènes', but she was fully aware of her family's economic struggles and the Bavarian aristocracy's waning political influence. Her marriage to the respected entrepreneur Hugo Bruckmann offered Elsa Cantacuzènes the financial means to retain an aristocratic lifestyle while her husband acquired sociocultural cachet and respectability in the match. But Elsa and Hugo Bruckmann's carefully staged image harboured troubling ideological undercurrents that would erupt onto the surface in the decades to come. Namely, the alignment of progressive cultural values with regressive politics that supported the German Empire's military culture, imperialism, anti-Semitism and authoritarianism. Although set in Berlin, Thomas Mann's novel *Buddenbrooks: The Decline of a Family* (1901) aptly critiqued this rapidly contracting upper-bourgeois world inhabited by the likes of Elsa and Hugo Bruckmann by chronicling the decline of a wealthy German merchant family over the course of four generations.¹⁰¹

4.11 Elsa Bruckmann's 'enhanced independence'

Elsa and Hugo Bruckmann were powerful advocates of Jugendstil from its very inception at the Munich Glaspalast in 1897. Hugo Bruckmann commissioned Martin Dülfer to design the new headquarters for his new publishing house and

Elsa Bruckmann invited Charles Rennie Mackintosh and Margaret Macdonald to collaborate with local designers and create a Jugendstil *Gesamtarrangement* for her dining-room-cum-salon in her new apartment. Hugo Bruckmann used his publishing empire to promote modern design through monographs and his journal *Dekorative Kunst*, while his wife used the material and intellectual parameters of her Thursday evenings to showcase the merits of Jugendstil design. Their marriage epitomized a commanding alliance between central Europe's old aristocracy and the German Empire's educated upper-middle classes. As a couple, they deployed local, national and international connections to promote modern architecture and design, and soon became powerful tastemakers of their day. The French sociologist Pierre Bourdieu argued fifty years ago that taste plays a key role in the modern world because it forms the basis for social judgement. Objects are actively implicated in these complex judgements as they reflect and materialize taste.[102] The Bruckmanns' Jugendstil home showcased its owners' progressive taste in terms of modern design and provided an ideal space to broker crucial alliances with Munich's cultural–political elite during Elsa Bruckmann's Thursday evenings.

Historians across a range of disciplines have long contended that eighteenth- and nineteenth-century salons imbued elite women with sociopolitical agency in an otherwise relatively limited sphere of action. Elsa Bruckmann's salon represented a more fluid and heterogeneous site. Elsa Bruckmann turned the 'private' and intimate space of her Jugendstil dining room into a salon that hosted readings and performances and 'publicly' declared the Bruckmanns' progressive cultural profiles. If culture occupies the space between experience and expectation, then the historically and geographically specific site of Elsa Bruckmann's salon played an important role in the projection of a distinctly modern identity. Elsa Bruckmann did not share the radical political views of her fellow Jugendstil patrons Sophia Goudstikker and Anita Augspurg, discussed in Chapter 2. The Bruckmanns' supported progressive design ethos anchored in modernity but, strictly speaking, Elsa Bruckmann was not a 'New Woman'. Elsa Bruckmann represented a different kind of modern woman: well educated and upper class with a devoted husband, a beautiful home, an impeccable appearance, great taste and considerable social clout. And, most importantly, she had a degree of independence and agency, even if these were generated by Hugo's wealth and cultural prestige. Design historian Penny Sparke coined the helpful expression 'enhanced independence' to describe this dynamic.[103]

Notes

1 H. Elgo, 'Glueck', *Pan* 2, no. 3 (1896–7): 219–20.

2 'Die Schottischen Künstler: Margaret Macdonald, Frances Macdonald, Chas. R. Mackintosh, T. Morris und J. Herbert McNair', *Dekorative Kunst* III (1899):

48–9; 'Glasgow-München', *Dekorative Kunst* III (1899): 69–76; 'C. R. Mackintosh, Glasgow', *Dekorative Kunst* IV (1899): 78–9.

3   Arjun Appadurai, *The Social Life of Things: Commodities in Cultural Perspective* (Cambridge: Cambridge University Press, 1986).

4   Pierre Bourdieu, *A Social Distinction of Taste* (London: Routledge, 1984). For a helpful feminist engagement with Bourdieu see Toril Moi, 'Appropriating Bourdieu: Feminist Theory and Pierre Bourdieu's Sociology of Culture', *New Literary History* 22, no. 4 (Autumn 1991): 1017–49.

5   *The Encyclopaedia Britannica*, 11th edn., vol. 5 (Cambridge: Cambridge University Press, 1910), 208.

6   Marie von Hellingrath, *Aus unserer Kindheit: Erinnerungen zum Anlass von Elsa Bruckmanns 70. Geburtstag am 23 Februar 1935*, unpublished manuscript, Bruckmannia Supplement (BS), Schachtel 15, Bayerische Staatsbibliothek (BSB).

7   The German Empire's educational systems for girls and its cultural–political impact on modern design practices are discussed in Chapter 3 of this book.

8   Anne Schlüter, *Pionierinnen – Feministinnen – Karrierefrauen? Zur Geschichte des Frauenstudiums in Deutschland, Frauen in Geschichte und Gesellschaft, Bd. 22* (Pfaffenweiler: Centaurus, 1992).

9   Michelle Facos, *Nationalism and the Nordic Imagination: Swedish Art of the 1890s* (Berkeley: University of California Press, 1998); Barbara Lane Miller, *National Romanticism and Modern Architecture in Germany and the Scandinavian Countries* (Cambridge: Cambridge University Press, 2000); Wilfred Jack Rhoden and E. E. Snyder, *Poetry, Politics and Pictures in the Nineteenth Century* (Bern: Peter Lang, 2013).

10 H. Elgo [Elsa Bruckmann Cantacuzène], 'Glück', *Pan* 2, no. 3 (November 1896): 219; Elsa Bruckmann Fürstin Cantacuzène, 'Vom vierblättrigen Kleeblatt', *Illustrirte Frauen-Zeitung* 24, no. 12 (1897): 95.

11 Hugo Bruckmann quoted in Wolfgang Martynkewicz, *Salon Deutschland: Geist und Macht, 1900–1945* (Berlin: Aufbau Verlag, 2011), 42.

12 For an excellent discussion of Eduard and Sophie Todesco see Elana Shapira, *Style and Seduction: Jewish Patrons, Architecture and Design in Fin-de-Siècle Vienna* (Waltham: Brandeis University Press, 2016), 22–45.

13 Sophie Todesco's father Philipp Gomperz (1782–1881) acquired his fortune through banking; her brother was the famous classicist Theodor Gomperz (1832–1912) and her nephew the equally renowned philosopher Heinrich Gomperz (1873–1942). *Österreichisches Biographisches Lexikon 1815–1850*, Bd. 4 (Vienna: Verlag der Österreichischen Akademie der Wissenschaften, 2012), 364.

14 Carl Schorske, *Fin-de-Siècle Vienna: Politics and Culture* (New York: Knopf, 1980). For Schorske's profound impact on the scholarship of Viennese modernism see Steven Beller, *Rethinking Vienna 1900* (New York: Berghahn, 2001) and *Vienna and the Jews: A Cultural History* (Cambridge: Cambridge University Press, 1989).

15 Renate Wagner-Rieger, *Die Ringstrasse: Bild einer Epoche*, 11 vols. (Wiesbaden: Steiner, 1969–81) and Wolfgang Kos and Ralph Gleis, *Experiment Metropole: 1873 Wien und die Weltausstellung* (Vienna: Czerin Verlag, 2014).

16 The exact address was Kärntner Strasse 51/Walfischgasse 2. Todesco made several shrewd investments along the Ring Street and famously owned the building housing Vienna's iconic Hotel Sacher. Monika Czernin, *Anna Sacher und ihr Hotel im Wien der Jahrhundertwende,* 3rd ed. (Munich: Albrecht Knaus Verlag, 2014).

17 Cornelia Reiter and Robert Stalla, *Theophil Hansen: Architekt und Designer* (Weitra: Bibliothek der Provinz, 2013).

18 Shapira, *Style and Seduction,* 22–45.

19 Ibid.

20 *Österreichisches Biographisches Lexikon,* 364.

21 Martynkewicz, *Salon Deutschland,* 27–30.

22 Ibid., 42.

23 Elsa Bruckmann Bruckmann, *Diary,* BS 15.

24 This was an interesting inversion of the legendary constellation in Victorian Britain whereby American heiresses married into British nobility. See, for example, Marian Fowler, *In a Gilded Cage: From Heiress to Duchess* (New York: St. Martin's Press, 1994).

25 The Bruckmann family initially owned a porcelain manufacture in Deutz but it failed to turn a profit due to several fires and mounting competition from France and Britain. Fritz sold the company in 1858 and founded his publishing house, which operates to this day. Erich Pfeiffer-Belli, *100 Jahre Bruckmann* (Munich: Bruckmann, 1958).

26 Munich was one of Europe's leading centres for photographic reproduction during the second half of the nineteenth century. Helmut Heß, *Der Kunstverlag Franz Hanfstaengl und die frühe fotografische Reproduktion: Das Kunstwerk und sein Abbild* (Munich: Akademischer Verlag, 2000).

27 Alphons recalled in his memoires that 'in those days, the colour postcard industry was in full bloom, and millions of such cards were ordered from me because their quality was first class'. Alphons Bruckmann, *Lebenserinnerungen* (1935), 45. Unpublished manuscript, BS 21.

For a history of picture postcards see Richard Carline, *Pictures in the Post: The Story of the Picture Postcard and its Place in the History of Popular Art* (London: Gordon Fraser Gallery, 1971); Anett Holzheid, *Das Medium Postkarte: Eine sprachwissenschaftliche und mediengeschichtliche Studie* (Berlin: E. Schmidt, 2011).

28 Michael Bringmann, *Friedrich Pecht (1914–1903): Maßstäbe der deutschen Kunstkritik zwischen 1850 und 1900* (Berlin: Mann, 1982); Iris Lauterbach, *Die Kunst für Alle (1885-1944): Zur Kunstpublistik vom Kaiserreich bis zum Nationalsozialismus* (Munich: Zentralinstitut für Kunstgeschichte, 2010); Beth Irwin Lewis, *Art for All? The Collision of Art and the Public in Late-Nineteenth Century Germany* (Princeton: Princeton University Press, 2003).

29 By this point in time, Meier-Graefe had already co-founded the modernist journal *Pan* (1895–1900) and was about to open his famous Paris gallery La Maison Moderne, which promoted International Art Nouveau (1899).

30 Hugo remained at the helm of the Bruckmann Publishing House until his death in 1941 and steered the company through several challenging economic times such as the First World War and the Great Depression of 1929.

31 Elsa Bruckmann Cantacuzène letters to Hugo, BS 3.

32 Dülfer's estate was destroyed in 1945, but Dieter Klein has painstakingly reconstructed Dülfer's professional biography: Dieter Klein, *Martin Dülfer: Wegbereiter der deutschen Jugendstilarchitektur* (Munich: Landratsamt für Denkmalspflege, 1993).

33 Klein, *Martin Dülfer*, 11.

34 Sabine Wieber, 'The German Interior at the end of the Nineteenth Century', in *Designing the Modern Interior: From the Victorians to Today*, ed. Penny Sparke (Oxford: Berg, 2009), 53–64.

35 He had previously collaborated with Riemerschmid on the Villa Bechtolsheim (Maria-Theresia Strasse 27), which is regarded as Germany's first Jugendstil buildings. Winfried Nerdinger, *Richard Riemerschmid: Vom Jugendstil zum Werkbund. Werke und Dokumente* (Munich: Prestel, 1982).

36 Rudolf Vogel, 'Moderne, wahre Baukunst', *Deutsche Bauhütte* 6 (1902), 329–95.

37 This excerpt also serves as a wonderful illustration of the workings of Historicism whereby any historical object could readily be copied. Jugendstil designers, of course, vehemently react against this practice. Letter from Elsa Bruckmann to Hugo Bruckmann, 29 July 1898, BS 2.

38 Roger Billcliffe, *Charles Rennie Mackintosh: The Complete Furniture Drawings and Interior Designs*, 4th ed. (Moffat: Cameron & Hollis, 2009), 47–50. The Hunterian Art Gallery, University of Glasgow, GLAHA 41799, 41800, and 41801.

39 University of Glasgow, The Hunterian, GLAHA 41801 and 41800.

40 Fred M. Walker, *The Song of the Clyde: A History of Clyde Shipbuilding* (Edinburgh: John Donald Publishing, 2011).

41 A virtually identical repoussé panel by Macdonald is owned by the Hunterian Art Gallery, GLAHA 41265.

42 For the fascinating relationship between the Glasgow Four and (Belgian) Symbolism see David Brett, *C.R. Mackintosh: The Poetics of Workmanship* (London: Reaktion Books, 1992), especially Chapter 3.

43 Little is known about Karl Bertsch, but the Bavarian National Museum holds a suite of furniture for a *Lady's Sitting Room* that he designed in 1907. Bertsch was a co-founder of the Munich Workshops for Domestic Interiors (1904), and his role as an advocate for modern furniture design warrants further research. Karl Mayr, 'Neue Räume der Werkstätten für Wohnungs-Einrichtungen Karl Bertsch, München', *Innen Dekoration* 15 (May 1904): 119–32.

44 Elsa Bruckmann Diary entries 11 and 14 January 1899, BS 15.

45 Laura Euler, *The Glasgow Style* (Atglen: Schiffer Publishing, 2008).

46 Perilla Kinchin, *Taking Tea with Mackintosh: The Story of Miss Cranston's Tea Rooms* (San Francisco: Pomegranate, 1998).

47 For example, David Stark, *Charles Rennie Mackintosh and Co. 1854 to 2004* (Mauchline: Stenlake Publishing 2004); Alan Crawford, *Charles Rennie Mackintosh* (London: Thames & Hudson, 1995); James Macaulay, *Charles Rennie Mackintosh: A Biography* (New York: W. W. Norton, 2010).

48 Janice Helland, 'Collaboration among the Four', *Charles Rennie Mackintosh*, ed. Wendy Kaplan (New York: Abbeville Press, 1996), 89–114.

49 Gleeson White, 'Some Glasgow Designers and Their Work', *The Studio* XI (July 1897): 86–100. See for example Macaulay, *Charles Rennie Mackintosh* or Thomas Howarth, *Charles Rennie Mackintosh and the Modern Movement*, 3rd ed. (London: Routledge, 1990).

50 *The Studio: An Illustrated Magazine for Fine and Applied art* was founded by Charles Holme in 1893 and only ceased publication in 1964. Bryan Holme, *The Studio: A Bibliography, the First Fifty Years 1893–1943* (London: Simms and Reed, 1978).

51 John Feather, *A History of British Publishing* (Abingdon: Routledge, 1988).

52 Kaplan, *Charles Rennie Mackintosh*, 19.

53 The term 'modern movement' was famously coined by Nikolas Pevsner, *Pioneers of the Modern Movement* (New York: Faber & Faber, 1936).

54 Hermann Muthesius, *Das englische Haus*, 3 vols. (Berlin: Ernst Wasmuth, 1904).

55 The University of Glasgow, 'Mackintosh Architecture: Context, Making and Meaning', accessed 17 March 2017, http://www.mackintosh-architecture.gla.ac.uk/catalogue/name/?nid=MuthHer#MuthHer3-back.

56 The Hunterian Art Gallery, GLAHA 41937.

57 Mackintosh quoted in 'Mackintosh Architecture: Context, Making and Meaning'.

58 Hermann Muthesius, 'Die Glasgower Kunstbewegung: Charles R. Mackintosh und Margaret Macdonald-Mackintosh', *Dekorative Kunst* 10 (March 1902): 193–221.

59 Else Bruckmann quoted in Martynkewicz, *Salon Deutschland*, 52.

60 Else Bruckmann Diary entry May 1899, BS 15.

61 Ibid.

62 Elsa Bruckmann Bruckmann, 'Das heutige Kunstgewerbe', *Illustrirte Frauen-Zeitung* 21, no. 1 (November 1899): 166–7.

63 Else Bruckmann Diary Entry 26 January 1899, BS 15.

64 Eva Maria von Bülow was Richard Wagner's first daughter and born when Cosima (1837–1930) was still married to the conductor and composer Hans von Bülow (1830–1894). For the complicated yet fascinating family history of the Wagner dynasty see Oliver Hilmes, *Cosimas Kinder: Triumph and Tragödie der Wagner-Dynastie* (Munich: Siedler, 2009).

65 Elsa Bruckmann does not mention the names of Levi's and Hildebrand's wives, which signals a fascinating historical gender bias. Irene Schäuffelen left no retrievable historical trace beyond her grave in Munich's Kirchhof Oberföhring cemetery. Her gravestone was made by her husband.

66 Houston Stewart Chamberlain, *Grundlagen des Neunzehnten Jahrhunderts* (Munich: Bruckmann Verlag, 1899). For Chamberlain's biography and the intellectual context of his theories see Geoffrey Field, *Evangelist of Race: The Germanic Vision of Houston Stewart Chamberlain* (New York: Columbia University Press, 1981); Udo Bermbach, *Houston Stewart Chamberlain: Wagners Schwiegersohn – Hitlers Vordenker* (Stuttgart: J. B. Metzler, 2015).

67 Yuri Slezkine, *The Jewish Century* (New Jersey: Princeton University Press, 2004).

68 Letter from Chamberlain to H. Bruckmann, 7 August 1898, BS 1.

69 Else Bruckmann Diary Entry 26 January 1899, BS 15.
70 Craveri quoted in Emily D. Bilski and Emily Braun, *Jewish Women and Their Salons: The Power of Conversation* (New Haven: Yale University Press, 2005), 3.
71 Martynkewicz, *Salon Deutschland*, 58.
72 Else Bruckmann Diary Entry 26 January 1899, BS 15.
73 Some of the key figures from the German Empire's culture elite who attended Elsa Bruckmann's salon were Rainer Maria Rilke, Heinrich Wölfflin, Count Keyserling, Rudolf Kassner, the Jewish author Karl Wolfskehl, Harry Graf Kessler, Alfred Schuler and Norbert von Heilingrath.
74 Charles Rennie Mackintosh and Margaret Macdonald married in 1900 but for ease of writing, they are referred to as 'the Mackintoshes', which is a term regularly employed by design historians.
75 Barbara Penner, Iain Borden and Jane Rendell, *Gender Space Architecture: An Interdisciplinary Introduction* (London: Routledge, 2000).
76 Peter Vergo, *Ein moderner Nachmittag. A Thoroughly Modern Afternoon* (Vienna: Böhlau, 2000), 18–40.
77 Benedetta Craveri, *The Age of Conversation,* trans. Teresa Waugh (New York: New York Review of Books, 2005); Dena Goodman, *The Republic of Letters: A Cultural History of the French Enlightenment* (Ithaca: Cornell University Press, 1994).
78 Sarah C. Maza, *Private Lives and Public Affairs: The Causes Célèbres of Pre-Revolutionary France* (Berkeley: University of California Press, 1993); Bilski and Braun, *Jewish Women and Their Salons*.
79 Jürgen Habermas, *Strukturwandel der Öffentlichkeit* (Neuwied: Luchterhand Verlag, 1962).
80 Ibid., 36.
81 Verena Heyden-Rynsch, *Europäische Salons: Höhepunkte einer versunkenen weiblichen Kultur* (Munich: Artemis & Winkler, 1992).
82 Petra Wilhelmy, *Der Berliner Salon im 19. Jahrhundert, 1780–1914* (Berlin: Walter de Gruyter, 1989); Peter Seibert, *Der literarische Salon: Literatur und Geselligkeit zwischen Aufklärung und Vormärz* (Stuttgart: Metzler, 1993).
83 'Jewish Women and their Salons: The Power of Conversation', The Jewish Museum, New York and the McMullen Museum of Art, Boston College. For the important link between nineteenth-century Jewish identity and salon culture see: Deborah Holmes, 'Nichts weniger als die Erneuerung der Weiblichkeit: Wiener Salonkultur ab der Jahrhundertwende', in *Hilde Spiel und der literarische Salon,* ed. Ingrid Schramm and Michael Hansel (Innsbruck: Studienverlag, 2011), 15–34; Clemens Peck, 'Theodor Herzl and the Utopia of the Salon in *Fin-de-Siècle* Vienna', trans. Deborah Holmes, *Austrian Studies* 24 (2016): 79–93.
84 Jolanta T. Pekacz, *Conservative Tradition in Pre-Revolutionary France: Parisian Salon Women* (New York: Peter Lang, 1999), 10.
85 Ibid.
86 Nancy W. Collins, 'The Problem of the Enlightenment Salon' (PhD Dissertation, University College of London, 2006), 2. See also Antoine Lilti, *The World of the*

Salons: Sociability and Worldliness in Eighteenth-Century Paris (New York: Oxford University Press, USA, 2015).

87 Amanda Vickery offers a salient argument for the recalibration of Habermas's separate spheres model in her essay 'Golden Age to Separate Spheres? A Review of the Categories and Chronology of English Women's History', *Historical Review* 36, no. 2 (1993): 383–414.

88 Johanna Meehan, *Feminists Read Habermas* (London: Routledge, 1995), 2.

89 For a recent historical overview of German Romanticism and its abiding impact on contemporary culture see Rüdiger Safranski, *Romanticism: A German Affair,* trans. R. Goodwin (Evanston: Northwestern University Press, 2015).

90 Stefan Nienhaus, *Geschichte der deutschen Tischgesellschaft* (Berlin: Walter de Gruyter, 2003).

91 Habermas, *Strukturwandel der Öffentlichkeit*, 238.

92 Immanuel Kant, *Anthropologie in pragmatischer Hinsicht,* Akademie Textausgabe, Bd. 7 (Berlin: Walter de Gruyter, 1972), 428.

93 Barbara Schilling, *Tischkultur in der bürgerlichen Gesellschaft des 19. Jahrhunderts: Die 'Gute Gesellschaft' ist, was und wie sie isst* (Munich: GRIN Verlag, 2008).

94 Mary C. Beaudry, 'Artifacts and Active Voices: Material Culture as Social Discourse', in *The Archaeology of Inequality*, ed. Randall H. McGuire and Robert Paynter (Oxford: Basil Blackwell, 1991), 150–91.

95 Elsa Bruckmann Diary, BS 15.

96 A discussion of the fascinating history of nineteenth-century hospitality exceeds the parameters of this chapter but suffice to note that it was a deeply classed and gendered construct.

97 David Blackbourn and Greoff Eley, *The Peculiarities of German History* (Oxford: Oxford University Press, 1994); John B. Lyon, *Out of Place: German Realism, Displacement and Modernity* (London: Bloomsbury Publishing, 2013); Thomas Nipperdey, *Deutsche Geschichte 1866-1918,* vol. 2 (Munich: Beck, 1992).

98 I thank Kjetil Fallan for drawing my attention to a current example of the problematic 'translation' of culturally specific concepts into different national contexts, namely, the Anglophone craze for the Scandinavian 'hygge'. This has been eloquently discussed by Malene Breunig and Shona Kallestrop, 'Translating Hygge: A Danish Design Myth and Its Anglophone Appropriation', *Journal of Design History* 33, no. 2 (2020): 158–74.

99 Celia Applegate, *A Nation of Provincials: The German Idea of Heimat* (Berkeley: University of California Press, 1990); Sabine Wieber, 'Designing the Nation: Neo-Northern Renaissance Interiors and the Politics of Identity in late Nineteenth-Century Germany, 1876–1888' (PhD Dissertation, The University of Chicago, 2004).

100 Linda L. Clark, *Women and Achievement in Nineteenth-Century Europe* (Cambridge: Cambridge University Press, 2008).

101 Mann attacked members of the upper bourgeoisie for turning their backs on the cultural–political values of liberalism that had engendered their social ascendancy in the first place. See also Wolfgang J. Mommsen, ed., *Bürgerliche Kulture und*

politische Ordnung: Künstler, Schriftsteller und Intellektuelle in der deutschen Geschichte 1830-1933 (Frankfurt: Fischer Verlag, 1980).

102 Pierre Bourdieu, *Distinction: A Social Critique of the Judgement of Taste* (Cambridge: Harvard University Press, 1984).

103 Penny Sparke, 'Your Place or Mine? The Client's Contribution to Domestic Architecture', in *Women's Places: Architecture and Design 1860–1960,* ed. P. Sparke and Brenda Martin (London: Routledge, 2003), 67.

PLATE 1 (ABOVE) Munich Hofbräuhaus, postcard *c.* 1900. Owned by author.

PLATE 2 (RIGHT) Josef Rudolf Witzel – Cover of the art and literary magazine *Jugend*, issue no. 16/1896. Courtesy Heidelberg University Library, Germany

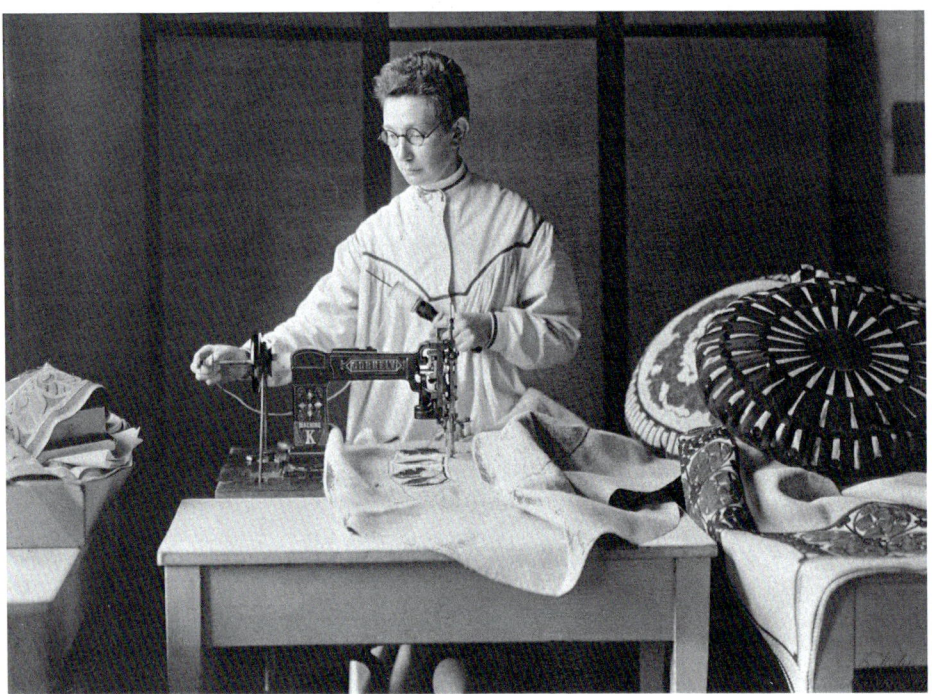

PLATE 3 MARGARETHE von Brauchitsch in her embroidery studio, photograph c. 1910. Theodor Hilsdorf Nachlass. Ullstein Bild Dtl./Contributor/Getty.

PLATE 4 MARGARETHE von Brauchitsch, tablecloth and pillows, 1909, in *Dekorative Kunst* 18 (1909–10): 27. Museum für Kunst und Gewerbe, Hamburg, MKDH Z D.

PLATE 5 (RIGHT) Photo-Studio Elvira, Grand Duchess Regent of Luxemburg, Maria Anna of Portugal with her children, 1903. https://commons.wikimedia.org/w/index.php?title=File:Maria_Anna_de_Luxembourg.jpg&oldid=486286454.

PLATE 6 (BELOW) Postcard of the Applied Arts Pavilion at the 'Bavarian Trade, Industry and Art Exhibition', Nuremberg 1906. Owned by author.

PLATE 7 (ABOVE) Debschitz School, metal workshop, 1905. Stadtmuseum Munich, Zentrales Bildarchiv.

PLATE 8 (RIGHT) Ernst Heilemann, Studentinnen, in *Simplicissimus* 4, no. 41 (6 January 1900): 332. Public Domain. Klassikstiftung Weimar.

PLATE 9 EMILIE Butters, vase, glazed and painted earthenware, Keramische Werkstätten Munich-Herrsching, 1912. Quittenbaum Kunstauktionen GmbH.

Elsa Bruckmann, geborene Fürstin Cantacuzène, um 1900

PLATE 10A AND 10B (ABOVE) Left: Hugo Bruckmann, Staatsbibliothek München, Handschriften Sammlung, Nachlass Elsa und Hugo Bruckmann (Bruckmanniana). Bayerische Staatsbibliothek / Bildarchiv. Right: Atelier Elisabeth, Gladbeck, Elsa Bruckmann, Photograph, *c*. 1895. Deutsches Literaturarchiv Marbach.

PLATE 11 (LEFT) Martin Dülfer, Bruckmann villa, Munich, 1898–9. Photograph by author.

PLATE 12 (RIGHT) Charles Rennie Mackintosh, smoker's cabinet, drawing, 1899. The Hunterian, University of Glasgow.

PLATE 13 (BELOW) Anna and Hermann Muthesius, drinking tea at the Priory, Hammersmith, London 1896. Nuremberg, Germanisches Nationalmuseum, Deutsches Kunstarchiv, NL Muthesius, Anna, 3652 (0008).

PLATE 14 BRUNO Paul, 'Der Münchner Jugendbrunnern', *Simplicissumus* 2, no. 10 (5 June 1897): 7 Staatliche Graphische Sammlung München, Inv.-Nr. Simpl. 1250.

5 REFORMERS
DRESSING THE PART

The fundamental principle of our dress reform must be the beauty of fitness and the beauty of form. And these ideals can only be realized by women who have the courage of their own convictions, and [who] are willing to stand out against the mighty current of conventionality.

MINNA CAUER, 1907[1]

In 1902, the architect Henry van de Velde published a lengthy discussion on what he called the 'new artistic principle in women's clothing' in the journal *Deutsche Kunst und Dekoration*.[2] In it, he argued that applied arts reformers must include dress in their quest for a modern style. Van de Velde's essay responded to a recent exhibition on *Künstlerkleider* (Artistic Dress) at the German Dressmakers' Meeting in Krefeld (4–13 August 1900). The exhibition was organized by van de Velde's close friend Friedrich Deneken (1857–1927), who was one of the German Empire's most progressive museum directors of the day.[3] Deneken used Germany's annual textile convention to boost Krefeld's textile industry and to advocate for a closer collaboration between Jugendstil designers and the garment industry.[4] To meet this objective, Deneken invited some of Germany's leading Jugendstil designers to apply their modern approaches to women's dress. His '*Sonder-Ausstellung moderner Damen-Kostüme nach Künstler-Entwürfen*' (Special Exhibition of Modern Ladies Costumes made from Artists' Designs) was the first of its kind in the German Empire and attracted considerable attention.

Van de Velde contributed six dresses to Deneken's exhibition that he had designed for his wife Marie-Louise 'Maria' Sèthe (1867–1943). Margarethe von Brauchitsch (Chapter 1) submitted a number of garments and modelled one of her coat designs for a photograph featured in van de Velde's essay. Other key contributors were members of the United Workshops Richard Riemerschmid, Franz August Krüger and Bernhard Pankok, as well as one of Germany's most vocal advocates of Artistic Dress, the Hamburg artist Alfred Mohrbutter (1867–1916). Two progressive fashion ateliers, Reinhard & Fia Wille (Berlin) and Reutlinger (Paris), also contributed, as did the immensely talented but, at the time, virtually unknown, Munich art student Elsa Oppler (1875–1965), who exhibited fifteen dresses (Figure 40).[5] Van de Velde declared that 'from today onwards, exhibitions of Ladies Garments are to be part of the category [*Kategorie*] art exhibition'.[6] The 1900 Krefeld exhibition recently served as a touchpoint for an exhibition on Artistic Dress at the Art Museum Krefeld (2018) and is compellingly discussed in Rebecca Houze's book on fashion and design reform in the Habsburg Empire (2015).[7] This chapter builds on this previous work but uses Deneken's exhibition as a point of entry into some of the rich debates around the role of dress within the German Empire's Life Reform movement. This approach repositions dress as a dynamic discourse and material practice that embodied many of the key trajectories of Jugendstil reform at the heart of this book. Jugendstil women engaged with Artistic Dress on many levels and literally wore their modernity on their sleeves. Moreover, this chapter shows that a critical study of dress opens up crucial new insights into the close interconnections, and indeed tensions, between the dress reformers' lofty ambitions and the German Empire's accelerating modernization.

FIGURE 40 a/b Else Oppler in one of her *Künstlerkleider*, c. 1900, in *Deutsche Kunst und Dekoration* 10 (1902): 366 Universitätsbibliothek Heidelberg, urn:nbn:de:bsz:16-diglit-63833.

5.1 What is Artistic Dress?

Deneken's exhibition showcased Künstlerkleider. The term is best translated as Artistic Dress, but the latter represents a vexing category. Design historian Robyne Calvert offers this useful definition:

> From roughly the mid-nineteenth century, Artistic Dress was an alternative sartorial style adopted by both men and women who wished to communicate their identification with artistic practices and philosophies that often ran counter to the status quo. For women, this style was expressed through a less structured look and cut of garment, resulting in a radical departure from the mainstream Victorian silhouette.[8]

The outfits exhibited in Krefeld were different from what is more commonly known in the scholarly literature and general parlance as Reform Dress. They are synchronous historical phenomena whose supporters shared many sociocultural ambitions, but Artistic Dress and Reform Dress should not be used interchangeably.[9] Artistic Dress originated in England, and German applied arts reformers kept a close watch on their Anglo-Saxon colleagues. Dress historians have long argued that Artistic Dress was 'invented' by the English Pre-Raphaelite Brotherhood (founded in 1848) and subsequently disseminated by the Arts and Crafts movement, by Aestheticism and, most importantly, by the Healthy and Artistic Dress Union founded in 1893.[10] Members of the Healthy and Artistic Dress Union included the painters George Frederic Watts (1817–1904) and Louise Jopling (1843–1933), the designer Walter Crane (1845–1915) and the founder of Liberty's department store Arthur Lasenby Liberty (1843–1917). Knowledge of these initiatives entered German reform circles through international exhibitions, reviews and more general discussions of European applied arts reform efforts in design journals. What started as an artistic practice during the 1850s was firmly entrenched in the popular imagination by the end of the nineteenth century.

In Germany, Artistic Dress represented an aspect of the country's nationwide design reform movement but it lacked the latter's unmistakable sociopolitical agenda. Supporters of Reform Dress prioritized health and social mobility while advocates of Artistic Dress were dedicated to infusing contemporary dress with Jugendstil design principles. The two were not mutually exclusive and Artistic Dress formed an aspect of the German Empire's dress-reform movement, but its advocates tended to be more concerned with aesthetics than politics. As a matter of fact, devotees of Artistic Dress moved in quite elite socio-economic circles. Henry van de Velde was one of Germany's chief spokesmen for Artistic Dress and revealed his unconscious bias against a more politically motivated engagement with Reform Dress when writing in 1902 that fashion suffered a first attack a few years ago; the first army formed in Germany under the banner of 'Reform Dress'. [...] But Reform Dress was only supported by principles of health; its proponents completely neglected beauty. [. . .] Reform Dress was somewhat puritan, dry and plain, all of which repels.[11]

While acknowledging a shared genealogy between the two, van de Velde was more concerned with warding off (French) fashion dictates than batting for women's rights.

5.2 Artistic Dress and German dress reform

The study of historical dress and textiles – in their material forms as well as their wider visual representations – offers a rich and interdisciplinary area of research that is now firmly established within academia. Josephine Miller and Lou Taylor, two early advocates of the scholarly engagement with historical clothing, rightly asserted that dress and textile history is 'a multi-faceted subject' that 'needs to be placed firmly within a cultural context, against a background of technological and industrial change, literary and aesthetic ideas'.[12] From this follows that changes in dress styles, especially during the latter part of the nineteenth century, did not simply result from new production methods (e.g. wire crinolines) and technologies (e.g. aniline dyes) but engendered shifting cultural, social and political constructions of femininity and masculinity. These gender norms were materially and conceptually embedded in clothing and fashionable taste, respectively. Jugendstil scholarship has been slow in acknowledging dress and textiles history's important contributions to the subject because of its persistent focus on the analysis of architecture, interiors, the applied arts and furniture. The long absence of dress in Jugendstil's historiography is also tied to museums and other collecting practices that tended to prioritize applied arts and furniture over fashionable dress and accessories, which were too often considered as ephemera. To make matters worse, garments and accessories have a more precarious lifespan and tended to be discarded by their owners. However, recent scholarly publications and exhibition endeavours have presented irrefutable arguments on the importance of dress within the complex negotiations of an increasingly fractured and dislocated external and internal world that characterized modernity.[13]

Within Jugendstil circles, Reform Dress *was Künstlerkleid.* All of the Jugendstil designers involved in Deneken's Krefeld exhibition conceived dress as an art form and individuality was their credo. Their embrace of *Künstlerkleid* was in part motivated by one of Jugendstil's core aims, namely, to level (at least on paper) the age-old hierarchies between the fine arts, architecture and the applied arts. Dress could be art and, vice versa, aesthetics had a role to play in the design of contemporary garments. Van de Velde powerfully argued this very point when asserting that 'clothing was the final frontier for artistic reform'.[14] But beyond Jugendstil circles, *Künstlerkleider* were viewed with caution and more radical factions of Germany's dress-reform movement considered *Künstlerkleider* as yet another aesthetic calcification of the female body. Gunta Beeg, for example, argued in 1901 that 'woman is not an inanimate object; nor is she a mere surface that can be adorned with ornament; she is herself form and line and movement, to which the gown must drape, colour, and adjust'.[15]

This photograph shows a typical *Künstlerkleid* of the day, made from light-brown Liberty velvet, embroidered with silk cord and featuring a Jugendstil pattern in silk appliqué around the hem, the neckline and the short sleeves (Figure 41). Most importantly, van de Velde's gown was constructed in such a way that no corset was required. Generous amounts of loose drapery fall straight from an empire neckline and the Liberty silk panels create a flowing line. Liberty fabrics were coveted by German designers of *Künstlerkleider* because they embodied the reform impulse and aesthetic appeal that they wanted to convey in their creations. By the mid-

FIGURE 41 a/b Henry van de Velde, tea gown, *c.* 1900, in *Deutsche Kunst und Dekoration* 10 (1902): 371. Universitätsbibliothek Heidelberg, urn:nbn:de:bsz:16-diglit-63833.

1890s, London's Liberty & Co department store in Regent Street was one of Europe's most fashionable shopping destinations.[16] Liberty's was an important site for the dissemination of Artistic Dress and had a strong connection to the Healthy and Artistic Dress Union through the architect-designer Edward William Godwin (1833–1886), who became Liberty's first artistic director in 1884 and created in-house apparel that remains hugely popular to this day.[17]

Virtually all dresses in Deneken's exhibition rejected a corseted silhouette, although it would be short-sighted to declare that all *Künstlerkleider* were without corsets.[18] In fact, some Artistic Dresses made at the height of British Aestheticism (1860–1900), which was a key inspiration for German *Künstlerkleider*, even had internal boning. This shows that whether a woman wore a corset or not, there was a desire among certain champions of German *Künstlerkleider* to not stray too far from a fashionable silhouette. Drapery was sometimes attached to dresses to offer an appearance of looseness while still maintaining a corseted form underneath.[19] Alfred Mohrbutter, for one, liked to corset some of his models to further accentuate the Jugendstil patterns on his dresses (Figure 42). But on the whole, the Krefeld exhibition showcased designs that renounced corsets and embraced a softer and more undulating line. Compared to a fashionable dress of the day, these garments were relatively plain with sparsely placed, but highly skilled, appliqué work or embroidery. The type of cloth dictated the garment's shape, and the fall of the folds was based on the cut of the dress rather than ingenious pleats and

FIGURE 42 Alfred Mohrbutter, Dress, c. 1900, in Heinrich Pudor, *Die FrauenReformkleidung* (1903): 42. Digitale Sammlung der Bauhaus-Universität-Weimar. https://digitalesammlungen.uni-weimar.de/viewer/resolver?urn=urn:nbn:de:gbv:wim2-g-916666

hidden darts. *Künstlerkleider* also tended to be structured in a more simple way and did not necessarily call for expert tailoring, which meant that they could be made by a range of technical skill levels ranging from homemaker to professional seamstresses. In these ways, *Künstlerkleider* strictly adhered to Jugendstil's dictate of material and functional integrity.

5.3 Dress and function

The garments in Deneken's exhibition had a double function. They were both *Künstlerkleider* and *Gebrauchskleider* (functional dress), meaning that they were artistically inspired while tailored to the everyday needs of modern women.[20] Maria van de Velde made this point in her foreword to the aforementioned album of Artistic Dress from the Krefeld exhibition: 'these dresses did not originate as exhibits [*Schaustücke*] but were designed by artists for specific ladies with their input.'[21] *Gebrauchskleider* were categorized according to strict social conventions and etiquette. Different times of day and circumstances called for different types of dresses. This is an important point to keep in mind because a dress's function dictated its aesthetic and its cut. This could be viewed as a literal manifestation of modernism's iconic declaration that 'form follows function', which was first advocated by the architect Louis Sullivan (1856–1924) in 1896 and later became common parlance via the Bauhaus.[22] Tea gowns, for example, were more informal and looser-fitting garments because women wore them in their homes. This is not to say that they represented a late-nineteenth-century equivalent of our current 'lounge wear'. Jugendstil women received visitors in these gowns, and they had to observe strict social etiquettes. Tea gowns cover a wide range of designs from very loosely fitting to garments with boning and long satin ribbons that look much more formal gowns with sacque-backs. Van de Velde's dress worn in the photograph discussed herein was a tea gown (Figure 41). Outdoor dress comprised more tailored garments that were often combined with a coat, such as Margarethe von Brauchitsch's example featured in Henry van de Velde's 1902 essay cited at the beginning of this chapter (Figure 43).

Lastly, *Gesellschaftskleider* (evening gowns) represented luxurious gowns that were worn to formal engagements and thus tended to be more embellished with different types of fabrics (satins, silks, cottons and chiffon). Another photograph from van de Velde's essay illustrate his take on two society dresses and a coat (Figure 44). The dress in the centre was probably corseted and points to the wide range of silhouettes that could be accommodated by German *Künstlerkleider*. Margarethe von Brauchitsch exhibited an extraordinary society dress in Deneken's Krefeld exhibition with a high waistline that was accentuated by a fabric belt, pleated chiffon sleeves and a flared silk skirt with a small train (Figure 45). Brauchitsch modelled her own design in this photograph, and she is

FIGURE 43 Margarethe von Brauchitsch, street dress 1902, in *Deutsche Kunst und Dekoration* 10 (1902): 365 Universitätsbibliothek Heidelberg, urn:nbn:de:bsz:16-diglit-63833.

FIGURE 44 Clara Möller and Else Oppler, three women in formal dress, 1904, in *Deutsche Kunst und Dekoration* 14 (1904–5): 455. Universitätsbibliothek Heidelberg, urn: nbn:de:bsz:16-diglit-63833.

FIGURE 45 Margarethe von Brauchitsch, formal dress, c. 1900, in *Album moderner, nach Künstler-Entwürfen ausgeführten Damenkleider*, 1900: plate 22. Bibliothek für Gestaltung Basel.

easily recognizable by her short hair that aligned the designer with Munich's more radical political factions discussed in Chapter 2. But Margarethe von Brauchitsch's most evocative design feature was on the back, where the bodice was accentuated by two organically shaped cut-outs that echoed in the back of the sleeves and recalled the Romanticism of a medieval gown.

5.4 Fashion/anti-fashion

Champions of German dress reform formulated a robust response to the perceived irrational, frivolous, physically damaging and sociopolitically oppressive profligacy of nineteenth-century fashion. Much has been published on modernism's conflicted relationship with fashion, and this chapter can only offer a very cursory glimpse into some of these discourses.[23] Needless to say, Jugendstil designers and their supporters (ranging from applied arts reformers to consumers) were ambivalent about fashion and fashionability. Aware that the German Empire's capitalist economy hinged on fashionable trends and that fashion tapped into deep-seated emotions of desire and belonging, design reform rhetoric targeted (Parisian) haute couture and its perceived degenerate force that were seen to impede the evolution of a truly modern style. This anti-French stance was underpinned by the German Empire's stark economic realities that saw its garment industry lagging far behind

Parisian haute couture and France's cloth and accessories production in general. In this context, Deneken's Krefeld exhibition might be viewed as a strategic attempt to position German design against French hegemony in the worlds of couture and fashion.

During the time period in question, fashion could be seen to epitomize modernity in Charles Baudelaire's sense of the word: in a constant state of flux and as a crucial marker of being of one's time.[24] But late-nineteenth-century observers of contemporary life were not univocal in their celebration of modernity and a mounting critique of fashion, that is, Paris-dictated haute couture, in particular, emerged within Germany's culturally progressive camps. Van de Velde, for example, argued that fashion misrepresented itself as modern but essentially enslaved women instead of moving humanity forward. Van de Velde mused in his 1959 autobiography that

> the evolution of women's clothing was exclusively subjected to the vagaries of fashion, which was never logical or sensible. Fashion is volatile, disloyal, coquettish and naturally dishonest. But at least she [fashion] openly admits her mistakes, which, ultimately, accounts for her charm and tempting attraction.[25]

Van de Velde's assessment of fashion predated Roland Barthes's astute distinction between fashion as a social construct and fashion as actual items of clothing. Barthes's formative book *The Fashion System* was first published in 1967 and opened up new ways of thinking about fashion as an abstract idea that was generated by the collusion of 'real garment' with 'image-clothing' (visual representation in fashion magazines) and 'written garment' (text) – all deployed to spark consumer desire.[26] Barthes's post-structural critique laid the groundwork for future fashion historians such as Christopher Breward, who defines fashion as a social process that is 'a market-driven cycle of consumer desire and demand; and it is a modern mechanism for the fabrication of the self'.[27] As mentioned earlier, this makes fashion both a historical phenomenon and a system of meaning-making.[28]

Breward aptly described the European fashion industry during the final decades of the nineteenth century as follows:

> Design innovation was a simple case of pushing the accepted boundaries of spectacle, subtly realigning bodily proportions, structural emphases, decorative patterns, colours and textures in a cyclical repertoire of historical referencing, sexual theatrics, and bravura examples of craft skill.[29]

Some of the late-nineteenth-century's highly fashionable body shapes promoted wasp waists and 'S-Curve' figures that were achieved by corsets, heavy skirts, flowing blouses, metal contraptions and all kinds of other sartorial engineering devices. During the 1890s, corsets were made of heavy cloth and whalebone or steel for structure. As discussed shortly, dress historians must not take this vilification of the corset by dress reformers at face value. Many women during the time period in question continued to wear corsets for support. Indeed, it has been shown that, when properly worn, corsets could help women with their posture.[30] And yet, dress-reform literature of the day attacked corsets across the board as being too tightly laced and creating an idealized body shape that featured an unnaturally small waist ('wasp waist') that visually accentuated a woman's hips, flattened her stomach and created an over-exaggerated bust that was sometimes described as a pigeon chest (Figure 46). If worn from a young age, the corset was believed to physically deform a woman's body or, at least, compromise her internal organs, lead to fainting spells and undermine her ability to bear children.[31] Dress reformers attacked the 'un-natural' silhouettes these contraptions created as irrational and follies of spectacle.[32] The famous German sociologist Georg Simmel (1858–1918), for example, wrote in 1895 that fashion was propelled by its appeal to women's vanity and their desire to imitate or copy: 'fashion offers a space for individuals who are internally and externally dependent and need guidance, but who crave reward, attention, and sense of being special.'[33] Although Simmel wrote of 'individuals', he meant women because he went on to distinguish women's weak psychology from that of their male counterparts.[34]

FIGURE 46 Maison Jeulin, Paris, promenade costume, 1902, in *Deutsche Kunst und Dekoration* 10 (1902): 386. Universitätsbibliothek Heidelberg, urn:nbn:de:bsz:16-diglit-63833.

5.5 Maria van de Velde and Alfred Mohrbutter

As tends to be the case with historical polemics of this kind, the spectrum between radical dress reform and Artistic Dress was rather more fluid than their respective rhetoric indicates. Maria van de Velde (1867–1943) is a good example of a Jugendstil woman who amalgamated the two positions in her practice as a design reform advocate and maker/wearer of Artistic Dress. She not only inspired many of her husband's Artistic Dress designs but actively contributed to discussions around the artistic value of dress within Jugendstil circles. She wrote a short, but compelling, essay in the lavishly illustrated catalogue for the Krefeld exhibition, where she forcefully rejected the ongoing tyranny of fashion:

> fashion forced itself on everyone with its entire repertoire of aberrations and trivialities. For fashion is the great aberration, the thing most responsible for all that ugliness that the century piled up. As it is dominated by caprice and chance, so all its creations unfailingly bear the characteristics of caprice and change.[35]

In response to this woeful state of affairs, Maria van de Velde called upon German artists to take seriously 'the art of clothing' and to develop practical solutions in the 'struggle against fashion'.[36] Just like German dress reformers, she vehemently rejected the ongoing tyranny of fashion that was seen to originate in Paris but spread across Europe like a wildfire. Maria van de Velde acknowledged that there were numerous obstacles to overcome, ranging from a lack of 'attractive basic materials' to untrained workers tasked with realizing complicated artistic designs.[37] But she remained optimistic that individual women 'will summon the courage to overthrow the rules of fashion' and dare 'to dress according to her own taste and to the character of her own personality in the effort to create a work of beauty'.[38] Maria van de Velde's text offers a fascinating insight into the ways in which a more radical dress-reform rhetoric infiltrated *Künstlerkleider* debates around the issue of French fashion dictates. Van de Velde called for the organization of regular exhibitions of Artistic Dress as a first step into the right direction because 'they would be a support and a guide for those women who want to break away from fashion . . . and they would assuredly win over the tailors by degrees for the artistic stimulus'.[39] This statement shows Maria van de Velde as a pragmatist who, maybe more so than her husband, was well aware of the German textile industry's deep economic investment in fashion and its ever-changing trends.

Maria van de Velde's concerns were shared by Deneken's close friend and fellow Jugendstil designer Alfred Mohrbutter (1867–1916), who contributed to the Krefeld exhibition and published a beautifully illustrated book on Artistic Dress in 1904 simply called *Das Kleid der Frau* (Women's Dress).[40] In it, Mohrbutter posited Artistic Dress as a viable alternative to fashion. He took his cue from Maria van de Velde and argued that Artistic Dress represented a response to Parisian haute couture. He also drew on Anna Muthesius's recently published book *Das Eigenkleid der Frau* (Woman's Own Dress; 1903), which will be considered later in this chapter. Mohrbutter urged women to free themselves from fickle fashion trends and become more actively involved in the styling of Artistic Dress. His publication was intended to offer Jugendstil women the tools to do so: 'the colours and their combinations, their moods have to be enlivened for our women. Not the colour combinations dictated by the [fashion] season, but colours that directly emerge from the taste, the character, the very being of a woman.'[41] Mohrbutter wanted to explain the underlying design principles of Artistic Dress and offered a 'how to' manual that showed specific dresses suggested multiple options for tailoring these to his readers' own needs and tastes. He also raised the important point that *Künstlerkleider* should be elevated to the status of applied arts because it offered opportunities to experiment with modern decoration and ornament.[42]

5.6 Artistic Dress and Jugendstil interiors

Maria van de Velde and Mohrbutter both suggested a connection between Jugendstil interiors and *Künstlerkleid*. The Munich art critic Karl Widmer cemented this link in an essay published in 1909 on the relationship between dress and domestic space.[43] He argued that Jugendstil designers should take dress seriously because of its potential to 'create a harmonious relationship between humans and their domestic spaces and furniture', which had deep historical roots that could be traced back to antiquity.[44] Widmer cited numerous examples from art history that, in his view, proved a close relationship between costume and the applied arts. He did not differentiate between men's and women's garments until he discussed historicism (c. 1860–90), at which point Widmer felt that men's clothing 'embodied the spirit of modern individuals' while women's dress was caught up in a 'historical masquerade'.[45] Here, he aligned himself with progressive reform circles when he applauded makers of clothing and applied arts objects who rejected fashionable market trends and remembered 'the chic of the simple and functional'[46] that, according to Widmer, was more readily found in everyday furniture and clothing than public spaces and formal toilettes.

Widmer's examination of the symbiotic relationship between attire and interiors signalled a reassessment of dress and textiles within Jugendstil debates. If, as discussed in previous chapters, the individual components of an aesthetically unified Jugendstil interior based on a Wagnerian *Gesamtkunstwerk* only come together within the experiential realm of the beholder, then Jugendstil dress played a crucial role in this process. It could even be argued that Jugendstil interiors were predicated on *Künstlerkleid* because the latter did not simply match Jugendstil interiors but embodied some of the very design principles that generated these spaces in the first place. The interconnection between *Künstlerkleid* and the interior was underscored by the use of architectural language in early-twentieth-century Reform Dress discourse. Henry van de Velde, for example, offered an architectural analysis of women's clothing that firmly embedded both practices within modernism.[47] Van de Velde adapted earlier discussions emerging from Britain that posited a link between architecture and dress. Edward William Godwin, for example, explained in 1884 that 'as architecture is the art and science of building, so dress is the art and science of clothing'.[48] Van de Velde reformulated Godwin's dictate to demand that Jugendstil designers should employ the same tectonic principles as architects when designing garments.[49]

The Viennese writer and critic Hermann Bahr lucidly expressed a similar idea in 1902 when observing that 'a house is beautiful if it is the necessary and appropriate form for the people that live in it. A dress is beautiful when it becomes the perfect skin for the person who wears it.'[50] Rebecca Houze showed that the Krefeld exhibition was extensively commented upon in Vienna and proved very influential on dress reform and Artistic Dress in the Habsburg Empire.[51] Jugendstil designers and their supporters fully embraced this mandate and embedded *Künstlerkleid* into their promotion of the aesthetically unified interior. Indeed, it could be argued that Jugendstil dress became Artistic Dress once activated within the modern interior (as place and space). Casting her mind back to one of Maria van de Velde's soirées, the German author Helene von Nostitz (1878–1944) evoked the important aesthetic relationship between Jugendstil interiors and Artistic Dress:

> And I still recollect, at one lecture, the strong impression I had of women seated around the black piano in the hall-like room wearing their garments and jewellery of the time that van de Velde had designed himself. Exotic batik material with a narrow neckline, generally green stones on simple, long chains, and men in dark suits in between. All of them stood out like silhouettes against the soft, restful walls on which a few dancers by [the painter] Ludwig von Hofmann formed the sole spots of colour. At such moments you really had a picture of the times in front of you, just as one did of the Rococo or Empire or Biedermeier periods in past centuries.[52]

As discussed in previous chapters, Jugendstil designers tried to overturn a number of hierarchies (art/design; handicraft/machine; public/private interior, etc.), but they remained entrenched in late-nineteenth-century gender constructions that anchored women in the domestic sphere and as consumers of fashion. Dress and textile historians have recently turned their attention to the notion of embodiment as a productive theoretical platform to articulate the relationship between historical bodies and material objects that takes seriously the processes of creating and making. Hilary Davidson explained the so-called embodied turn as 'the trend for scholars of history to appreciate and incorporate embodied, experiential, implicit or tacit knowledges gained through the making and doing into their study of history'.[53] Her theoretically grounded approach offers a productive point of entry into the study of the historical experience of Jugendstil women at the centre of this book, although the term 'making' is expanded here to accommodate a much broader range of activities than the physical production of objects. It also includes knowledge generation, subjectivity construction, network creation and political activism.

5.7 Health and beauty

The relationship between Jugendstil design and the German Empire's dress-reform movement was not always straightforward but the two shared key concerns around health and beauty.[54] The architect Paul Schultze-Naumburg (1869–1949) famously called for a re-design of women's dress based on new medical knowledge of the human body. He offered his views in a critically celebrated book on *The Culture of the Female Body as a Foundation of Women's Clothing* (1901) that included erotic photographs of naked bodies, which he used to juxtapose healthy and deformed physiques.[55] His publication was partially based on Anna Kuhnow's 1893 repudiation of the corset in her influential treatise *Women's Clothing from the Perspective of Hygiene*.[56] Schultze-Naumburg outright rejected corsets from a medical perspective and differentiated between the beautiful 'natural body' and the degenerate 'fashionable body'. His ideal body was inspired by classical statues like the Uffizi Gallery's *Venus de Urbino*. Schultze-Naumburg proposed three basic designs for Reform Dresses that, in his view, accentuated a woman's natural body. They were (1) garments that fell loosely off the shoulder and fastened with a strap at either shoulder, bust or hip; (2) two-piece 'suits' with a tailored skirt and jacket; (3) 'blouse-dresses', that is, a blouse worn with a sleeveless gown over top.[57] These three dress shapes recalled Godwin's earlier suggestions made in the context of Britain's Healthy and Artistic Dress Union, whose journal *Aglaia* was well familiar to German dress reformers. Like Godwin, Schultze-Naumburg emphasized that body and dress should engage in a harmonious dialogue and individual garments should reflect their function (entertaining at home, walking, riding a bicycle, etc.).

Jugendstil designers responded to Schultze-Naumburg's publication by creating garments that fitted more loosely, used natural fabrics (cotton and linen) and were draped over an un-corseted body in a flowing line extending from the shoulders to the ankles – although as alluded to earlier in this chapter, the un-corseted body was maybe more rhetorical than true-to-life (Figure 47). This photograph shows a *Gesellschaftskleid* designed by Schultze-Naumburg. It featured a relatively simple

FIGURE 47 Paul Schultze-Naumburg, reform dress, *Deutsche Kunst und Dekoration* 11 (1902): 168. Universitätsbibliothek Heidelberg, urn:nbn:de:bsz:16-diglit-63833.

cut and delicate appliqué work. This photograph signalled Schultze-Naumburg's adherence to one of Jugendstil's core principles: the insistence on material integrity or *Materialgerechtigkeit*. Accordingly, a garment's cut should draw attention to its fabric, use no more than two different types of cloth and should avoid superfluous decoration at all cost. Seamstresses across the German Empire experimented with new construction methods and cutting techniques that were aimed at minimal intervention into the natural drape of the cloth. The Berlin seamstress Hedwig Buschmann, for example, explained that she rarely used scissors because she wanted the beauty of the material to be as uncompromised as possible.[58] This had the added practical effect that precise sizing was less of an issue and a wider range of women's physiques could be accommodated.

5.8 German life reform

German dress reform was deeply anchored in the late-nineteenth-century *Lebensreform* (Life Reform) movement. German Life Reform essentially offered a response to the negative repercussions of the German Empire's relatively late industrialization and urbanization.[59] Lack of suitable living space in large cities, the plight of Germany's working classes, deficient hygiene, unhealthy lifestyles, pollution and the destruction of natural habitats were but some of the causes taken up by Life Reformers. Advocates came from diverse parts of Germany's sociopolitical spectrum, but they shared a fundamental conviction that a return to a 'more natural' way of life would recalibrate the physical and psychic well-being of modern individuals. How this equilibrium could be achieved divided opinions and numerous initiatives were proposed: homeopathy, vegetarianism, alcohol abstinence, landownership reform, nature and heritage (Heimat) conservation, youth movements and sports clubs, alternative pedagogies, garden cities, communal living and spiritualism including occult practices. Many of its followers were committed to class and gender equality (as far as the ideological and political horizons of the late nineteenth century allowed) and supported the women's movement's demand for equal access to education and the vote. Many of these utopian endeavours focused on new conceptions of the human body that celebrated health and nature. The corset was targeted by dress reformers and Life Reformers who both called for liberation of the female body from its physical and social constraints. The most radical Life Reformers rejected clothing altogether and formed nudist colonies.[60] Even though communal living and alternative lifestyles lay at the core of this radical recalibration of the German Empire's bourgeois world, it is important to emphasize that Life Reform did not automatically equate progressive politics. Indeed, for some, the discourse around health and the natural body, as well as the search for an authentically German identity rooted in folk culture, soon metamorphosed into National Socialist ideologies and were subsequently corrupted by the Nazi Party (1933–45).[61]

5.9 Dress reform and Germany's women's movement

The *'Internationaler Kongress für Frauenwerke und Frauenbestrebungen'* (International Congress for Women's Work and Efforts) was held in Berlin in 1896 and featured two panel discussions on the question of women's dress. The German gynaecologist Carl Spener led one discussion and the renowned feminist Sera Proelss the other, who discussed women's health and rights, respectively.[62] This pairing of a physician and a women's rights advocate encapsulated two of German dress reform's key concerns; namely, women's well-being, physical mobility (made possible through new types of dress) and sociopolitical emancipation. The Congress raised much awareness and some consternation in the German Empire's popular press, and the event led to the founding of *Allgemeine Verein für Verbesserung der Frauenkleidung* (Association for the Improvement of Women's Dress) the following year. The association was headquartered in Berlin and had eleven chapters across Germany, including one in Munich. Its members were committed to propagating women's clothing that was 'healthy – beautiful – practical' and demanded 'a simplification of undergarments. Relieve the strain on hips. Preservation of the body's natural form. Self-determined design of modern garments. Shortening of street-wear.'[63] It might be useful to remind readers that a garment worn by bourgeois women in public weighed on average 4.5 kilograms and arguably not only impeded physical movement but also posed dangers to women's health and well-being. Crinolines, for example, were sensationalized in the contemporary press for catching fire.[64]

Members of the Association for the Improvement of Women's Dress were adamant that 'the movement is not simply a fashionable current, as it has so often been labelled by its ill-informed opponents, but organically grew out of the needs of our time. This is why we will win, even if this entails a long battle.'[65] In a fascinating account of Germany's dress-reform movement written for a British newspaper, Minna Cauer argued in 1907 that true liberation could be achieved only if women were permitted to dress as they liked rather than following fashion dictates. Cauer was a close friend of Anita Augspurg (Chapter 2) and moved in Germany's most important women's movement circles.[66] In a nod to her contemporary Georg Simmel, Cauer acknowledged that it was necessary to achieve educational and professional equality before women were capable of making truly liberated choices: 'this question of dress reform will never be settled until women assert their independence and strike out for themselves on commercial and professional lines.'[67] She stressed that dress reform was driven by a recalibration of health and beauty. 'The best of our women have united to denounce the old-fashioned "*Künstlerkleider*" – which may have given us a *fashionable* figure, but never yet a *beautiful* one. The human frame is tortured out of all semblance of beauty.'[68] Cauer expressed what architectural historian Mark Wigley would later sum up in his reinstatement of dress in Henry van de Velde's modernism: 'to be modern was to be mobile and to have this mobility registered in one's dress.'[69]

5.10 Jugendstil women and dress reform

Jugendstil women actively participated in dress reform on a number of different fronts: as political activists agitating for emancipation and suffrage; as linchpins in alternative communities set up within the Life Reform Movement; as strategists and thinkers publishing across a wide range of the printed press; as designers and makers; and as consumers. Unsurprisingly, their efforts and initiatives have been largely written out of design history's accounts of Jugendstil. More often than not, women are mentioned as wives and muses of key Jugendstil architects and designers rather than protagonists in their own rights. But Maria van de Velde and Lili Behrens, for example, did not simply model Jugendstil garments designed by their husbands. They acted as creative collaborators across a range of fascinating artistic and marital configurations.[70] They realized their husbands' designs, accessorized and styled the garments into Artistic Dress and played a key role in staging many of the photographs that design historians now draw on. Hermann Muthesius' wife Anna Trippenbach (1870–1961) enacted this model of an active creative collaboration with her husband. Readers already encountered the couple in the previous chapter on Elsa Bruckmann (Chapter 4). They were living in the London Borough of Hammersmith (1896–1904) and served as important conduits between the English Arts and Crafts movement and continental Art Nouveau. Anna Trippenbach was a renowned concert singer before she married her husband in 1895 and moved among Germany's progressive cultural and intellectual circles. Anna Muthesius gave up her artistic career to marry her husband, but she became actively involved in dress reform and published her seminal book *Das Eigenkleid der Frau* in 1903.

5.11 Anna Muthesius and Else Oppler

Das Eigenkleid der Frau is a fascinating text on a number of levels, least of all because it attested to the thriving relationship between German Jugendstil and the Glasgow Four discussed previously.[71] Anna Muthesius's book originally featured a binding designed by Frances McNair that employed the design language and typography associated with the Glasgow School of Art, including stylized female figures and Glasgow's iconic rose (also present in the Elsa Bruckmann dining room's stencil work). The book itself included photographs of the Macdonald sisters, Anna Muthesius herself as well as Elsie and Mary Newbery in Artistic Dress (Figure 48).[72] Anna Muthesius translated Schultze-Naumburg's somewhat hermetic discourse into a more practical and appealing text. She also followed her architect husband's call for functional and material honesty in design. She acknowledged that the relationship between the female body and clothing had to be fundamentally reconceived through an emphasis on individuality. The word *Eigenkleid* in her book title denoted both 'individual dress' and 'dress endorsed by women'. Anna Muthesius's word choice was fascinating because it accommodated the dual meaning of speaking to the women's movement's reform impulses (as in 'a dress of one's own') *and* the material properties of a particular garment in the sense that any woman could make her own Artistic Dress.

Muthesius proposed that a garment should be tailored to its wearer's physique rather than manipulating a women's body to fit a fashionable silhouette. It should also be made of less expensive or luxurious cloth and should be quite sturdy. If women followed these basic design principles, they could break free from Parisian fashion dictates and make their own sartorial choices: 'Reform Dress simply represents the framework for an artistic conception of dress [. . .]. One must therefore not think of Reform Dress as a template, on the contrary, each

FIGURE 48 Frances McNair in formal dress, in Anna Muthesius, *Das Eigenkleid der Frau* 1903. © Glasgow School of Art Library, purchased with assistance from Friends of the National Libraries.

woman has to dress according to her own individuality.' Muthesius suggested that this 'individuality' was anchored in the face, which served as the starting point for any subsequent sartorial choices including hair, hats, accessories and so on.[73] Her advice was very specific, and much of her book reads like a 'how to' manual. She recommended, for example, that women with round faces and rosy cheeks should pin their hair up in braids while women with finer features should part their hair and keep it straight.[74] Short women could add a train to their tea gowns because it optically elongated their bodies while tall women could put horizontal embellishments onto their dress as to interrupt long lines.[75]

In 1904, Anna Muthesius reviewed a *Künstlerkleid* exhibition at the Kaufhaus (department store) Wertheim in Berlin that was organized by her friend and fellow Jugendstil woman, Else Oppler (1875–1965).[76] The department store was housed in a spectacular Jugendstil building designed by Alfred Messel in 1896–7 and located along one of Berlin's premier shopping streets, the Leipzig Strasse. Oppler is a fascinating historical figure, and her multidimensional career begs to be reassessed by design historians.[77] She studied under Maximilian Dasio at the Munich Association of Women Artists (1898–1901), discussed in Chapter 3, under van de Velde in Berlin (1901) and under Josef Hoffmann in Vienna (1901). There, she met and became close friends with the modernist designer Lilly Reich (1885–1947). Oppler won a silver medal for her embroideries at the 'First International Exhibition of Decorative Arts' in Turin (1902) and ran an applied arts school for women in Nuremberg, where she met the architect and designer

Peter Behrens (1868–1940), who became her teacher and lifelong friend. After the success of her Artistic Dress exhibition at the Kaufhaus Wertheim, she was hired as its first in-house artistic director for women's fashion. She left the Kaufhaus Wertheim in 1909 and returned to teaching. She opened Germany's first school for window dressing in Berlin, the *Höhere Schule für Dekorationskunst* and became a sought-after costume and set designer on silent movies during the 1920s. Oppler published throughout her career and placed a fascinating essay in *The Independent* (1905), based in London, in which she repeated familiar arguments about hygiene, aesthetics and ethics that formed the keystones of German dress reform.[78]

5.12 Artistic Dress and the department store

Oppler's exhibition at the Kaufhaus Wertheim drew considerable attention. This was only the second time a department store had opened its sales floors to *Künstlerkleider* – the Hohenzollern Kaufhaus (Berlin) having done so on a smaller scale the previous year.[79] In her review, Muthesius repeated aspects of her previous argument in *Das Eigenkleid*, but she coined the intriguing term 'anti-fashion dress' (*Anti-Modekleid*) to describe German efforts to defy Parisian fashion trends.[80] She observed that many 'free-thinking' women wanted to wear Artistic Dress but did not have the sewing skills, the taste, the time or the financial resources to do so. If dress reform was to have any impact, then, according to Muthesius, the 'art of dressing' must be made more accessible and needed to move out of the discursive realm – 'essays and lectures by taste-theorists'[81] – and into practice. Muthesius praised Oppler's visionary strategy of dressing twelve shop assistants in Artistic Dress that virtually turned them into live models. The event lasted for two weeks, and each shop assistant underwent several dress changes throughout her shift. Muthesius congratulated the Kaufhaus Wertheim's management for supporting such 'a determined and capable artist'.[82] Oppler designed many of the dresses herself (fifteen to be precise) and asked some of her Jugendstil friends to send garments. Margarethe von Brauchitsch, Frieda Petersen, Rudolf and Fia Wille, Else von Hahn and Alfred Mohrbutter happily complied with her request and the event offered a beautiful overview of the most recent developments in *Künstlerkleid* design (Figure 49).

Muthesius was particularly complimentary about Oppler's dresses because the designer had taken into account all of the stipulations put forth by dress reformers: no corset; harmony between type of cloth and form; expert tailoring; individuality; functionality (which included paying attention to its wearer's age); and aesthetic value. By this point in time, Oppler was at the top of her game and her dresses were featured in key Jugendstil dress publications such as Mohrbutter's *Das Kleid der Frau* (Woman's Dress; 1904). Muthesius also praised the advanced

FIGURE 49 Else Oppler, summer street dress, in *Deutsche Kunst und Dekoration* 14 (1904): 456. Universitätsbibliothek Heidelberg, urn:nbn:de:bsz:16-diglit-63833.

technical abilities of German seamstresses evident in the garments modelled at the Wertheim event, but she bemoaned the widespread lack of access to the right kinds of material for Artistic Dress such as Liberty cottons, silks, velvets, lace and trimmings that had to be procured from England and France:

> If we could go to any store and purchase good colours and cloth manufactured in Germany and thus affordable, then a great service would be done to *Eigenkleid* because it would not only be found in the grand toilette of rich women, but also be made by local seamstresses at home.[83]

This quote signals that Muthesius was well aware of the fact that most Artistic Dresses were unaffordable for most women across the German Empire and ran the risk of becoming yet another elite extravagance rather than a serious critique of haute couture fashion.

Despite Muthesius's complaint, Oppler's exhibition at the Kaufhaus Wertheim bears witness to the fact that the German department store represented a key site for the dissemination of Jugendstil design ranging from furniture and decorative objects to tableware, jewellery and *Künstlerkleider*. Women from across the German Empire's social stratum frequented these new 'consuming temples'[84] to acquire the materials and inspirations needed to dress and live as modern women. Department stores, in general, have long been considered by social commentators and scholars as a quintessential 'site of modernity' because it, literally and metaphorically, brought into focus key aspects of modern urban society. Godela Weiss-Sussex and Ulrike Zitzlsperger recently described the 'phenomenon' department store as a 'kaleidoscopic entity – an economic type of retail and an architectural reality, a space for emancipatory possibilities and a site of aesthetic education'.[85] The literature on department stores is vast and emerges from many different disciplines ranging from architecture and urban studies, economics and consumer studies, modern languages, sociology, gender studies, fashion history, material and visual culture studies to name but a few. This chapter closes with a brief look at the importance of a specific Munich department store, the Kaufhaus Oberpollinger, as a key site for the dissemination of modern design. Here Jugendstil women – be they designers, makers in the broadest sense, or consumers – had the opportunity to showcase and encounter the latest developments in progressive design practices (as well as more conservative and fashionable trends) while they could freely socialize. This made the department store a deeply circumspect, if not outright dangerous, site for some. Conservative critics, driven by Germany's rising anti-Semitism and a blatant fear of emancipated women, outright dismissed the department store as a frivolous space populated by female pleasure seekers.[86] This indicates that anxieties about Jews, 'liberated' women, urban spaces and consumption were intertwined and generated much debate.[87]

5.13 The Kaufhaus Oberpollinger and the Warenhaus Hermann Tietz

Despite this sense of unease, the German department store represented a vital conduit for the dissemination and popularization of Jugendstil design. In February of 1905, two Munich department stores opened their doors to shoppers in brand-new, custom-designed buildings: the Kaufhaus Oberpollinger located on one of Munich's premier shopping streets, the Neuhauser Strasse, and the Warenhaus Hermann Tietz prominently positioned across from the city's main train station (Figures 50 and 51).[88] Both stores were designed by the prominent Munich architect Max Littmann (1862–1931). Their exteriors are historicist, but their interiors offered customers a thoroughly modern shopping experience. Littmann employed the latest building techniques such as reinforced steel and concrete to create large open spaces that complied with fire regulations and facilitated a spectacular consumer experience. The façades were covered in limestone. Both stores were spatially organized around a magnificent *Lichthof* (a large central courtyard illuminated from above by a spectacular glass and iron cupola) that lent itself to comparisons with sacred spaces of cathedrals and was

FIGURE 50 Max Littmann, department store Tietz, in *Deutsche Bauzeitung* 39, no. 53 (1905): 326. Brandenburgische Technische Universität Cottbus-Senftenberg.

FIGURE 51 Max Littmann, department store Oberpollinger, *Deutsche Bauzeitung* 39, no. 54 (1905): 338. Brandenburgische Technische Universität Cottbus-Senftenberg.

FIGURE 52 Max Littmann, department store Tietz, Lichthof, *Deutsche Bauzeitung* 39, no. 53 (1905): 335. Brandenburgische Technische Universität Cottbus-Senftenberg.

derived from French department store architecture (Figure 52). The designation of department stores as either temples or churches can be traced back to Emile Zola's novel *Au bonheur des dames* (The Ladies Paradise), first serialized in *Gil Blas* in 1883:

> The department store tends to replace the church. It marches to the religion of the cash desk, of beauty, of coquetry, and fashion. [Women] go there to pass the hours as they used to go to church: as an occupation, a place of enthusiasm where they struggle between their passion for clothes and the thrift of their husbands; in the end all the drama of life with the hereafter of beauty.[89]

Littman used renowned local artists (Heinrich Düll, Georg Pezold, Julius Seidl, Jakob Brandl) to come up with the buildings' sculptural scheme. Scholars from across a range of disciplines have paid close attention to the 'phenomenon department store'. Design historians can build on this rich foundation for their analysis of historical design practices within department stores (down to the arrangement of the vitrine's content) and patterns of consumption, not to mention the fascinating dialogue between the building's interiors and exteriors.[90]

5.14 Shopping

Seminal research by Erika Rappaport and Theresa McBride reveals that late-nineteenth-century women were seen by their contemporaries as Europe's premier shoppers.[91] As previously discussed, German middle-class women were responsible for running the family home and were seen to have the leisure time to fill with shopping. The German Empire's department stores modelled themselves on earlier French examples such as Au Bon Marché (1852) and Au Printemps (1865), whose owners pioneered new sales techniques.[92] These quintessentially modern sites targeted female shoppers. They had lavish tea rooms and restaurants, offered a vast range of goods at fixed prices (low-profit margins but large turnover) and actively encouraged browsing through their luxurious and frequently changing displays. Shopping was transformed from the act of purchasing a specific item into a multisensory activity anchored in a specific site, namely, the department store. Women could walk around specialized departments, choose items to look at and maybe even try them on without feeling pressured to make a purchase. Historian Elaine S. Abelson described the perceived connection between women, shopping, pleasure and desire department stores as follows:

> Women had to walk a tightrope between real needs, defined by practical use, and stimulated wants created by a suggestive ambience, lavish display, and often manipulated prices ... The categories were not clear cut, they overlapped and collapsed into each other, and in a setting that was dependent on high consumption and quick turnover, confusion about what was in fact a real need or a symbolic need was encouraged.[93]

Abelson's assessment of the shopping experience is indebted to Guy Debord's formative definition of modern consumption as 'a matter not of basic items bought for definite needs, but of visual fascination and remarkable sights of things not found at home'.[94] The modern department store turned consumption into a cultural practice because the transaction was as important as the product.[95]

Modern consumer culture in late-nineteenth-century Germany changed how shoppers acquired and used goods. Historians Konrad Jarausch and Michael Geyer propose that consumer society is defined by the following:

> the availability of an ample range of goods for a multiplicity of consumers, a system of mass media that allows for the collective attribution of meaning to objects, the differentiation of a world of objects and their meaning ... [and] a wholesale shift in the self-definition of society from production to consumption, from work to leisure, and, one might add, from producing destruction to create waste.[96]

But consumer culture did not simply unleash oppressive capitalist forces that subjugated consumers; it also challenged the German Empire's social hierarchies and gender relations. Gender historians have long drawn attention to the fact that the modern city as a whole and the department store as one of its quintessential sites offered the potential to enact female autonomy and creativity.[97] While women still needed chaperones to walk through the city to not be perceived as prostitutes, department stores offered amenities where women could socialize without peril (tea parlours, luncheon rooms, hairdressers). Here, new gender identities could be negotiated outside of the domestic realm. Needless to say, sociocultural discourses of the day tried to control these potentially emancipatory forces by arguing that department stores enticed and seduced women by tapping into their irrational nature and unleashing a distinctly feminine *Kauflust* (desire to shop) or, worse, a pathological *Kaufwahn* (compulsion to shop).[98]

On 14 June 1905, the Kaufhaus Oberpollinger advertised an imminent special exhibition of Reform Dress and reform underwear that 'followed the intentions of Munich's Association for the Improvement of Women's Dress'. Undoubtedly, Oberpollinger's management was aware of their Berlin competitor's exhibition of *Künstlerkleider* the previous year and quickly followed suit. Interestingly, its organizers prioritized Reform Dress over *Künstlerdress*. It is important to remember that the cultural–economic rivalries between Berlin and Munich were very much alive. This provided all the more impetus for the Kaufhaus Oberpollinger, which from a Berlin perspective was little more than a provincial outpost, to assert its status as taste maker and supporter of progressive design practices. The timing of this exhibition was meticulously calibrated as the Kaufhaus Oberpollinger had only just moved into its glorious new building on the Neuhauser Strasse. This event received much less press attention than Oppler's staging at the Kaufhaus Wertheim, but this might be due to the fact that the exhibition was not marketed as an artistic intervention into Reform Dress design and thus did not garner the same kind of interest from art and design journals. But the Oberpollinger event clearly evidences that by 1905, department stores served as one of Germany's most important sites for the popularization and sale of modern dress covering the gamut from *Künstlerkleid* to Reform Dress. Late-nineteenth-century department stores across the German Empire became crucial conduits in the process of moving artistically inspired garments from the confines of artists' studios and exclusive sewing ateliers into the popular imagination and purchasing habits.

Sadly, the fruitful collaboration between progressive Jugendstil designers, women's rights advocates and new 'consuming temples' was relatively short-lived. It failed to achieve its lofty aim of revolutionizing women's dress and liberating German women from the perceived tyranny of French haute couture. A cultural–political division crept into Germany's dress-reform movement during the years leading up to the First World War. Advocates of *Künstlerkleider* continued to argue for a close collaboration of Jugendstil designers with Germany's clothing industry

FIGURE 53 Madame Poiret modelling clothing designed by her husband Paul Poiret, 1913. Library of Congress Prints and Photographs Division, Washington DC. LC-USZ62-56751.

to produce healthy, beautiful and modern dresses. Members of Germany's women's movement, on the other hand, began to question this collaboration as impractical at best and repressive at worst. They demanded practical dresses ('car coats', tweeds, etc.) in which they could work, protest and reject being viewed as beautiful objects. On an economic level, it was difficult to produce artistically inspired Reform Dresses that were affordable for German women beyond the upper echelons of society. This was not helped by the fact that a number of Jugendstil designers, among them Henry van de Velde, submitted designs that had to be made by highly skilled seamstresses in small-scale studios. The founding of the German Werkbund in 1907 tried to find a middle ground between these polarized views.

But in an ironic twist of fate – since the French fashion industry was one of the primary targets of German dress reform – it took French couturiers like Coco Chanel, Paul Poiret or Madelaine Vionnet to turn artistically inspired Reform Dress into mainstream fashion (Figure 53). The prominent Berlin art collector Paul Westheim presciently responded to Paul Poiret's work at the Berlin Fashion Week of 1910 when observing that

> Our ideas for the Reform Dress dissipate into nothing compared to these Poiretish creations – as they really must be called. [. . .] What we are still lacking and for which there is no antidote is that astounding instinct which – even

irrespective of Poirot – has made the French art of dressmaking the best of all that we have today in the field of applied arts.⁹⁹

Notes

1 Minna Cauer, 'Dress Reform in Germany', *The Independent* 63 (July 1907): 997.
2 Henry van de Velde, 'Das neue Kunst-Prinzip in der modernen Frauen-Kleidung', *Deutsche Kunst und Dekoration* 10 (1902): 363–71.
3 Deneken worked under Julius Brinckmann at the Museum for Art and Industry in Hamburg. He was appointed as inaugural director of Krefeld's Kaiser-Wilhelm Museum in 1897, where he built a world-class collection of modern art and design. During his tenure (1897–1922), he regularly travelled to Paris and introduced German audiences to the Post-Impressionists (von Gogh, Cézanne, Signac and Gauguin), Toulouse-Lautrec's posters, Art Nouveau glassware (Tiffany, Gallé) and furniture (Henry van de Velde). None of these acquisitions were without controversy, but Deneken remained committed to the historical avant-garde. Rainer Stamm, *Farbwelten: Von Monet bis Yves Klein: Werke der klassischen Moderne aus den Kunstmuseen Krefeld* (Bremen: Kunstsammlungen Bottcherstrasse and Paula Modersohn-Becker Museum, 2009), 9–19.
4 Krefeld was Germany's late-nineteenth-century centre for silk production. Herbert Kisch, *From Domestic Manufacture to Industrial Revolution: The Case of the Rhineland Textile Districts* (Oxford: Oxford University Press, 1989).
5 Deneken invited Glasgow's Macdonald sisters, who sadly declined. This is especially unfortunate given the extraordinary designs featured by these two in Anna Muthesius's influential book *Das Eigenkleid der Frau* (1903), for which Frances Macdonald also designed the cover. Anna Muthesius, *Das Eigenkleid der Frau* (Krefeld: Kramer & Tree, 1903).
6 Henry van de Velde, *Die künstlerische Hebung der Frauentracht* (Krefeld: Kramer & Baum, 1900), 8.
7 Ina Ewers-Schultz and Magdalena Holzhey, *Tailored for Freedom: The Artistic Dress around 1900 in Fashion, Art and Society* (Munich: Hirmer Verlag, 2018); Rebecca Houze, *Textiles, Fashion, and Design Reform in Austria-Hungary before the First World War* (Farnham: Ashgate, 2015).
   There are certain points of convergence between my work and Houze's chapter on Viennese dress reform because, as she makes clear, some of her historical actors drew on German discourses that are the object of my study.
8 Robyne Calvert, 'Manly Modes: Artistic Dress and the Styling of Masculine Identity', *Visual Culture in Britain* 16, no. 2 (2015): 224.
9 Early German dress reform (1870s) was focused on men and their liberation from severely restricting hats, but its advocates' focus soon shifted to women's corsets. By the 1890s, Reform Dress was predominantly associated with women. This is not to suggest that progressive men did not purchase and wear modern dress, but a discussion of men's dress falls outside *Jugendstil Women's* scope. See Christopher Breward, *The Hidden Consumer: Masculinities, Fashion and City Life 1860–1914*

(Manchester: Manchester University Press, 1999); Tim Edwards, *Men in the Mirror: Men's Fashion, Masculinity, and Consumer Society* (London: Cassell, 1997); Laura Ugolini, *Men and Menswear: Sartorial Consumption in Britain 1880–1939* (Aldershot: Ashgate, 2007).

10 Robyne Calvert, 'Fashioning the Artist: Artistic Dress in Victorian Britain, 1848–1900' (PhD Dissertation, University of Glasgow, 2012).

11 Van de Velde, 'Das neue Kunst-Prinzip in der modernen Frauen-Kleidung', 366.

12 Josephine Miller, 'The Study of Dress and Textiles', in *Design History: A Student's Handbook*, ed. Hazel Conway (London: Harper Collins Academic, 1987), 15. Lou Taylor, *The Study of Dress History* (Manchester: Manchester University Press, 2002). For a fascinating account of the history of scholarly engagement with dress and textiles, see L. Taylor, 'Fashion, Textiles and Dress History: A Personal Perspective', University of Brighton, Research & Enterprise, accessed 4 February 2021, http://arts.brighton.ac.uk/arts/alumni-and-associates/the-history-of-arts-education-in-brighton/fashion,-textiles-and-dress-history-a-personal-perspective-by-lou-taylor.

13 Houze, *Textiles, Fashion, and Design Reform in Austria-Hungary before the First World War*; Ewers-Schultz and Holzhey, *Tailored for Freedom*.

14 Van de Velde quoted in Mark Wigley, *White Walls, Designer Dresses* (Cambridge, MA: MIT Press, 1995), 11.

15 Gunta Beeg, 'Zur künstlerischen Reform der Mode', *Illustrirte Frauen-Zeitung* 28, no. 21 (1 November 1901): 76.

16 *Liberty's 1875–1975: An Exhibition to Mark the Firm's Centenary* (London: Victoria & Albert Museum, 1975); Alison Adburgham, *Liberty's: A Biography of a Shop* (London: George Allen and Unwin, 1975).

17 Aileen Reed, 'Edward William Godwin (1833–1886): Towards an Art-Architecture' (PhD Dissertation, University of London, 1999); *Architect-Designers from Pugin to Mackintosh* (London: Fine Arts Society, 1981).

18 *Album moderner, nach Künstler-Entwürfen ausgeführter Damenkleider* (Düsseldorf: Wolfrum, 1900).

19 Conversation with Robyne Calvert, Glasgow School of Art, 15 June 2020.

20 This brief discussion of different types of Artistic Dress takes its cue from Houze's helpful analysis of the Krefeld exhibitions' categories of modern dress. Houze, 'Fashion and its Discontent', in *Textiles, Fashion, and Design Reform in Austria-Hungary before the First World War*, 209–11.

21 Maria van de Velde qtd. in van de Velde, 'Das neue Kunst-Prinzip in der modernen Frauen-Kleidung', 364.

22 'Whether it be the sweeping eagle in his flight, or the open apple-blossom, the toiling work-horse, the blithe swan, the branching oak, the winding stream at its base, the drifting clouds, over all the coursing sun, *form ever follows function*, and this is the law.' Louis Sullivan, 'The Tall Office Building Artistically Considered', *Lippincott's Magazine* (March 1896): 408.

23 For a more in-depth discussion, see, for example, Louise Wallenberg and Andrea Kollnitz, *Fashion and Modernism* (London: Bloomsbury, 2018); Ulrich Lehmann, *Tigersprung: Fashion in Modernity* (Cambridge, MA: MIT Press, 2000).

24 'Modernity is the transient, the fleeting, the contingent; it is one half of art, the other being the eternal and the immovable. [. . .] You have no right to despise this transitory fleeting element, the metamorphoses of which are so frequent, nor to dispense with it.' Charles Baudelaire, 'The Painter of Modern Life' (1863), in *The Nineteenth-Century Visual Culture Reader,* ed. Vanessa R. Schwartz and Jeannene M. Przyblyski (London: Routledge, 2004), 40.

25 Henry van de Velde, *Geschichte meines Lebens* (Munich: Piper Verlag, 1962), 153.

26 Roland Barthes, *The Fashion System* (Berkeley: University of California Press, 1967).

27 Christopher Breward and Caroline Evans, *Fashion and Modernity* (Oxford: Berg, 2005), 3.

28 Christopher Breward, *Fashion, Oxford History of Art* (Oxford: Oxford University Press, 2003), 49.

29 Ibid., 66.

30 Valerie Steel wrote an excellent history of the corset that opened up new ways of historicizing its usage and reputation. Valerie Steele, *The Corset: A Cultural History* (New Haven: Yale University Press, 2001). Bernadette Banner offers a fascinating reassessment of the Victorian corset *What Did Victorian Corsets Actually Look Like: Examining Corsets from the Symington Collection*, You Tube video, 11:31, posted 12 October 2019, https://www.youtube.com/watch?v=5QUEf-8BKyE. I thank Robyne Calvert for pointing me to this resource.

31 Heinrich and Anna Jäger, *Hygiene der Kleidung* (Stuttgart: E. H. Moritz, 1906); Carl Spener, *Die jetzige Frauenkleidung und Vorschläge zu ihrer Verbesserung* (Berlin, 1897).

32 Karin Schrott, *Das normative Korsett* (Würzburg: Königshausen & Neumann, 2005); Steele, *The Corset*; Patricia Ober, *Der Frauen neue Kleider: Das Reformkleid und die Konstruktion des modernen Frauenkörpers* (Kempten: Schlier, 2005).

33 Georg Simmel, 'Zur Psychologie der Mode: Soziologische Studie', *Die Zeit: Wiener Wochenschrift für Politik, Volkswirtschaft, Wissenschaft und Kunst,* 42, no. 12.10 (1895): 23.

34 Ibid.

35 Anna Muthesius, 'Introduction', in *Album moderner, nach Künstler-Entwürfen ausgeführter Damenkleider: As Exhibited at the Great General Exhibition of the Clothing Industry, Krefeld 1900*, trans. Iain Boyd Whyte, *Art in Translation* 10, no. 4 (2018): 375–6.

36 Whyte, *Art in Translation*, 377.

37 Ibid.

38 Ibid.

39 Ibid.

40 Alfred Mohrbutter, *Das Kleid der Frau: Ein Beitrag zur künstlerischen Gestaltung des Frauenkleides* (1904; reprint, Hannover: Schäfer, 1985).

41 Ibid., 12. For a more detailed discussion of Alfred Mohrbutter see Anna-Maria Ganzenbacher, 'Mieder und Reformkleid: Zum Wandel der Damenmode von 1900 bis 1918' (Master's Thesis, University of Graz, 2009).

42 Ibid.

43 Karl Widmer, 'Kleid und Wohnraum', *Innendekoration* 20, no. 7 (1909): 237–41.
44 Ibid., 240.
45 Ibid.
46 Ibid., 241.
47 For a superb discussion of the long-ignored impact of dress design/discourse on modernist architecture, see Wigley, *White Walls, Designer Dresses*.
48 E.W. Godwin, *Dress and its Relation to Health and Climate* (1884) quoted in Mark Wigley, 'White-out: Fashioning the Modern', *Assemblage* 22 (December 1993): 13.
49 Van de Velde, *Die künstlerische Hebung der Frauentracht*, 23.
50 Hermann Bahr quoted in Houze, 214.
51 See Houze, 'Fashion and its Discontent', in *Textiles, Fashion, and Design Reform*, 185–247.
52 Helene von Nostitz quoted in Antje Neumann, 'The Textile Designer and Gesamtkünstler Henry van de Velde and his Weimar Circle', in *Tailored for Freedom*, 31.
53 Hilary Davidson, 'The Embodied Turn: Making and Remaking Dress as an Academic Practice', *Fashion Theory* 23, no. 3 (2019): 330.
54 Key publications on Reform Dress are Brigitte Stamm, 'Das Reformkleid in Deutschland' (PhD Dissertation, Technische Universität Berlin, 1976); Patricia A. Cunningham, *Reforming Fashion, 1850–1914: Politics, Health, Art* (Kent: Kent State University Press, 2003).
55 Paul Schultze-Naumburg, *Die Kultur des weiblichen Körpers als Grundlage der Frauenkleidung* (Jena: Eugen Diederichs, 1901). The photographs of naked women become increasingly erotic as his narrative unfolds, and he often zoomed in on his models' pubic areas and breasts. One might relate their visual idiom to Germany's thriving trade in erotic postcards and photographs. For a fruitful theoretical discussion of these issues within a Viennese context see Gemma Blackshaw, 'Dead Men and their Naked Truths', in *The Nakeds,* ed. Mary Doyle and Kate Macfarlane (Manchester: Cornerhouse, 2014), 12–29.
56 Anna Kuhnow, *Die Frauenkleidung vom Standpunkte der Hygiene: Vortrag für Frauen gehalten zu Leipzig am 14. Februar 1893* (Leipzig: Hobbing, 1893). Kuhnow (1859–1923) was one of Germany's first approbated (in Zurich) female physicians who ran gynaecological clinics in Leipzig (1890–1900) and Berlin (1900–23). She also designed her own Reform Dress and (unsuccessfully) petitioned Saxony's Ministry of Culture to outlaw the wearing of corsets in schools, accessed 30 March 2020, https://research.uni-leipzig.de/agintern/frauen/kuhnow.htm.
57 Schultze-Naumburg, *Die Kultur des weiblichen Körpers*, 113–20.
58 Hedwig Buschmann quoted in Ober, *Der Frauen neue Kleider,* 139.
59 Life Reform was a cross-European phenomenon. For an excellent discussion of German Life Reform across a wide spectrum of causes and politics, see Diethart Kerbs and Jürgen Reuleck, *Handbuch der deutschen Reformbewegung 1880–1933* (Wuppertal: Peter Hammer Verlag, 1998); Wolfgang R. Krabbe, *Gesellschaftsveränderungen durch Lebensreform* (Göttingen: Vandenhoeck & Ruprecht, 1974).

60 The painter Hugo Höppener (1868–1948) known as 'Fidus' and his teacher Karl Wilhelm Diefenbach (1851–1913) are Germany's most famous examples of this manifestation. *The Prophet: The World of Karl Wilhelm Diefenbach* (Vienna: Wien Museum, 2011).

61 For a discussion of the complicated relationship between interwar Life Reform movements and National Socialism, see Wolfgang Hardtwig, *Utopie und politische Herrschaft im Europa der Zwischenkriegszeit* (Munich: Oldenbourg Verlag, 2003).

62 *Der Internationale Kongress für Frauenwerke und Frauenbestrebungen in Berlin 19.-26. September 1896: Eine Sammlung der auf dem Kongress gehaltenen Vorträge und Ansprachen* (Berling: 1897). See also Ute Gerhard, *Unerhört: Die Geschichte der Frauenbewegung* (Reinbek: Rowolt, 1990).

63 Constitution of the 'Verein für Verbesserung der Frauenkleidung', quoted in Ober, *Der Frauen neue Kleider*, 30.

64 Kerbs and Reuleck, *Handbuch der deutschen Reformbewegung 1880–1933*, 92. For a fascinating discussion of the physical perils of fashion, see Alison Matthews, *Fashion Victims: The Dangers of Dress Past and Present* (London: Bloomsbury, 2015).

65 *Vereinsblatt: Die neue Frauentracht* (Munich: Georg Callwey, 1903), n.p.

66 Minna Cauer, 'Towards Emancipation: Women in Modern European History, A Digital Exhibition and Encyclopedia', accessed 20 June 2020, http://hist259.web.unc.edu/minna-cauer-1841-1922/.

67 Cauer, 'Dress Reform in Germany', 995.

68 Ibid., 994.

69 Wigley, *White Walls, Designer Dresses*, 10.

70 Bibiana Obler, *Intimate Collaborations* (New Haven: Yale University Press, 2014); Sabine Wieber, 'Martha Vogeler and the Worpswede Artists' Colony, 1894–1905', in *Künstlerinnen: Neue Perspektiven auf ein Forschungsfeld der Vormoderne*, ed. Brigitte Munch and Andreas Tacke (Petersberg: Michael Imhof Verlag, 2017), 199–210.

71 Muthesius, *Das Eigenkleid der Frau*.

72 The Newbery sisters' dresses were designed by their mother Jessie Newbery, who was married to the director of the Glasgow School of Art, Francis 'Fra' Newbery and who founded the School's famous embroidery class. The book also included two dresses designed by the Scottish illustrator Jessie M. King (1875–1949). Anna and Hermann Muthesius's son Eckhart recalled that the couple met the Glasgow Four while they were in England. Eckhart Muthesius, *Hermann Muthesius 1861–1927* (London: Architectural Association, 1979), 4–5. Jessie Rowat Newbery (1864–1948) was born into one of Paisley's shawl manufacturing families, and her family embraced radical politics, which allowed her to get a proper education at the Glasgow School of Art (1884–8). She was a member of 'Glasgow-Girls', a name given to a group of progressive women artists and designers emerging from the Glasgow School of Art. Liz Arthur, *Glasgow Girls: Artists and Designers 1890-1930* (Dumfries: Kirkcudbright, 2000).

73 Muthesius, *Das Eigenkleid der Frau*, 24.

74 Ibid., 29.

75 Ibid.

76 Anna Muthesius, 'Die Ausstellung künstlerischer Frauenkleider im Waren-Haus Wertheim Berlin', *Deutsche Kunst und Dekoration* 14 (1904): 441–56.

77 Claus Pese published an online biography of Else Oppler, accessed 5 May 2020, https://claus-pese.de/else-oppler/.

78 Else Oppler, 'The German Dress Reform Movement', *The Independent* 59 (July–December 1905): 487–93.

79 Schultze-Naumburg was in charge of overseeing the organization of the Hohenzollern-Kaufhaus exhibition. Max Osborn, 'Ausstellungen für Frauen-Kleidung in Wiesbaden und Berlin', *Deutsche Kunst und Dekoration* 11 (1902): 165–6.

80 Muthesius, *Das Eigenkleid der Frau*, 441.

81 Ibid., 442.

82 Ibid.

83 Ibid., 448.

84 Paul Lerner, *Consuming Temple: Jews, Department Stores and the Consumer Revolution in Germany, 1880–1940* (Cornell University Press, 2015).

85 Godela Weiss-Sussex and Ulrike Zitzlsperger, *Das Berliner Warenhaus/The Berlin Department Store: Geschichte und Diskurse/History and Discourses* (Frankfurt: Peter Lang, 2013), 8.

86 Indeed, the question why and how women were so closely associated with consumption and shopping as a leisure activity has long occupied scholars. See, for example, Christopher Breward, *The Hidden Consumer: Masculinities, Fashion and City Life, 1860–1914,* Studies in Design and Material Culture (Manchester: Manchester University Press, 1999); Monica Neve, *Sold! Advertising and the Bourgeois Female Consumer in Munich, 1900–1914* (Konstanz: Franz Steiner Verlag, 2010).

87 Otto Weininger's notorious book *Sex and Character* (1903) served as an important point of reference for these debates. See Sander Gilman, *Difference and Pathology: Stereotypes of Sexuality, Race and Madness* (Ithaca: Cornell University Press, 1985) as well as *Freud, Race and Gender* (Princeton: Princeton University Press, 1995).

88 Bruno Specht, 'Die beiden neuen Warenhäuser in München', *Deutsche Bauzeitung* 39, no. 54 (July 1905): 325–35 and *Deutsche Bauzeitung* 39, no. 56 (July 1905): 337–42.

89 Emile Zola, *The Ladies' Paradise*, trans. John Calder (London: Alma Classics, 2013), 88.

90 Paul Göhre, *Das Warenhaus* (Frankfurt: Rütten & Loening, 1907); Bill Lancaster, *The Department Store: A Social History* (London: Leicester University Press, 1995); Gudrun M. König, *Konsumkultur: Inszinierte Warenwelt um 1900* (Vienna: Böhlau, 2009); Helmut Frei, *Tempel der Kauflust: Eine Geschichte der Warenhauskultur* (Leipzig: Edition Leipzig, 1997). Weiss-Sussex and Zitzlsperger, *Das Berliner Warenhaus*, 199–222; Daniel Morat et al., *Weltstadtvergnügen: Berlin 1880–1930* (Göttingen: Vandenhoeck & Ruprecht, 2016).

91 Erika Rappaport, *Shopping for Pleasure: Women in the Making of London's West End* (New Haven: Princeton University Press, 2001); Theresa M. McBride, 'A Woman's World: Department Stores and the Evolution of Women's Employment, 1870–1920', *French Historical Studies* 10, no. 4 (Autumn 1978): 664–83.

92 Christoph Gruneberg and Max Hollein, *Shopping: A Century of Art and Consumer Culture* (Ostfildern: Hatje Cantz, 2002); Jan Whitaker, *The Department Store: History, Design, Display* (London: Thames & Hudson, 2011).

93 Elaine S. Abelson, *When Ladies go a Thieving: Middle Class Shoplifters in the Victorian Department Store* (Oxford: Oxford University Press, 1989), 35. See also Rachel Bowlby, *The Invention of Modern Shopping* (London: Faber & Faber, 2000).

94 Guy Debord quoted in Rappaport, *Shopping for Pleasure*, 11.

95 Lerner, *Consuming Temple*, 12.

96 Janausch and Geyer quoted in Ibid.

97 Rappaport, *Shopping for Pleasure*, 3.

98 The prominent German psychiatrist Emil Kraepelin already discussed *Kaufsucht* as a pathology in 1901, and Georg Simmel offered an early sociological analysis in *Philosophie des Geldes* (Berlin: Duncker & Humboldt, 1900). Emil Kraepelin, *Einführung in die Psychiatrische Klinik* (Leipzig: J. A. Barth Verlag, 1901).

99 Westheim quoted in Isa Fleischmann-Heck, 'Making an Appearance: The Fashion Frenzy and "New Style" in Women's Clothing around 1900', in *Tailored for Freedom*, 89.

6 CONCLUSION

The German poet and essayist Lu Märten (1879–1970) published a small booklet entitled *Die Künstlerin* (The Female Artist) in 1914, which might be viewed as a progenitor of feminist art history.¹ Märten was a committed Social Democrat and concentrated her political activism on bettering the living and working conditions of contemporary women. These politics drove *Die Künstlerin*'s narrative, which offered a revaluation of women artists throughout history from a distinctly sociocultural viewpoint.² In her introduction, Märten made it crystal clear that she was not interested in rehashing the tired old question over women's artistic abilities. Instead, she reframed the debate by placing women's creativity within a larger social framework that disclosed the inequitable valuation of women's domestic tasks and professional ambitions throughout time:

> I emphasise, that I am purposely not posing the question or even paying attention to the contention, whether women can make art, be a genius etc. Instead, I assume that they are and examine the mental and social restriction that prevent [them] from living out their genius.³

Märten was well ahead of her time when she argued that women's work was twice devalued; once in the prioritization of men's work outside the home and then again, in the dismissal of domestic responsibilities as labour in the first place.⁴ She denounced the German Empire's utter lack of 'a routine societal recognition of women as intellectual or creative energy forces'.⁵ She concluded her polemic by demanding that women be supported in their quest to become artists and productive members of society: 'all problems experienced by today's women artists and workers are societal problems that demand a societal solution – all else about "nature" and "predestination" etc. is nothing but verbiage.'⁶

Märten's sobering assessment of the role of women on the cusp of the First World War recalled that the German reform impulses of the previous decades did not bring the anticipated changes within the German Empire's conservative sociopolitical landscape and power structures. This book on Jugendstil women explored a vital time frame in German design history (1895–1907) that promised new opportunities and possibilities for women artists and designers, as well as modern (middle-class) women across Wilhelmine society. Jugendstil was more than simply a style or a movement; it was a way of life that embraced modernity in all of its facets, and its supporters projected the dawn of a new age. Jugendstil design was guided by a series of modern aesthetic and artistic principles that were aimed at reforming German society as a whole. This included a recalibration of traditional gender roles that carved out more agency for Jugendstil women, be they designers, makers, teachers/students, patrons or salonnièrers. As discussed in the Introduction, the term 'Jugendstil' was originally associated with the illustrations and ornamentation pioneered by two Munich magazines: *Die Jugend* and *Simplicissumus*. But it soon came to represent an entire generation of artists, designers and their supporters who revolted against Munich's art–institutional fabric, against historicism and against social conventions that were perceived to stand in the way of a truly modern society.

This book on *Jugendstil Women and the Making of Modern Design* opened with the birth of Jugendstil at the 'Seventh International Art Exhibition' in 1897 as a design language that was moored in the aesthetically unified interior, celebrated craftsmanship of the highest standard and advocated truthful construction principles as well as material integrity (*Materialgerechtheit*). The exhibition garnered considerable critical and public attention, but it failed to generate official support from Munich's institutional art world, which led to the founding of the private initiative *Vereinigte Werkstätten für Kunst im Handwerk* in 1898. The United Workshops represented Germany's first design cooperative that was organized along Arts and Crafts principles emerging from Britain, and it took progressive supporters of applied arts reform by storm. Its members, including several women like *Margarethe von Brauchitsch*, designed and made modern furniture and applied arts objects for a growing upper-middle-class market and proved highly successful among clients from Munich's cultural elites like *Else Bruckmann*. The United Workshops were busy meeting market demands and sending Jugendstil objects to the German Empire's many applied arts exhibitions (Dresden, Berlin, Munich, Nuremberg) and as far afield as Paris and St Louis (World's Fairs). These commitments prevented the design cooperative from properly fulfilling one of its statutory objectives of educating and training modern artists, crafts(wo) men and designers. The private *Lehr- und Versuchs-Ateliers für angewandte und freie Kunst* (*Debschitz School*) was founded by Hermann Obrist and Wilhelm von Debschitz in 1902 to fill this educational void. The school was workshop-based and implemented a new pedagogy for 'all those who were dissatisfied with other methods of learning'.[7] The Debschitz School offered a viable alternative to Munich's established art and design worlds. Its curriculum grounded students in the basic principles of form, line and colour before they could progress to a more specialized engagement with materials and construction methods in workshops for ceramics, metal, textiles and wood. Crucially, this educational institution admitted female students and trained them alongside their male counterparts, which enabled women like *Emilie Butters* to enter professional careers and actively participate in the German Empire's rich exhibition culture.

Jugendstil Women and the Making of Modern Design presented a series of case studies that investigate the diverse roles of modern women in the inception of Munich Jugendstil as Germany's culturally and historically unique contribution to the cross-European phenomenon of International Art Nouveau. This book was motivated by a commitment to move away from conventional accounts of Munich Jugendstil that chiefly focus on (male) designers. It aimed to present a more inclusive and, hopefully, multifaceted story of this key moment in German art and design history. This approach integrates new stories and perspectives into design history that do not simply supplement the narrative with women, but question and reshape the analytical structures of Jugendstil historiography in the first place. The so-called *Frauenfrage* (Women's Question) was at the centre of many cultural, economic and sociopolitical debates around 1900 and left material traces in German applied arts reform and its search for a new design language. This book has shown how debates over women's access to education, female suffrage, sexual difference and their economic position outside of the marital home impacted modern design. Political activists like *Anita Augspurg* and *Sophia Goudstikker*, for example, challenged traditional gender roles and supported progressive design practices because they believed that the two were closely interconnected; a connection that even a politically more conservative, indeed reactionary, individual like *Elsa Bruckmann* recognized. Jugendstil women actively participated in the German Empire's dress-reform movement as either advocates of *Künstlerkleider* (*Anna Muthesius* and *Else Oppler*) or consumers of these sartorial responses to the perceived tyranny of French haute couture.

The Paris Universal Exposition in 1900 marked the highpoint of Jugendstil and International Art Nouveau respectively. But the event also popularized its design language to such a degree that it became a fashionable commodity and, subsequently, a mass phenomenon. As discussed in Chapter 1, machine production was not an issue per se for Jugendstil designers, but mass production was another question altogether. Cheaply produced wares based on copies of original designs that had been published in progressive journals such as *Die Jugend, Deutsche Kunst und Dekoration* and *Dekorative Kunst* began to flood the market and ignited debates around the viability of Jugendstil as a truly modern style. Critics, patrons and designers themselves gradually turned their backs on Jugendstil and the term gradually took on negative connotations. Jugendstil was increasingly viewed by the German Empire's most progressive cultural circles as consumerist, enslaved to fashion and of little or no aesthetic value. In 1901, the Cologne architect Otto Schulze (1863–?) wrote an essay entitled 'Jugendstil Sins' in which he defended

Jugendstil designers against speculating industrialists who misappropriated the term to sell their mass-produced wares.⁸ But Schulze's need to write this essay in the first place signalled a steady turn of the tide against Jugendstil. The Munich critic Hanns von Gumppenberg (1866–1928), who wrote under the clever pseudonym of Professor *Tiefenbohrer* (Deep Drill, leaving his readers in little doubt that he offered in-depth and intellectually rigorous cultural criticism), did not mince his words in 1903 when he declared that 'Jugendstil is the label for each wallpaper, each tie-fabric, each calico whose pattern is half ugly and half Japanese', the latter, of course, making reference to the fashionability of Japonisme.⁹

The *'Dritte Deutsche Kunstgewerbe Ausstellung'* (Third German Applied Arts Exhibition) held in Dresden at the same time as Nuremberg's 'Bavarian Applied Arts, Trade and Industry' exhibition (1906), discussed in Chapter 3, was in part conceived as a robust response to these reverberating criticisms of Jugendstil design (Figure 54). ¹⁰ This national exhibition featured three sections: fine arts, which included aesthetically unified interiors labelled as *Raumkunst* (Room Art), *Kunsthandwerk* (Applied Arts) and *Kunstindustrie* (Manufacture). The event was organized by the Dresden Applied Arts Association, and it was intended to ward off the aforementioned threat of viewing Jugendstil as simply another fashion trend. Organizers faced these negative rumblings head-on and developed an exhibition programme that brought together artists, designers, applied arts schools, manufacturers and small-scale industrialists in the hope of initiating a

FIGURE 54 Poster for the 'Third National Applied Arts Exhibition' in Dresden, 1906, *Deutsche Kunst und Dekoration* 18 (April–September 1906): 463. Universitätsbibliothek Heidelberg, urn:nbn:de:bsz:16-diglit-63833.

dialogue between the stakeholders on the grounds of mutual economic benefits. Karl Schmidt (1873–1948), head of the *Dresdner Werkstätten für Handwerkskunst Karl Schmidt* (Dresden Workshops for Handicraft) and co-organizer of the 1906 exhibition, envisioned an 'artists' economy in the applied arts' that renegotiated the relationship between artist, designer, crafts(wo)man and industry.[11] Design historians sometimes evoke this event as the first Werkbund exhibition avant la lettre.[12] The Werkbund was founded in Munich in 1907 as a national organization that advocated a mutually beneficiary collaboration between architecture, the applied arts and industry. Under its two intellectual leaders, Hermann Muthesius and Henry van de Velde, the Werkbund was committed to imbue industrially manufactured goods (industrial, commercial and household) with a design vision and solid craftsmanship. It goes without saying that Werkbund politics over design reform were deeply gendered and architectural historian Despina Stratigakos explored how women's call for gender equality in their everyday lives and their professional practices was mediated by the Werkbund.[13] She essentially argued that the Werkbund's promise of aesthetic unity was unable to reconcile 'masculine' reason with 'feminine' spirit.[14]

The 1906 Dresden exhibition gradually opened a new chapter in progressive German design discourse and practices while hailing the end of some of Jugendstil's core design principles. The founding of the German Werkbund in 1907, therefore, offers a natural closing point for this book's narrative. The Werkbund's core value of 'quality' advocated a simpler and more *sachliche* (objective) design language that rejected ornamentation and celebrated functional form.[15] Jugendstil designers and makers crafted unique objects that put their subjective artistic vision into material form. They were admired and bought by the German Empire's cultural elites. The Werkbund, on the other hand, targeted Germany's lower middle classes with its machine-made furniture and objects. Interestingly, Richard Riemerschmid bridged the two; he was one of the original founders of the United Workshops and his iconic *Maschinenmöbel* (machine-made furniture) were exhibited to great critical acclaim at the 1906 Dresden exhibition (Figure 55). Riemerschmid's career underlines the fact that the Werkbund emerged out of, and existed alongside, the United Workshops. The two shared core principles and they were both committed to design reform, but they appealed to different markets and embraced different aesthetics. The Werkbund finally achieved one of Jugendstil's unfulfilled ambitions, namely, to produce true *Nutzkunst* (functional art). But even within the Werkbund's circles, the issue around the employ of the machine remained unresolved and led to the famous debate between Hermann Muthesius and van de Velde at the Cologne Werkbund Exhibition in 1914. During a much-anticipated exchange between the two architects, Muthesius championed standardized design and mechanical mass production while van de Velde held on to the notion of artistic individuality and creative expression.[16] This split between Expressionism and

FIGURE 55 Richard Riemerschmid, 'Affordable Dining Room Furniture', Raumkunst at the 1906 Dresden Exhibition, *Deutsche Kunst und Dekoration* 18 (April–September 1906): 640. Universitätsbibliothek Heidelberg, urn:nbn:de:bsz:16-diglit-63833.

Rationalism was temporarily assuaged by Muthesius 'winning' the argument, but these frictions continued to boil underneath the surface and weakened the Werkbund's authority.

Jugendstil received its final death knell with the outbreak of the First World War on 28 July 1914, which devastated Europe's rich artistic and cultural landscape. Jugendstil's noble reform ambitions were lost amidst the chaos wrought by this military conflict. Its tumultuous sociopolitical aftermath destroyed the economic fabric that had generated and supported Munich Jugendstil. A number of Jugendstil critics and designers lost their lives in the war, and many of its patrons forfeited their financial resources and/or social capital. German women were finally granted voting rights by the Weimar Republic's *Rat der Volksbeauftragten* (Council of People's Deputies) on 30 November 1918. Applied Arts Schools and Fine Arts academies opened their doors to female students soon after. Two key goals of Germany's women's movement – female suffrage and equal access to post-secondary education – were achieved at long last. And yet, the women's question was far from being settled, and gender inequalities continue to plague German society to this very day.

What happened to the Jugendstil women at the heart of this book? They all survived the First World War. Some have been forgotten by history because they left no archival trail after their involvement with Jugendstil reform. Anna Muthesius's career, for example, became entirely subsumed into her husband's architectural practice. Others returned to their design practices, their political activism, their pedagogical missions and their cultural politicking. Else Oppler-Legband launched a second career as a successful stage and film-set designer after the First World War, and became Peter Behren's *Arbeitsgefährtin* (work partner) in the 1920s. The two collaborated on a number of exhibition projects such as a terrace house for the 1927 German Werkbund Exhibition in Stuttgart (Weissenhof Estate) or the *Ring der Frauen* (Circle of Women) pavilion at the 1931 *Bauausstellung* (Trade Fair for the German Building Industry) in Berlin.[17] Her career was cut short by the National Socialists' Nuremberg Laws (1935) and, as a woman of Jewish descent, she was forced to flee the country. As briefly discussed in Chapter 2, Anita Augspurg and Lida Gustava Heymann also had to leave Germany because their politics had earned them a place on the Nazi Party's blacklist. Their beautiful Jugendstil façade on the Photo-Studio Elvira was destroyed by Munich's Nazi officials to make way for the Tag der Deutschen Kunst parade in 1937. Like *Margarethe von Brauchitsch*, several of the Jugendstil women discussed across the pages of this book became members of the German Werkbund (1907). They reinvented themselves within the Werkbund's edicts of *Sachlichkeit* (objectivity) and *Typisierung* (standardization), and actively contributed to what historian Frederic Schwartz described the revaluation of 'the nature of culture in a consumer-oriented capitalist economy'.[18]

The Munich salonnière *Else Bruckmann* offers a different, and more problematic, lens into the Jugendstil women's afterlives. During the time period covered by this book, Elsa and Hugo Bruckmann actively supported International Modernism in art and design. After Elsa Bruckmann hosted Houston Steward Chamberlain at her inaugural salon, the couple espoused problematic ideas of ethnic and cultural purity that would eventually be consolidated under Germany's Nazi Regime. Between 1914 and 1933, the Bruckmanns became increasingly entangled with Bavaria's Radical Right. Their initial dabbling in Social Darwinism and biological theories of race (both of which were cross-European phenomena at the time) morphed into xenophobic nationalism and racist anti-Semitism. After the Bruckmanns moved into their grand Palais on the Karolinerplatz in 1908, their political worldviews contracted. Elsa Bruckmann became an ardent supporter of National Socialism after hearing Adolf Hitler speak at the Munich Circus Krone in 1921.[19] Indeed, she has recently been identified as introducing Adolf Hitler to Paul Troost, Hitler's first state architect, at one of her Thursday evenings.[20]

Chamberlain's reading at Elsa Bruckmann's first salon in January of 1899 might be viewed with historical hindsight as planting the seed for the Bruckmanns' eventual support of National Socialism. His racist theories undoubtedly fuelled early-twentieth-century manifestations of a kind of 'Germanic' chauvinism that was later consolidated by National Socialist ideology.[21] The place of National

Socialism in German history has occupied historians since Hitler's defeat in 1945, and it is often difficult to extricate early-twentieth-century German culture from the roots of National Socialism.[22] However, one should be careful to not draw simplistic causalities between late-nineteenth-century 'crypto-fascism' and the Nazi State or rehash the 1986 'Historians' Quarrel' over Germany's exceptional historical trajectory (*Sonderweg*) into totalitarianism.[23] It is undisputed that the Third Reich must be contextualized within the parameters of a broader historical lens. However, the Wilhelmine Empire (1871–1918) and the Weimar Republic (1918–33) also warrant attention as distinct political constellations with their own cultural, economic, social and political dynamics and parameters.

My book analyses a specific place (Munich) and time (1895–1907) to trace the diverse cultural roles played by Jugendstil women during this relatively short, but exceptionally dynamic, time frame. Historical specificity and geographical locale are two key anchors of this study. Some of the cultural–political trajectories that emerge from engaging with Jugendstil women raise questions about the ways in which ideological components of Nazism might be traced. The potential links and continuities between Jugendstil – and turn-of-the-last-century life reform movements more generally – and Nazi ideology are compelling. They warrant further analysis, and it is important that these questions are pursued. However, a different kind of study is needed to effectively excavate the interconnections between Jugendstil and National Socialism. *Jugendstil Women* treats Elsa Bruckmann's salon on the Nymphenburg Street (1899–1908), for example, as a site of cultural production that revealed the rich, and often contradictory, artistic, intellectual and sociopolitical worlds of the German Empire rather than serving as a prelude to the National Socialist Regime's erosion of civilization. Consequently, my book opens up questions rather than offering new research on the entanglement between the two.

By 1912, Jugendstil as a dynamic design language that promised sociocultural reform and embodied modernity had run its course. Richard Riemerschmid, who by this point in time was serving as the director of the *Königliche Kunstgewerbe Schule* (Royal Applied Arts School) in Munich, commented on the applied arts exhibits at the most recent Bavarian Trade Exhibition as follows: 'the great *Kunstgewerbler* (designers) live splendidly in spite of the fact that the 1912 Bavarian Trade Exhibition distressingly resembles their own official funeral.'[24] This observation must be understood in the context of the aforementioned Werkbund conflict, during which Riemerschmid as the maker of *Maschinenmöbel* obviously supported standardization, but it also signalled that Munich Jugendstil designers were out of touch with the times. This relegated Jugendstil to design history's sidelines and discarded its supporters in its wake.

Until the 1950s, Jugendstil was predominantly viewed by art and design historians as 'an artistic fashion trend that was supported by wealthy patrons who were simply interested in an individual aesthetic that signalled their social exclusivity.'[25] During the interwar period (1919–33), progressive German architects and designers erased ornament and decoration from their buildings and material objects while avant-garde artists embraced *Neue Sachlichkeit* (New Objectivity), Expressionism or Abstraction. Jugendstil had been rendered completely irrelevant, and its decorative design language was cast as modernism's binary opposite. The decorative was rejected by International Modernism as entrenched in fashion, pathetically feminine and devoid of substance. This spectre continued to haunt art and design history for much of the twentieth century and is nicely encapsulated by art historian T. J. Clark's observation in 1999 that during the 1890s, 'the decorative was a pretend solution to modernism's problems'.[26] This biased historiography posed a serious problem for the legacy of this book's Jugendstil women. They were targeted by modernism as its binary 'other' and were seen to stand for everything that modernist architecture and design was not. In this context, Bruno Paul's caricature *'Der Münchner Jugend Brunnen'* (Munich's Fountain of Youth), published in *Simplicissumus* in 1897, proved eerily prescient (Plate 14).[27] It shows a group of women positioned at either side of an elaborately ornamented fountain. The women on the left are dressed in contemporary garments; some might even be wearing reform dress, and are about to drink from the fountain only to emerge on the right as a randomly scattered bunch of women in *Künstlerkleidern* and with loose hair. Their shapes and form are weakened by the fountain's water. Paul's illustration offered a satirical view of Munich Jugendstil and women's quest for emancipation. Sipping from the fountain of youth turned them into rubber-limbed, rudderless misfits whose bodies were contorted into seemingly impossible shapes reminiscent of Jugendstil ornament and far from acting with purpose and reason.

International Modernism became design history's dogma. The women at the centre of this book gradually sank into oblivion. Their archives were lost – they were simply not deemed important enough to be kept by family members, let alone deposited into city archives. Art historian Marsha Meskimmon titled her fascinating study of women artists in the Weimer Republic *We Weren't Modern Enough*.[28] In the case of the Jugendstil women at the heart of this book, it was less of a question of not being modern enough but, with hindsight, these women hitched their wagon to what, in the larger scheme of design history, turned out to be the 'wrong' kind of modernism. But for a brief period of just over ten years, Jugendstil held the promise of a truly modern design language. The progressive women who supported Jugendstil in the various ways discussed in the book's five case studies strategically used design to position themselves at the epicentre of cultural and sociopolitical reform. Sadly, these cultural pioneers first fell into disrepute and then were outright forgotten. Their important contributions to the production, dissemination and consumption of Munich Jugendstil should finally be acknowledged by design historians.

Each of the women discussed in this book activated design in a different *Handlungsfeld* (field of action) that ranged from designing, making, collecting, commissioning and educating to politicking and facilitating. Design historian John Potvin recently argued that 'while agency is a distinctly human attribute, the role played by design and material objects cannot be underestimated in the way agency is activated or thwarted'.[29] The pioneering women discussed in this book deployed Jugendstil objects (in the broadest sense of the word) to carve out new roles for themselves within Munich sociocultural fabric and, in the process, became active agents in the making of modern design.

Notes

1. Lu Märten, *Die Künstlerin,* Kleine Monographien zur Frauenfrage, ed. Adele Schreiber (Munich: Albert Langen Verlag, 1914).
2. This method would much later be formalized as 'social art history' by the likes of T. J. Clark, Griselda Pollock and Linda Nochlin. T. J. Clark, *Image of the People: Gustave Courbet and the Second French Republic 1848–1851* (London: Thames & Hudson, 1973); Griselda Pollock, *Mary Cassatt: Painter of Modern Women* (London: Thames & Hudson, 1977); Linda Nochlin, *Realism: Style and Civilization* (London: Pelican Books, 1971).
3. Märten, *Die Künstlerin,* reprint (Bielefeld: Aisthesis, 2001), 10.
4. Ibid., 15.
5. Ibid., 25.
6. Ibid., 106.
7. Debschitz quoted in Helga Schmoll-Eisenwerth, 'Die Münchner Debschitz Schule', in *Kunstschulreform 1900–1933*, ed. Hans M. Wingler (Berlin: Gebrüder Mann, 1977), 71.
8. Otto Schulze, 'Jugendstil Sünden', *Kunst und Handwerk* 52 (1901–2): 198–202.
9. Gumppenberger quoted in Anne Goebel, 'Knospen, Blüten und andere Skandale', Süddeutsche Zeitung (26 August 2014), accessed 17 June 2020, https://www.sueddeutsche.de/muenchen/jugendstil-in-muenchen-knospen-blueten-und-andere-skandale-1.2103139.
10. The two previous national applied arts exhibitions took place in Munich in 1876 and 1888. Munich was planning to host a third iteration of this national event but organizers could not agree on a time frame and eventually abandoned all plans.
11. Karl Schmidt quoted in John V. Maciuika, *Before the Bauhaus: Architecture, Politics and the German State, 1890–1920* (Cambridge: Cambridge University Press, 2005), 138.
12. Ibid., 137.
13. Despina Stratigakos, 'Women and the Werkbund: Gender Politics and German Design Reform, 1907–14', *Journal of the Society of Architectural Historians* 62, no. 4 (December 2003): 490–511.
14. Ibid., 505–6.
15. Joan Campbell, *The German Werkbund: The Politics of Reform in the Applied Arts* (Princeton: Princeton University Press, 1978); Frederick J. Schwartz, *The Werkbund:*

Design Theory and Mass Culture before the First World War (New Haven: Yale University Press, 1996); Mark M. Jarzombek, 'The Kunstgewerbe, the Werkbund, and the Aesthetics of Culture in the Wilhelmine Period', *Journal of the Society of Architectural Historians* 53, no. 1 (1994): 7–19.

16 Katherine M. Kuenzli, 'Architecture, Individualism, and Nation: Henry van de Velde's 1914 Werkbund Theater Building', *The Art Bulletin* 94, no. 2 (2012): 251–73.

17 Peter Behrens, 'Terrassen am Hause', in *Bau und Wohnung. Die Bauten der Weissenhofsiedlung in Stuttgart, errichtet 1927 nach Vorschlägen des Deutschen Werkbundes im Auftrage der Stadt Stuttgart und im Rahmen der Werkbundausstellung 'Die Wohnung'*, ed. Deutscher Werkbund (Stuttgart: Wedekind, 1927) and 'Das Haus Ring der Frauen', in *Deutsche Bauausstellung 9 Mai–2 August 1931* (Berlin: n.p., 1931).

18 Schwartz, *The Werkbund*, 216.

19 The Bruckmanns joined the National Socialist Party in 1930, but their entry was backdated to 1925 so that their early support could be acknowledged through low membership numbers (91 and 92). 'Munich Biographies: Elsa Bruckmann Bruckmann', NS Dokumentationszentrum Munich, accessed 15 June 2017, https://www.ns-dokuzentrum-muenchen.de/dauerausstellung/muenchner-biographien/detail/?tx_ttnews%5Btt_news%5D=15&cHash=f1f6bb05e3275f719bf2950bc8f12511.

20 Despina Stratigakos, *Hitler at Home* (New Haven: Yale University Press, 2015), 15.

21 Adolf Hitler was an early admirer and the Nazi Party's chief ideologue Alfred Rosenberg cast Chamberlain as a prophet of Germany's Aryan future. Alfred Rosenberg, *Houston Stewart Chamberlain als Vekünder und Begründer einer deutschen Zukunft* (Munich: Bruckmann Verlag, 1927).

22 The scholarly literature in this field is vast and cannot be adequately reflected here but see for example Konrad Jarausch and Michael Geyer, *Shattered past: Reconstructing German Histories* (Princeton: Princeton University Press, 2003); David Blackbourne and Geoff Eley, *The Peculiarities of German History: Bourgeois Politics and Society in Nineteenth Century Germany* (New York: Oxford University Press, 1984); Fritz Stern, *The Politics of Cultural Despair: A Study in the Rise of the Germanic Ideology* (Berkeley: University of California Press, 1961); Woodruff D. Smith, *Politics and the Science of Culture in Germany, 1840–1920* (New York: Oxford University Press, 1991).

23 The term 'crypto-fascism' was first used by the eminent German historians Richard Hamann and Joost Hermand, *Epochen deutscher Kultur von 1870 bis zur Gegenwart*, 5 vols. (Frankfurt: Fischer Verlag, 1977). For the 'Historikerstreit' see Jürgen Kocka, 'German History before Hitler: The Debate about the German Sonderweg', *Journal of Contemporary History* 23, no. 1 (January 1988): 2–16.

24 Riemerschmid quoted in Friedrich Prinz and Marita Krauss, *München: Museenstadt mit Hinterhöfen. Die Prinzregentenzeit 1886-1912* (Munich: Beck Verlag, 1988), 243.

25 Richard Hamann and Jost Hermand, *Stilkunst um 1900* (Munich: Akademie Verlag, 1973), 246.

26 T. J. Clark, *Farewell to an Idea: Episodes from a History of Modernism* (New Haven: Yale University Press, 1999), 131. The dismissal of the decorative has recently been redressed by two important art historical publications. Katherine M. Kuenzli, *The Nabis and Intimate Modernism: Painting and the Decorative at the Fin-de-Siècle* (Burlington: Ashgate, 2010); Allison Morehead, *Nature's Experiments and the Search for Symbolist Form* (University Park: Penn State

University Press, 2012). This problem still demands German design history's attention. A notable exception is Robin Schuldenfrei, *Luxury and Modernism: Architecture and the Object in Germany 1900–1933* (Princeton: Princeton University Press, 2020).

27 Bruno Paul, 'Der Münchner Jugendbrunnen', *Simplicissimus* 10 (5 June 1897): 76.

28 Marsha Meskimmon, *We Weren't Modern Enough: Women Artists and the Limits of German Modernism* (New York: I. B. Tauris, 1999).

29 John Potvin, 'Introduction: Reassessing Design through Agency', in *Design & Agency*, ed. John Potvin and Marie-Ève Marchand (London: Bloomsbury Visual Arts, 2020), 1.

BIBLIOGRAPHY

Architect-Designers from Pugin to Mackintosh. London: Fine Arts Society, 1981.
'C. R. Mackintosh, Glasgow'. *Dekorative Kunst* 4 (1899): 78–9.
'Das Bürgerliches Gesetzbuch 1900 und die Rechte der Frauen'. 1 January 1900. https://www.zeitklicks.de/kaiserzeit/zeitklicks/zeit/alltag/frau-und-familie/das-buergerliche-gesetzbuch-1900-und-die-rechte-der-frauen/.
'Das Neue Schauspielhaus in München'. *Dekorative Kunst* 8 (1901): 366–71.
'Dekorative Stickereien'. *Die Kunst* 1, no. 2 (1900): 347.
Der Internationale Kongress für Frauenwerke und Frauenbestrebungen in Berlin 19.-26. September 1896: Eine Sammlung der auf dem Kongress gehaltenen Vorträge und Ansprachen. Berlin: 1897.
'Die localen Verhältnisse der Münchner Akademie der Künste'. *Allgemeine Zeitung* (28 November 1872): 1.
'Die Schottischen Künstler: Margaret Macdonald, Frances Macdonald, Chas. R. Mackintosh, T. Morris und J. Herbert McNair'. *Dekorative Kunst* 3 (1899): 48–9.
Documentation Centre Nazi Party Rally Grounds. Accessed 30 July 2019. https://museums.nuernberg.de/documentation-center/.
'Erste Ausstellung der Münchner Vereinigung für angewandte Kunst im Studiengebäude des Königl. National-Museums'. *Catalogue 1905*, n.p.
'Erste Kunst- und Kunstgewerbe-Ausstellung in Darmstadt 1898: Abteilung B: Moderne Kleinkunst und Zimmer-Ausstattung'. *Deutsche Kunst und Dekoration* 3 (1898/9): 105–14.
'Glasgow-München'. *Dekorative Kunst* 3 (1899): 69–76.
'Kleine Nachrichten'. *Kunst und Handwerk* 54 (1903/1904): 25.
'Landesausstellungen in Nürnberg 1906'. http://www.nuernberginfos.de/nuernberg-mix/landesausstellungen.html.
'Lehrwerkstätte der Vereinigten Werkstätten für Kunst im Handwerk'. *Kunst und Handwerk* 51, no. 6 (1901): 188.
'Mackintosh Architecture: Context, Making and Meaning'. *The University of Glasgow*. https://www.mackintosh-architecture.gla.ac.uk/
'Minna Cauer (1841–1922)'. *Towards Emancipation: Women in Modern European History. A Digital Exhibition & Encyclopedia*. http://hist259.web.unc.edu/minna-cauer-1841-1922/.
'München 1869–1958: Aufbruch zur Modernen Kunst'. Munich: Haus der Kunst, 1958.
'Munich Biographies: Elsa Bruckmann'. *NS Dokumentationszentrum Munich*. https://www.ns-dokuzentrum-muenchen.de/dauerausstellung/muenchner-biographien/detail/?tx_ttnews%5Btt_news%5D=15&cHash=f1f6bb05e3275f719bf2950bc8f12511.

Nachlass Kurt Breysig, DE-611-BF-981. Handschriftenabteilung, Staatsbibliothek zu Berlin: Preussischer Kulturbesitz.

'Nürnbergs Industriekultur'. http://www.nuernberginfos.de/industriekultur-nuernberg.html.

'Praterinsel: Familie Geschichte der Familie Riemerschmid'. https://web.archive.org/web/20071008023106/http://www.praterinsel.org/index.htm?page=/afp/riemer.htm

'Programm des Verbandes fortschrittlicher Frauenvereine'. https://www.digitales-deutsches-frauenarchiv.de/akteurinnen/verband-fortschrittlicher-frauenvereine#footnote3_lmd4by2.

'Unser Preisausschreiben'. *Dekorative Kunst* 6, no. 12 (1903): 477–80.

Verein für Faueninteressen e.V. https://www.fraueninteressen.de/.

Vereinsblatt: Die neue Frauentracht. Munich: Georg Callwey, 1903.

Abelson, Elaine S. *When Ladies go A-Thieving: Middle Class Shoplifters in the Victorian Department Store.* Oxford: Oxford University Press, 1989.

Abrams, Lynn. 'Martyrs or Matriarchs? Working-Class Women's Experience of Marriage in Germany before the First World War'. *Women's History Review* 1, no. 3 (1992): 357–76.

Abrams, Lynn and Elisabeth Harvey, *Gender Relations in German History: Power, Agency and Experience from the Sixteenth to the Twentieth Century.* Durham: Duke University, 1997.

Ackerl, Isabella. 'Wiener Salonkultur um die Jahrhundertwende: Ein Versuch'. In *Die Wiener Jahrhundertwende: Einflüsse, Umwelt, Wirkungen.* Edited by Jürgen Nautz and Richard Vahrenkamp, 694–708. Vienna: Böhlau, 1993.

Adams Stein, Jesse. *Hot Metal: Material Culture and Tangible Labour.* Manchester: Manchester University Press, 2016.

Adamson, Glenn. *The Invention of Craft.* London: Bloomsbury Academic, 2013.

Adburgham, Alison. *Liberty's: A Biography of a Shop.* London: George Allen and Unwin, 1975.

Afuhs, Eva and Andreas Strobl. *Hermann Obrist: Sculpture, Space, Abstraction around 1900.* Zurich: Scheidegger & Spiess, 2009.

Ahlers-Hestermann, Friedrich. *Stilwende: Aufbruch der Jugend um 1900.* Berlin: Gebrüder Mann, 1941.

Albisetti, James C. 'Could Separate be Equal? Helene Lange and Women's Education in Imperial Germany'. *History of Education Quarterly* Fall (1982): 301–17.

Alexander, Zeynep Çelik. 'Jugendstil Vision: Occultism, Gender and Modern Design Pedagogy'. *Journal of Design History* 22, no. 3 (2009): 203–26.

Alexander, Zeynep Çelik. *Kinaesthetic Knowing: Aesthetics, Epistemology, Modern Design.* Chicago: Chicago University Press, 2017.

Alfred Mohrbutter. *Das Kleid der Frau: Ein Beitrag zur künstlerischen Gestaltung des Frauenkleides* (1904). Reprint. Hannover: Schäfer, 1985.

Anderson, Harriet. *Utopian Feminism: Women's Movements in Fin-de-Siècle Vienna.* New Haven: Yale University Press, 1992.

Anger, Jenny. 'Forgotten Ties: The Suppression of the Decorative in German Art and Theory, 1900–1915'. In *Not at Home: Suppression of Domesticity in Modern Art and Architecture.* Edited by Christopher Reed, 130–46. London: Thames & Hudson, 1996.

Angioni, Alexandra, Gabriele Bodri and Jakobus Wilhelm. 'Anerkannt und doch vergessen? Margarete Junge, Gertrud Kleinhempel, Charlotte Krause und die Dresdener Werkstätten für Handwerkskunst'. *Dresdner Hefte. Gartenstadt Hellerau: Der Alltage einer Utopie* 15, no. 51 (1997): 13–19.

Appadurai, Arjun. *The Social Life of Things: Commodities in Cultural Perspective.* Cambridge: Cambridge University Press, 1986.

Applegate, Celia. *A Nation of Provincials: The German Idea of Heimat*. Berkeley: University of California Press, 1990.
Arnold, Klaus Peter. *Vom Sofakissen zum Städtebau: Die Geschichte der Deutschen Werkstätten und der Gartenstadt Hellerau*. Dresden: Verlag der Kunst, 1993.
Arthur, Liz. *Glasgow Girls: Artists and Designers 1890–1930*. Dumfries: Kirkcudbright, 2000.
Ash, Mitchell G. *Gestalt Psychology in German Culture, 1890–1967*. Cambridge: Cambridge University Press, 1995.
Attfield, Judy and Pat Kirkham. *A View from the Interior*. London: The Women's Press, 1989.
Aurnhammer, Achim and Wolfgang Brungart. *Stefan George und sein Kreis: Ein Handbuch*. Berlin: de Gruyter, 2012.
Aynsley, Jeremy and Charlotte Grant. *Imagined Interiors: Representing the Domestic Interior Since the Renaissance*. London: V&A Publishing, 2006.
Azzouni, Safia and Uwe Wirth. *Dilettantismus als Beruf*. Berlin: Kulturverlag Kadmos, 2010.
Balzer, Isabel. 'Exhibiting Unified Germany: 1871–1889'. PhD Dissertation, Northwestern University, 1997.
Banner, Bernadette. *What did Victorian Corsets Actually Look Like: Examining Corsets from the Symington Collection*. YouTube video, 11:31. Posted 12 October 2019. https://www.youtube.com/watch?v=5QUEf-8BKyE.
Bartesch, Hermine. 'Die Kunststickerei auf der Pariser Weltausstellung'. *Kunstgewerbeblatt*, 12, no. 6 (1901): 105.
Bartesch, Hermine. Mathilde Fiedler and Helene Wesley. *Die moderne Damenschneiderei in Wort und Bild*. Leipzig: Killinger, 1918.
Barthes, Roland. *The Fashion System*. Berkeley: University of California Press, 1967.
Bartmann, Dominik. *Anton von Werner*. Munich: Hirmer Verlag, 1993.
Barton, Gregory A. 'The Historian's Task'. *British Scholar* 2, no. 1 (September 2009): 1–3.
Bauakte 10, 240. *Lokalbaukommission*. Stadtarchiv Munich.
Baudelaire, Charles. 'The Painter of Modern Life' (1863). In *The Nineteenth-Century Visual Culture Reader*. Edited by Vanessa R. Schwartz and Jeannene M. Przyblyski, 37–42. London: Routledge, 2004.
Bäumer, Gertrud. 'Das lebendige Haus'. *Die Frau* 31, (1924): 7. Reprinted in *In Hof-Atelier Elvira 1887–1928: Ästheten, Aristokraten*, 113. Munich: Stadtmuseum, 1985.
Bäumer, Gertrud and Helene Lange. *Handbuch der Frauenbewegung*. 5 vols. Berlin: W. Moeser, 1901–1906.
Baumgartner, Marianne. *Der Verein der Schriftstellerinnen und Künstlerinnen in Wien (1885–1938)*. Wien: Böhlau, 2015.
Beaudry, Mary C. 'Artifacts and Active Voices: Material Culture as Social Discourse'. In *The Archaeology of Inequality*. Edited by Randall H. McGuire and Robert Paynter, 150–91. Oxford: Basil Blackwell, 1991.
Beaudry, Mary C. *Findings: The Material Culture of Needlework and Sewing*. New Haven: Yale University Press, 2006.
Bebel, August. *Die Frau und der Sozialismus* (1879). Reprint. Bonn: Dietz Verlag, 1990.
Beet, Gunta. 'Zur künstlerischen Reform der Mode'. *Illustrirte Frauen-Zeitung* 28, no. 21.3 (1 November 1901): 76.
Behrens, Peter. 'Das Haus "Ring der Frauen" auf der Deutschen Bauausstellung, Berlin 1931'. *Die Baugilde* 13, no. 13 (1931): 1085.
Behrens, Peter. 'Terrassen am Hause'. In *Bau und Wohnung. Die Bauten der Weissenhofsiedlung in Stuttgart, errichtet 1927 nach Vorschlägen des Deutschen*

Werkbundes im Auftrage der Stadt Stuttgart und im Rahmen der Werkbundausstellung 'Die Wohnung'. Edited by Deutscher Werkbund. Stuttgart: Wedekind, 1927.
Beller, Steven. *Rethinking Vienna 1900*. New York: Berghahn, 2001.
Beller, Steven. *Vienna and the Jews: A Cultural History*. Cambridge: Cambridge University Press, 1989.
Benjamin, Walter. 'Theses on the Philosophy of History'. In *Illuminations*. Edited by Hannah Arendt, 253–64. New York: Schocken Books, 1968.
Bennet, Tony and Patrick Joyce. *Material Powers: Cultural Studies, History and the Material Turn*. London: Routledge, 2010.
Bennette, Rebecca A. *Fighting for the Soul of Germany: The Catholic Struggle for Inclusion after Unification*. Harvard: Harvard University Press, 2012.
Berger, Renata. *Malerinnen auf dem Weg ins 20. Jahrhundert: Kunstgeschichte als Sozialgeschichte*. Cologne: DuMont, 1982.
Berlepsch-Valendas, Hans Eduard von. 'Endlich ein Umschwung'. *Deutsche Kunst und Dekoration* 1 (1897/8): 1–12.
Bermbach, Udo. *Houston Stewart Chamberlain: Wagners Schwiegersohn – Hitlers Vordenker*. Stuttgart: J.B. Metzler, 2015.
Berneike, Christiane. 'Nichts ist Unmöglich: Anita Augspurg, eine Biographische Recherche'. *FrauenMediaTurm*. https://frauenmediaturm.de/historische-frauenbeweg ung/nichts-ist-unmoeglich-anita-augspurg-eine-biographische-recherche/.
Beyerle, Tulga and Klára Nemecková. *Gegen die Unsichtbarkeit: Designerinnen der Deutschen Werkstätten Hellerau 1898–1938*. Munich: Hirmer Verlag, 2019.
Billcliffe, Roger. *Charles Rennie Mackintosh: The Complete Furniture, Furniture Drawings and Interior Designs*. 4th Edition. Moffat: Cameron & Hollis, 2009.
Bilski, Emily D. and Emily Braun. *Jewish Women and Their Salons: The Power of Conversation*. New York: Jewish Museum, 2005.
Blackbourn, David and Greoff Eley. *The Peculiarities of German History*. Oxford: Oxford University Press, 1994.
Blackshaw, Gemma. 'Dead Men and Their Naked Truths'. In *The Nakeds*. Edited by Mary Doyle and Kate Macfarlane, 12–29. Manchester: Cornerhouse, 2014.
Bloom-Hiesinger, Kathryn. *Art Nouveau in Munich*. Munich: Prestel, 1988.
Bock, Marion. 'Hedwig Kettler: Eine Wegbereiterin gymnasialer Mädchenbildung'. *Hannoversche Geschichtsblätter* 44 (1990): 53–70.
Bode, Wilhelm von. 'Hermann Obrist', *Pan* 5, no. 1 (1896): 318–34.
Bode, Wilhelm von. 'Künstler im Kunsthandwerk: Die Abteilung der Kleinkunst in den Internationalen Ausstellungen zu München und Dresden, 1897'. *Pan* 3, no. 2 (1897): 113.
Bode, Wilhelm von. *Kunst und Kunstgewerbe am Ende des 19. Jahrhunderts. Neue Ausgabe*. Berlin: Cassirer, 1901.
Bodenhausen, Eduard von. 'Entwicklungslehre und Aesthetik'. *Pan* 5, no. 4 (1900): 236–41.
Bothe, Rolf. *Das frühe Bauhaus und Johannes Itten*. Ostfildern-Ruit: Hatje, 1994.
Bourdieu, Pierre. *A Social Distinction of Taste*. London: Routledge, 1984.
Brandow-Faller, Megan. *The Female Secession: Art and the Decorative at the Viennese Women's Academy*. University Park: Pennsylvania State University Press, 2020.
Brandow-Faller, Megan. 'An Art of Their Own: Reinventing Frauenkunst in the Female Academies and Artist Leagues of Late-Imperial and First Republic Austria, 1900–1930'. PhD dissertation, Georgetown University, Washington, DC, 2010.
Braun, Irene. 'Alte und Neue Stickereien'. *Kunst und Handwerk* 50, no. 12 (1899/1900): 381–95.

Bredt, Ernst Wilhelm. *München als Kunststadt*. Berlin: Marquardt, 1907.
Brett, David. *C.R. Mackintosh: The Poetics of Workmanship*. London: Reaktion Books, 1992.
Breward, Christopher and Caroline Evans. *Fashion and Modernity*. Oxford: Berg, 2005.
Breward, Christopher and Caroline Evans. *Fashion*. Oxford History of Art. Oxford: Oxford University Press, 2003.
Breward, Christopher and Caroline Evans. *The Hidden Consumer: Masculinities, Fashion and City Life 1860-1914*. Manchester: Manchester University Press, 1999.
Bringmann, Michael. *Friedrich Pecht (1914-1903): Maßstäbe der deutschen Kunstkritik zwischen 1850 und 1900*. Berlin: Mann, 1982.
Bröcker, Nicola, Gisela Moeller and Christine Salge. *August Endell, 1871-1925: Architekt und Formkünstler*. Imhof: Petersberg, 2012.
Brooker, Peter et al. *Oxford Critical and Cultural History of Modernist Magazines*. Oxford: Oxford University Press, 2013.
Browne, Clare and Jennifer Wearden *Samplers from the Victoria and Albert Museum*. London: Victoria & Albert Museum Publications, 1999.
Bruckmann, Elsa. 'Das heutige Kunstgewerbe'. *Illustrirte Frauen-Zeitung* 21, no. 1 (November 1899): 166-7.
Bruns, Brigitte. 'Das dritte Geschlecht von Ernst von Wolzogen'. In *Hof-Atelier Elvira 1887-1928: Ästheten, Aristokraten*, 171-90. Munich: Stadtmuseum, 1985.
Burger, Angelika. 'Textile Kunstwerke einer unabhängigen Unternehmerin'. In *Ab nach München: Künstlerinnen um 1900*. Edited by Antonia Voit, 320-3. Munich: Süddeutsche Zeigung GmbH, 2014.
Butler, Judith. *Gender Trouble: Feminism and the Subversion of Identity*. New York: Routledge, 1990.
Calhoun, Bonnie. 'Shaping the Public Sphere: English Coffeehouses and French Salons and the Age of Enlightenment'. *Colgate Academic Review* 3 (Spring 2008): 75-99.
Calvert, Robyne Erica. 'Fashioning the Artist: Artistic Dress in Victorian Britain, 1848-1900'. PhD Dissertation, University of Glasgow, 2012.
Calvert, Robyne Erica. 'Manly Modes: Artistic Dress and the Styling of Masculine Identity'. *Visual Culture in Britain* 16, no. 2 (2015): 223-42.
Campbell, Joan. *The German Werkbund: The Politics of Reform in the Applied Arts*. Princeton: Princeton University Press, 1978.
Cantacuzène, Fürstin Elsa. 'Vom vierblättrigen Kleeblatt'. *Illustrirte Frauen-Zeitung* 24, no. 12 (1897): 95.
Carline, Richard. *Pictures in the Post: The Story of the Picture Postcard and its Place in the History of Popular Art*. London: Gordon Fraser Gallery, 1971.
Carruthers, Annette. *The Arts and Crafts Movement in Scotland*. New Haven: Yale University Press, 2013.
Cauer, Minna. 'Dress Reform in Germany'. *The Independent* 63 (July 1907): 993-7.
Chamberlain, Houston Stewart. *Grundlagen des Neunzehnten Jahrhunderts*. Munich: Bruckmann Verlag, 1899.
Chatwick, Whitney. *Women, Art and Society*. 3rd Edition. London: Thames & Hudson, 2002.
Clark, Linda L. *Women and Achievement in Nineteenth-Century Europe*. Cambridge: Cambridge University Press, 2008.
Clark, T. J. *Farewell to an Idea: Episodes from a History of Modernism*. New Haven: Yale University Press, 1999.

Clark, T. J. *Image of the People: Gustave Courbet and the Second French Republic 1848–1851*. London: Thames & Hudson, 1973.

Collins, Nancy W. 'The Problem of the Enlightenment Salon'. PhD Dissertation, University College London, 2006.

Colomina, Beatriz. *Privacy and Privacy: Modern Architecture as Mass Media*. Cambridge: MIT Press, 1994.

Coxon, Ann. *Anni Albers*. Munich: Hirmer Verlag, 2018.

Craveri, Benedetta. *The Age of Conversation*. Translated by Teresa Waugh. New York: New York Review of Books, 2005.

Crawford, Alan. *Charles Rennie Mackintosh*. London: Thames & Hudson, 1995.

Crowe, Sarah et al. 'The Case Study Approach'. *BMC Medical Research Methodology* 11, no. 100 (2011). https://doi.org/10.1186/1471-2288-11-100.

Cullen, Anthea. *The Angel in the Studio: Women in the Arts and Crafts Movement*. London: Astragal, 1979.

Cummins, Elizabeth and Wendy Kaplan. *The Arts and Crafts Movement*. London: Thames & Hudson, 1991.

Cunningham, Patricia A. *Reforming Fashion, 1850–1914: Politics, Health, Art*. Kent: Kent State University Press, 2003.

Curtis, Robin and Richard George Elliott. 'An Introduction to Einfühlung'. *Art in Translation* 6, no. 4 (December 2014): 353–76.

Czernin, Monika. *Anna Sacher und ihr Hotel im Wien der Jahrhundertwende*. 3rd Edition. Munich: Albrecht Knaus Verlag, 2014.

D.R. 'Die Mitglieder der 'Lehr- und Versuchs-Ateliers für Angewandte und Freie Kunst, Wilhelm von Debschitz, München' auf der Bayerischen Jubiläums-Landesausstellung Nünrberg 1906'. *Dekorative Kunst* 14 (1906): 345–64.

D.R. 'Moderne Stickereien von Margarete von Brauchitsch'. *Deutsche Kunst und Dekoration* 16 (1905): 498.

Daly Goggin, Maureen and Beth Fowkes Tobin. *Women and Things, 1750–1950*. Aldershot: Ashgate, 2009.

Daniel Morat, Daniel et al. *Weltstadtvergnügen: Berlin 1880–1930*. Göttingen: Vandenhoeck & Ruprecht, 2016.

David, Helge. 'Ein fliessender Teppich: Zur Ästhetik von August Endell'. In *August Endell, 1871–1925: Architekt und Formenkünstler*. Edited by Nicola Bröcker, Gisela Moeller and Christiane Salge, 69–76. Petersberg: Michael Imhof Verlag, 2012.

Davidson, Hilary. 'The Embodied Turn: Making and Remaking Dress as an Academic Practice'. *Fashion Theory* 23, no. 3 (2019): 330.

Davis, Whitney. 'Style and History in Art History'. In *The Uses of Style in Archaeology*. Edited by Margaret Wright Conkey and Christine Ann Hastorf, 18–31. Cambridge: Cambridge University Press, 1990.

De Grazia, Victoria and Ellen Furlough. *The Sex of Things: Gender and Consumption from a Historical Perspective*. Berkeley: University of California Press, 1996.

De Lauretis, Teresa. *Technologies of Gender: Essays on Theory, Film and Fiction*. Bloomington: Indiana University Press, 1987.

Dearstyne, Howard and David Spaeth. *Inside the Bauhaus*. New York: Rizzoli, 1986.

Debschitz, Wilhelm von. 'Eine Methode des Kunstunterrichts'. *Dekorative Kunst* 12 (1904): 207–27.

Derenda, Maria. *Kunst als Beruf: Käthe Kollwitz und Elena Luksch-Makowskaja*. Frankfurt: Campus Verlag, 2018.

Deyseve, Yvette. *Der Künstlerinnen-Verein München e.V. und seine Damen Akademie*. Munich: Herbert Utz Verlag, 2005.

Dollard, Catherine. *The Surplus Woman: Unmarried in Imperial Germany, 1871–1918*. New York: Berghahn, 2009.
Dreger, Moritz. 'Die Textilausstellung des Leipziger Kunstgwerbemuseums'. *Kunst und Kunsthandwerk* 5 (1902): 169–76.
Dülfer, Martin. *Illustrirter Katalog der VII. Internationalen Kunstausstellung im königlichen Glaspalaste*. Munich: Rudolf Mosse, 1897.
Edwards, Tim. *Men in the Mirror: Men's Fashion, Masculinity, and Consumer Society*. London: Cassell, 1997.
Eisler, Rudolf. 'Anschauung'. In *Nachschlagwerk zu Immanuel Kant* (1930). https://www.textlog.de/31941.html.
Eley, Geoff, Jennifer L. Jenkins and Tracie Matysik. *German Modernities from Wilhelm to Weimar: A Contest of Futures*. London: Bloomsbury Academic, 2016.
Elferich, Christa. 'Die Gründungsgeschichte (1894–1899) des Vereins für Fraueninteressen'. In *Evas Töchter: Münchner Schriftstellerinnen und die moderne Frauenbewegung 1894–1933*. Edited by Ingvild Richardsen, 47–63. Munich: Volk Verlag, 2018.
Elgo, H. 'Glueck'. *Pan* 2, no. 3 (1896/7): 219–20.
Endell, August. 'Architektonische Erstlinge'. *Dekorative Kunst* 6 (1900): 304.
Endell, August. *Um die Schönheit: Eine Paraphrase über die Münchener Kunstausstellung*. Munich: 1896.
Erdmann Neumeister. *Thomas Manns frühe Erzählungen: Der Jugendstil asl Kunstform im frühen Werk*. Bonn: Bouvier Verlag Grundmann, 1972.
Euler, Laura. *The Glasgow Style*. Atglen: Schiffer Publishing, 2008.
Ewers-Schultz, Ina and Magdalena Holzhey. *Tailored for Freedom: The Artistic Dress around 1900 in Fashion, Art and Society*. Munich: Hirmer Verlag, 2018.
Faber, Monika. *Madame d'Ora*. New York: Prestel, 2020.
Facos, Michelle. *Nationalism and the Nordic Imagination: Swedish Art of the 1890s*. Berkeley: University of California Press, 1998.
Feather, John. *A History of British Publishing*. Abingdon: Routledge, 1988.
Fernandez, Ocón María. *Ornament und Moderne: Theoriebildung und Ornamentdebatte im deutschen Architekturdiskurs, 1850–1930*. Berlin: Reimer Verlag, 2004.
Fiedler-Bender, Gisela. *Otto Eckmann*. Krefeld: Kaiser-Wilhelm Museum, 1977.
Field, Geoffrey. *Evangelist of Race: The Germanic Vision of Houston Stewart Chamberlain*. New York: Columbia University Press, 1981.
Fisch, Stefan. 'Die Prinzregentenstrasse: Moderne Stadtplanung zwischen Hof. Verwaltung und Terraininteressen'. In *München: Museenstadt mit Hinterhöfen*, Edited by Prinz and Kraus, 82–9. Munich: C.H. Beck, 1988.
Fleischmann-Heck, Isa. 'Making an Appearance: The Fashion Frenzy and 'New Style' in Women's Clothing around 1900'. In *Tailored for Freedom: The Artistic Dress around 1900 in Fashion, Art and Society*. Edited by Ina Ewers-Schultz and Magdalena Holzhey, 78–90. Munich: Hirmer Verlag, 2018.
Foth, Heike. 'Fotografie als Frauenberuf'. In *Hof-Atelier Elvira 1887–1928: Ästheten, Aristokraten*. Edited by Rudolf Herz and Bettina Bruns, 153–70. Munich: Stadtmuseum, 1985.
Foucault, Michel. *Discipline and Punish: The Birth of the Prison*. New York: Pantheon.
Fowler, Marian. *In a Gilded Cage: From Heiress to Duchess*. New York: St. Martin's Press, 1994.
Frei, Helmut. *Tempel der Kauflust: Eine Geschichte der Warenhauskultur*. Leipzig: Edition Leipzig, 1997.
Freimann, Max. *Über den physiologischen Stumpfsinn des Mannes*. Berlin: Carl Wiegand, 1905.

Friedman, Alice T. *Women and the Making of the Modern House: A Social and Architectural History*. New York: Harry N. Abrams, 1998.
Friedrichs-Friedlaender, Carola. *Architektur als Mittel politischer Selbstdarstellung im 19. Jahrhundert: Die Baupolitik der Wittelsbacher*. Miscellanea Bavarica Monacensia. Munich: Stadtarchiv, 1980.
Fritsch, Matthias. *The Promise of Memory: History of Politics in Marx, Benjamin and Derrida*. Albany: State University of New York Press, 2006.
Fuchs, Georg. 'Hermann Obrist 1862–1927'. *Dekorative Kunst* 35 (1926/7): 323.
Fuchs, Georg. 'Hermann Obrist'. *Pan* 1, no. 5 (1895/6): 318–25.
Gaehtgens, Thomas W. *Anton von Werner: Die Proklamierung des Deutschen Kaiserreichs*. Frankfurt: Fischer, 1990.
Ganzenbacher, Anna-Maria. 'Mieder und Reformkleid: Zum Wandel der Damenmode von 1900 bis 1918'. MA Thesis, University of Graz, 2009.
Ganzer, Inga. 'Spuren Ostasiens: August Endell im Kontext der Japanrezeption nach 1900'. In *August Endell, 1871–1925: Architekt und Formenkünstler*. Edited by Nicola Bröcker, Gisela Moeller and Christiane Salge 91–101. Petersberg: Michael Imhof Verlag, 2012.
Garb, Tamar. *Bodies of Modernity: Figure and Flesh in Fin-de-Siècle France*. New York: Thames and Hudson, 1998.
Garb, Tamar. *The Body in Time: Figures of Femininity in Late Nineteenth-Century France*. Seattle: University of Washington Press, 2008.
Gebhard, Heinz. *Königlich Bayerische Hof-Photographie 1838–1918*. Munich: Verlag Richter, 1979.
Gebhardt Fink, Sabine and Matthias Vogel. *Hermann Obrist: Im Netzwerk der Künste und Medien um 1900*. Berlin: Kunstverlag Kadmos, 2013.
Gerhard, Ute. *Unerhört: Die Geschichte der Frauenbewegung*. Reinbek: Rowolt, 1990.
Gilman, Sander. *Difference and Pathology: Stereotypes of Sexuality, Race and Madness*. Ithaca: Cornell University Press, 1985.
Gilman, Sander. *Freud, Race and Gender*. Princeton: Princeton University Press, 1995.
Gmelin, Leopold. *Deutsche künstlerisches Handwerk zur Zeit der Weltausstelling in Chicago 1893*. Munich: Bayerischer Kunstgewerbe Verein, 1893.
Goebel, Anne. 'Knospen, Blüten und andere Skandale'. *Süddeutsche Zeitung* (26 August 2014). https://www.sueddeutsche.de/muenchen/jugendstil-in-muenchen-knospen-bl ueten-und-andere-skandale-1.2103139.
Göhre, Paul. *Das Warenhaus*. Frankfurt: Rütten & Loening, 1907.
Goodman, Dena. *The Republic of Letters: A Cultural History of the French Enlightenment*. Ithaca: Cornell University Press, 1994.
Goodman, Nelson. *Ways of Worldmaking*. Indianapolis: Hackett Publishing, 1978.
Götz, Norbert and Clementine Schack-Simitzis. *Die Prinzregentenzeit*. Munich: C.H. Beck, 1988.
Götze, Carl. *Kunsterziehung: Ergebnisse und Anregungen des Kunsterziehungstages in Dresden am 28. und 29. September 1901*. Leipzig: R. Voigtländer, 1902.
Goudstikker, Sophie. 'Ika Freudenberg und die Frauenbewegung in München'. *Die Frau* 9, no. 5 (February 1902): 291–3.
Grand, Sarah. 'The new Aspect of the Woman Question'. *North American Review* 158 (1894): 270–6.
Greenhalgh, Paul. *Art Nouveau: 1890–1914*. London: Victoria and Albert Museum, 2000.
Greensted, Mary. *The Arts and Crafts Movement in Britain*. Oxford: Shire, 2018.
Gruneberg, Christoph and Max Hollein. *Shopping: A Century of Art and Consumer Culture*. Ostfildern: Hatje Cantz, 2002.

Günther, Georg. 'Es liegt Mord und Selbstmord vor: Die Stuttgarter Künstlertragödie Obrist-Sutter von 1910'. In *Musik in Baden-Württemberg*. Edited by Georg Günther and Reiner Nägele, 79–130. Stuttgart: J.B. Metzler, 2000.

Günther, Sonja. *Interieurs um 1900*. Munich: Fink Verlag, 1971.

Haase, Gisela. *Jugendstil in Dresden: Aufbruch in die Moderne*. Dresden: Staatliche Kunstsammlung, 1999.

Habermas, Jürgen. *Strukturwandel der Öffentlichkeit: Untersuchungen zu einer Kategorie der bürgerlichen Gesellschaft*. Revised Edition. Frankfurt: Suhrkamp, 1991.

Haebler, Oskar. *Moderne Flächenkunst*. Plauen: 1905.

Haenel, Erich. 'Raumkunst'. In *Das Deutsche Kunstgewerbe 1906: Die Dritte Deutsche Kunstgewerbe Ausstellung Dresden, 1906*. Edited by Fritz Schumacher. Munich: Verlagsanstalt Bruckmann, 1906.

Hamann, Richard and Joost Hermand. *Epochen deutscher Kultur von 1870 bis zur Gegenwart*. 5 Volumes. Frankfurt: Fischer Verlag, 1977.

Hamann, Richard and Joost Hermand. *Stilkunst um 1900*. Munich: Akademie Verlag, 1973.

Hand, Stacy. 'Embodied Abstraction: Biomorphic Fantasy and Empathy Aesthetics in the Work of Herman Obrist, August Endell and Their Followers'. PhD Dissertation, University of Chicago, 2008.

Hanebutt-Benz, Eva-Maria. *Jugendstil Keramik*. Frankfurt: Museum für Kunsthandwerk, 1980.

Hansen, Fritz. 'Zur Frauenfrage in der Photographie'. *Photographisches Wochenblatt Berlin* 1 (1898): 3.

Hardtwig, Barbara. *Mass und Freiheit: Textilkunst im Jugendstil von Behrens bis Olbrich*. Munich: Hirmer Verlag, 2009.

Hardtwig, Wolfgang. *Utopie und politische Herrschaft im Europa der Zwischenkriegszeit*. Munich: Oldenbourg Verlag, 2003.

Hartwig, Josef. *Leben und Meinung des Bildhauers Josef Hartwig*. Frankfurt: Kunstgewerbeverain, 1955.

Hartzell, Freyja Thorbjorn. 'A Ghost in the Machine Age: The Westerwald Stoneware Industry and German Design Reform'. *The Journal of Modern Craft* 2, no. 3 (2009): 251–77.

Hartzell, Freyja Thorbjorn. 'Delight in Sachlichkeit: Richard Riemerschmid and the Thingliness of Things'. PhD Dissertation, Yale University, 2013.

Haruhiko Fujita, Haruhiko. *Words for Design: Comparative Etymology and Terminology of Design and its Equivalents*. Vols. 1–3. Osaka: Japan Society for the Promotion of Science, 2007–2009.

Heiss, Nikolaus. *Mathildenhöhe Darmstadt*. Regensburg: Schnell & Steiner, 2018.

Heisserer, Dirk. *Wo die Geister Wandern: Eine Topographie der Schwabinger Bohème um 1900*. Munich: Diederichs, 1993.

Helland, Janice. 'Collaboration among the Four'. In *Charles Rennie Mackintosh*. Edited by Wendy Kaplan, 89–114. New York: Abbeville Press, 1996.

Hellingrath, Marie von. *Aus unserer Kindheit: Erinnerungen zum Anlass von Elsas 70. Geburtstag am 23 Februar 1935*. Unpublished Manuscript. Bruckmannia Supplement (BS). Munich: Bayerische Staatsbibliothek.

Herber, Anne-Kathrin Herber. 'Frauen an deutschen Kunstakademien im 20. Jahrhundert. Ausbildungsmöglichkeiten für Künstlerinnen at 1919 unter besonderer Berücksichtigung der süddeutschen Kunstakademien'. PhD, Universität Heidelberg, 2009.

Hermand, Jost. *Jugendstil*. Darmstadt: Wissenschaftliche Buchgesellschaft, 1971.

Hermann Obrist: Sculpture, Space, Abstraction around 1900. Edited by Museum Bellerive. Chicago: University of Chicago Press, 2017.

Hertz, Deborah. *Die jüdischen Salons im alten Berlin.* Munic: DTV, 1995.

Heß, Helmut. *Der Kunstverlag Franz Hanfstaengl und die frühe fotografische Reproduktion: Das Kunstwerk und sein Abbild.* Munich: Akademischer Verlag, 2000.

Heskett, John. *German Design 1870–1918.* New York: Tapliner, 1986.

Heyden-Rynsch, Verena von der. *Europäische Salons: Höhepunkte einer versunkenen weiblichen Kultur.* Düsseldorf: Artemesis & Winkler, 1997.

Heymann, Lida Gustava. *Erlebtes – Erschautes: Deutsche Frauen kämpfen für Freiheit, Recht und Frieden, 1850–1940.* Meisenheim: Anton Hain, 1972.

Heynen, Hilde and Gülsüm Baydar. *Negotiating Domesticity: Spatial Production of Gender in Modern Architecture.* London: Routledge, 2005.

Hilmes, Oliver. *Cosimas Kinder: Triumph and Tragödie der Wagner-Dynastie.* Munich: Siedler, 2009.

Hofmeister, Barbara and Rüdiger Joppien. *Europäischer Jugendstil.* Hamburg: Museum für Kunst und Gewerbe, 1991.

Hoffmann, Hans-Christoph. *Darmstadt und der Jugendstil.* Bremen: Mader, 1981.

Hollweck, Ludwig. *Was war wann in München: Stadtgeschichte in Jahresporträts.* Munich: Wilhelm Umverhau, 1972.

Holme, Bryan. *The Studio: A Bibliography, The First Fifty Years, 1893–1943.* London: Simms and Reed, 1978.

Holmes, Deborah. 'Nichts weniger als die Erneuerung der Weiblichkeit: Wiener Salonkultur ab der Jahrhundertwende'. In *Hilde Spiel und der literarische Salon.* Edited by Ingrid Schramm and Michael Hansel, 15–34. Innsbruck: Studienverlag, 2011.

Holmes, Val. *The Encyclopedia of Machine Embroidery.* London: Batsford, 2003.

Hölz, Christoph. *Schön und Gut: Positionen des Gestaltens.* Munich: Förderbank Bayern, 2002.

Holzheid, Anett. *Das Medium Postkarte: eine sprachwissenschaftliche und mediengeschichtliche Studie.* Berlin: E. Schmidt, 2011.

Hopper, John. 'The Embroidery of Margarete von Brauchitsch'. *The Textile Blog.* https://thetextileblog.blogspot.com/.

Houze, Rebbeca. *Textiles, Fashion, and Design Reform in Austria-Hungary Before the First World War.* Farnham: Ashgate, 2015.

Howard, Jeremy. *Art Nouveau: International and National Styles in Europe.* Manchester: Manchester University Press, 1996.

Howarth, Thomas. *Charles Rennie Mackintosh and the Modern Movement.* 2nd Edition. London: Routledge, 1977.

Hunter, Clare. *Threads of Life: A History of the World through the Eye of a Needle.* London: Hodder & Stoughton, 2019.

Jäger, Anna and Heinrich. *Hygiene der Kleidung.* Stuttgart: E.H. Moritz, 1906.

Jarausch, Konrad and Michael Geyer. *Shattered Past: Reconstructing German Histories.* Princeton: Princeton University Press, 2003.

Jarzombek, Mark M. 'The Kunstgewerbe, the Werkbund, and the Aesthetics of Culture in the Wilhelmine Period'. *Journal of the Society of Architectural Historians* 53, no. 1 (1994): 7–19.

Jefferies, Matthews. *Imperial Culture in Germany, 1871–1918.* Basingstoke: Palgrave, 2003.

Jelavich, Peter. *Munich and Theatrical Modernism.* Cambridge, MA: Harvard University Press, 1985.

Jensen, Robert. *Marketing Modernism in Fin-de-Siècle Europe.* Princeton: Princeton University Press, 1996.

Johnson, Julie. *The Memory Factory: The Women Artists of Vienna 1900*. West Lafayette: Purdue University Press, 2012.
Kale, Steven. *French Salons: High Society and Political Stability from the Old Regime to the Revolution of 1848*. Baltimore: John Hopkins University Press, 2006.
Kandinsky, Wassily. *Punkt und Linie zur Fläche*. Leipzig: Bauhaus Press, Hesse und Becker, 1926.
Kant, Immanuel. *Anthropologie in pragmatischer Hinsicht* (1798). Akademie Textausgabe, Band 7. Berlin: Walter de Gruyter, 1972.
Kempton, Richard. *Art Nouveau: An Annotated Bibliography*. Los Angeles: Hennessey & Ingalls, 1977.
Kerbs, Diethart and Jürgen Reulecke, *Handbuch der deutschen Reformbewegung, 1880–1933*. Wuppertal: Peter Hammer Verlag, 1998.
Kerkhoff, Ulrich. *Theodor Fischer: Eine Abkehr vom Historismus oder ein Weg zur Moderne*. Stuttgart: Karl Krämer Verlag, 1987.
Kettle, Alice and Jane McKeating, *Machine Stitch: Perspectives*. London: A&C Black, 2010.
Kinchin, Perilla. *Taking Tea with Mackintosh: The Story of Miss Cranston's Tea Rooms*. San Francisco: Pomegranate, 1998.
Kirkham, Pat. *The Gendered Object*. Manchester: Manchester University Press, 1996.
Kisch, Herbert. *From Domestic Manufacture to Industrial Revolution: The Case of the Rhineland Textile Districts*. Oxford: Oxford University Press, 1989.
Klahr, Douglas. 'Munich as Kunststadt, 1900–1937: Art, Architecture and Civic Identity'. *Oxford Art Journal* 34, no. 2 (2011): 179–201.
Klein, Dieter. *Martin Dülfer: Wegbereiter der deutschen Jugendstilarchitektur*. Munich: Bayerisches Landesamt für Denkmalpflege, 1981.
Koch, Michael. *Jugendstil im Bayerischen Nationalmuseum*. Dresden: Arnoldsche Art Publishers, 2010.
Kocka, Jürgen. 'German History before Hitler: The Debate about the German Sonderweg'. *Journal of Contemporary History* 23, no. 1 (January 1988): 2–16.
König, Gudrun M. *Konsumkultur: Inszinierte Warenwelt um 1900*. Vienna: Böhlau, 2009.
Kos, Wolfgang and Ralph Gleis, *Experiment Metropole: 1873 Wien und die Weltausstellung*. Vienna: Czerin Verlag, 2014.
Kraepelin, Emil. *Einführung in die Psychiatrische Klinik*. Leipzig: J.A. Barth Verlag, 1901.
Krabbe, Wolfgang R. *Gesellschaftsveränderungen durch Lebensreform*. Göttingen: Vandenhoeck & Ruprecht, 1974.
Krauss, Marita. *Wirtshäuser in München um 1900*. Munich: Buchendorfer Verlag, 1997.
Krempe, Ulrich and Susanne Meyer-Büser. *Garten der Frauen: Wegbereiter der Moderne in Deutschland*. Hannover: Sprengel Museum, 1996.
Kuenzli, Katherine M. 'Architecture, Individualism, and Nation: Henry van de Velde's 1914 Werkbund Theater Building', *The Art Bulletin* 94, no. 2 (2012): 251–73.
Kuenzli, Katherine M.. *The Nabis and Intimate Modernism: Painting and the Decorative at the Fin-de-Siècle*. Burlington: Ashgate, 2010.
Kuhnow, Anna. *Die Frauenkleidung vom Standpunkte der Hygiene: Vortrag für Frauen gehalten zu Leipzig am 14. Februar 1893*. Leipzig: Hobbing, 1893.
Kunstschöpfungen von Hermann Götz: Ausgeführte Arbeiten und Entwürfe. 3 vols. Dresden: Gerhard Kühtmann, 1903.
Lancaster, Bill. *The Department Store: A Social History*. London: Leicester University Press, 1995.
Landes, Joan B. *Women and the Public Sphere in the Age of the French Revolution*. Ithaca: Cornell University Press, 1988.

Lane Miller, Barbara. *National Romanticism and Modern Architecture in Germany and the Scandinavian Countries*. Cambridge: Cambridge University Press, 2000.

Langenstein, York. *Der Münchner Kunstverein im 19. Jahrhundert*. Miscellanea Bavarica Monacensia. Munich: Uni Druck, 1983.

Large, David Clay. *Where Ghosts Walked: Munich's Road to the Third Reich*. New York: W.W. Norton & Company, 1997.

Larson, Barbara. *The Art of Evolution: Darwin, Darwinism and Visual Culture*. Chicago: Chicago University Press, 2016.

Lauterbach, Iris. *Die Kunst für Alle (1885-1944): Zur Kunstpublistik vom Kaiserreich bis zum Nationalsozialismus*. Munich: Zentralinstitut für Kunstgeschichte, 2010.

Lefebvre, Henri. *The Production of Space*. Translated by Donald Nicholson-Smith. Oxford: Blackwell, 1991.

Lehmann, Ulrich. *Tigersprung: Fashion in Modernity*. Cambridge, MA: MIT Press, 2000.

Lenman, Robin. 'Art and Tourism in Southern Germany, 1850-1930'. In *The Arts, Literature and Society*. Edited by Arthur Marwick, 163-80. London: Routledge, 1990.

Lenman, Robin. *Artists and Society in Germany, 1840-1914*. Manchester: Manchester University Press, 1997.

Lenman, Robin. *Die Kunst, die Macht und das Geld: Zur Kulturgeschichte des kaiserlichen Deutschlands*. Frankfurt: Campus Verlag, 1994.

Leonhardt, Brigitte and Dieter Zühlsdorff. *Friedrich Adler: Zwischen Jugendstil und Art Deco*. Stuttgart: Arnoldsche Verlagsgesellschaft, 1994.

Lerner, Paul. *Consuming Temple: Jews, Department Stores and the Consumer Revolution in Germany, 1880-1940*. Ithaca: Cornell University Press, 2015.

Levy, Mervyn. *Liberty Style: The Classic Years 1898-1910*. New York: Rizzoli, 1986.

Lewis, Beth. *Art for All? The Collision of Art and the Public in Late-Nineteenth Century Germany*. Princeton: Princeton University Press, 2003.

Liberty's 1875-1975: An Exhibition to Mark the Firm's Centenary. London: Victoria & Albert Museum, 1975.

Lichtwark, Alfred. 'Die Ausstellung der Akademie III'. *Gegenwart* 23 (1883): 301-66.

Lieb, Stefanie. *Was ist Jugendstil: Eine Analyse der Jugendstilarchitektur 1890-1910*. Darmstadt: Primus, 2010.

Lilti, Antoine. *The World of the Salon: Sociability and Worldliness in Eighteenth-Century Paris*. Oxford: Oxford University Press, 2015.

Lipps, Theodor. *Ästhetik: Psychologie des Schönen und der Kunst*. Hamburg: L. Voss, 1903.

Logan, Mary. 'Hermann Obrist's Embroidered Decorations', *The Studio* 12, no. 56 (1897): 96-105.

Long, Christopher. 'The Origins and Context of Adolf Loos's 'Ornament and Crime'. *The Journal of the Society of Architectural Historians* 68, no. 2 (June 2009): 200-23.

Loos, Adolf. 'Schulausstellung der Kunstgewerbeschule, 30. Oktober 1897'. In *Sämtliche Schriften*. Edited by Franz Glück, 139-43. Wien: Herold Druck- und Verlagsgesellschaft, 1962.

Loos, Adolf. *Ornament and Crime: Selected Essays*. Translated by Michael Mitchell. Riverside: Ariadne, 1998.

Ludwig, Horst. *Kunst, Geld und Politik um 1900 in München*. Berlin: Gebrüder Mann Verlag, 1986.

Lybeck, Marti M. *Desiring Emancipation: New Women and Homosexuality in Germany, 1890-1933*. Albany: State University Press, 2014.

Lyon, John B. *Out of Place: German Realism, Displacement and Modernity*. London: Bloomsbury Publishing, 2013.

Macaulay, James. *Charles Rennie Mackintosh*. New York: W.W. Norton, 2010.

Maciuika, John V. *Before the Bauhaus: Architecture, Politics and the German State, 1890–1920*. Cambridge: Cambridge University Press, 2005.

Makela, Maria. 'New Women, New Men, New Objectivity'. In *New Objectivity: Modern German Art in the Weimar Republic*. Edited by Stephanie Barron, 51–63. Los Angeles: Los Angeles County Museum of Art, 2015.

Makela, Maria. *The Munich Secession: Art and Artists in Turn-of-the-Century Munich*. Princeton: Princeton University Press, 1990.

Mann, Rosemarie. 'Ernst Haeckel, Zoologie und Jugendstil', *Berichte zur Wissenschaftsgeschichte* 13 (1990): 1–11.

Mann, Thomas. 'Gladius Dei'. In *Stories of Three Decades*. Translated by H. T. Lowe-Porter, 181–93. New York: Knopf, 1951.

Marcus, Jane. *Art and Anger: Reading Like a Woman*. Columbus: Ohio University Press, 1988.

Mariny, Anke. 'Die Bildende Künstlerin - Ein Kopfarbeiter besonderer Art'. In *Profession ohne Tradition: 125 Jahre Verein Bildender Künstlerinnen*. Edited by Karoline Müller and Jörn Merkert, 367–375. Berlin: Berlinische Galerie, 1992.

Märten, Lou. *Die Künstlerin, Kleine Monographien zur Frauenfrage*. Edited by Adele Schreiber. Munich: Albert Langen Verlag, 1914.

Martin, Biddy. *Women and Modernity: The (Life)Styles of Lou Andreas-Salomé*. Ithaca: Cornell University Press, 1991.

Martin, Brenda and Penny Sparke. *Women's Places: Architecture and Design 1860–1960*. London: Routledge, 2003.

Martynkewicz, Wolfgang. *Salon Deutschland: Geist und Macht, 1900–1945*. Berlin: Aufbau Verlag, 2011.

Matthews, Alison. *Fashion Victims: The Dangers of Dress Past and Present*. London: Bloomsbury, 2015.

May, Walther. *Goethe, Humboldt, Darwin, Haeckel*. Berlin: Steglitz, 1906.

Mayr, Karl. 'Neue Räume der Werkstätten für Wohnungs-Einrichtung Karl Bertsch - München'. *Innen-Dekoration* 15, no. 5 (May 1904): 119–37.

Maza, Sarah C. *Private Lives and Public Affairs: The Causes Célèbres of Pre-Revolutionary France*. Berkeley: University of California Press, 1993.

Mazón, Patricia M. *Gender and the Modern Research University: The Admission of Women to German Higher Education, 1865–1914*. Stanford: Stanford University Press, 2003.

McBride, Theresa M. 'A Woman's World: Department Stores and the Evolution of Women's Employment, 1870–1920'. *French Historical Studies* 10, no. 4 (Autumn 1978): 664–83.

McKellar, Susie and Penny Sparke. *Interior Design and Identity*. Manchester: Manchester University Press, 2004.

Meehan, Johanna. *Feminists Read Habermas: Gendering the Subject of Discourse*. London: Routledge, 1995.

Melk-Haen, Christina. *Hans Eduard von Berlepsch-Valandas: Wegbereiter des Jugendstils in München und Zürich*. Zurich: Denkmalpflege Amt, 1993.

Menke, Beate. *Die Riemerschmid-Innenausstattung des Hauses Thieme Georgenstrasse 7*. Munich: Schriften aus dem Institut für Kunstgeschichte der Universität München 37, 1990.

Meskimmon, Marsha. *We Weren't Modern Enough: Women Artists and the Limits of German Modernism*. London: I.B. Tauris, 1999.

Meskimmon, Marsha and Shearer West. *Visions of the Neue Frau: Women and the Visual Arts in Weimar Germany*. Aldershot: Ashgate, 1995.

Metzger, Rainer. *Munich: Its Golden Age or Art and Culture 1890–1920*. London: Thames & Hudson, 2009.

Michel, Wilhelm. 'Ein Frühstücksraum von Margarete von Brauchitsch', *Deutsche Kunst und Dekoration* 15 (1905): 255–61.
Miller, Josephine. 'The Study of Dress and Textiles'. In *Design History: A Student's Handbook*. Edited by Hazel Conway, 15–38. London: HarperCollins Academic, 1987.
Mims, Martina. 'August Endell's Construction of Feeling'. PhD dissertation, Columbia University, New York, 2013.
Möbius, Paul Julius. *Über den physiologischen Schwachsinn des Weibes*. 2nd Edition. Halle: Marhold, 1901.
Möckl, Karl. *Die Prinzregentenzeit: Gesellschaft und Politik während der Ära des Prinzregenten Luitpold in Bayern*. Munich: R. Oldenbourg, 1972.
Moi, Toril. 'Appropriating Bourdieu: Feminist Theory and Pierre Bourdieu's Sociology of Culture'. *New Literary History* 22, no. 4 (Autumn 1991): 1017–49.
Mollenhauer, Bernd. *Jugendstil in München*. Munich: Hirschkäfer Verlag, 2014.
Morehead, Allison. 'The Nabis and Intimate Modernism: Painting and the Decorative at the Fin-de-Siècle' by Katherine M. Kuenzli'. *CAA Reviews* (August 2012). http://www.caareviews.org/reviews/1848#.XkVPXhP7QW8.
Morehead, Allison. *Nature's Experiments and the Search for Symbolist Form*. University Park: Penn State University Press, 2012.
Muller, Ulrike. *Bauhaus Women: Art, Handicraft, Design*. Paris: Flammarion, 2015.
Murphy, Mary A. 'The Theory and Practice of Counting Stiches as Stories: Material Evidence of Autobiography in Needlework'. *Women's Studies* 32, no. 5 (2003): 641–55.
Muscheler, Ursula. *Mutter, Muse und Frau Bauhaus*. Berlin: Berenberg, 2018.
Muthesius, Anna. 'Die Ausstellung künstlerischer Frauenkleider im Waren-Haus Wertheim Berlin'. *Deutsche Kunst und Dekoration* 14 (1904): 441–56.
Muthesius, Anna. 'Introduction'. In *Album moderner, nach Künstler-Entwürfen ausgeführter Damenkleider: As Exhibited at the Great General Exhibition of the Clothing Industry, Krefeld 1900*. Translated by Iain Boyd Whyte. *Art in Translation* 10, no. 4 (2018): 375–6.
Muthesius, Anna. *Das Eigenkleid der Frau*. Krefeld: Kramer & Tree, 1903.
Muthesius, Eckhart. *Hermann Muthesius 1861–1927*. London: Architectural Association, 1979. 4–5.
Muthesius, Hermann. 'Die Glasgower Kunstbewegung: Charles R. Mackintosh und Margaret Macdonald-Mackintosh'. *Dekorative Kunst* 10 (March 1902): 193–221.
Muthesius, Hermann. 'Kunst und Maschine'. *Dekorative Kunst* 10 (1902): 142.
Muthesius, Hermann. *Das englische Haus*. 3 Volumes. Berlin: Ernst Wasmuth, 1904.
Muthesius, Stefan. 'Das Münchner Kunstgewerbe und das künstlerische Wohn-Interieur: Gabriel von Seidl und Georg Hirth'. In *Postitionen des Gestaltens seit 1850*. Edited by Christoph Hölz, 155–66. Munich: Deutscher Kunstverlag, 2002.
Muthesius, Stefan. *The Poetic Home: Designing the Nineteenth-Century Domestic Interior*. London: Thames & Hudson, 2009.
Naumann, Friedrich. 'Der Geist im Hausgestühl'. In *Preisbuch Dresdner Hausgeräthe, 1906*. Dresden: Dresdner Werkstätten für Handwerkskunst, 1906.
Nerdinger, Winifried. *Richard Riemerschmid: Vom Jugendstil zum Werkbund. Werke und Dokumente*. Munich: Prestel, 1982.
Neumann-Adrian, Edda and Michael. *Münchens Lust am Jugendstil: Häuser und Menschen um 1900*. Munich: Buchendorfer Verlag, 2005.
Neumann, Antje. 'The Textile Designer and Gesamtkünstler Henry van de Velde and his Weimar Circle'. In *Tailored for Freedom: The Artistic Dress around 1900 in Fashion, Art and Society*. Edited by Ina Ewers-Schultz and Magdalena Holzhey, 30–6. Munich: Hirmer Verlag, 2018.

Neve, Monika. *Sold! Advertising and the Bourgeois Female Consumer in Munich, 1900–1914*. Konstanz: Franz Steiner Verlag, 2010.
Nielsen, Astrid. *Jugendstil in Dresden: Aufbruch in die Moderne*. Dresden: Minerva, 1999.
Nienhaus, Stefan. *Geschichte der deutschen Tischgesellschaft*. Berlin: Walter de Gruyter, 2003.
Nipperdey, Thomas. *Deutsche Geschichte 1866–1918*. Volume 2. Munich: Beck, 1992.
Noberg-Schulz, Christian. *Existence, Space & Architecture*. London: Studio Vista, 1971.
Nochlin, Linda. 'Why Have There Been No Great Women Artists?'. *Art News* (January 1971): 22–39 and 67–71.
Nochlin, Linda. *Realism: Style and Civilization*. London: Pelican Books, 1971.
Norton, Robert Edward. *Secret Germany: Stefan George and His Circle*. Ithaca: Cornell University Press, 2002.
Ober, Patricia. *Der Frauen neue Kleider: Das Reformkleid und die Konstruktion des modernen Frauenkörpers*. Kempten: Schlier, 2005.
Obler, Bibiana K. *Intimate Collaborations: Kandinsky and Münter, Arp and Taeuber*. New Haven: Yale University Press, 2014.
Obrist, Hermann. 'Ein künstlerischer Kunstunterricht'. In *Der Lotse: Hamburgische Wochenschrift für deutsche Kultur* 1, no. 23 (23 February 1901): 682–6.
Obrist, Hermann. 'Stellungsnahme zum Thema Kunstschulen'. *Kunst und Künstler* 5, no. 5 (1907): 206–10.
Obrist, Hermann. *Ein glückliches Leben: Eine Biographie des Künstlers, Forschers und Alleingängers Hermann Obrist*. Obrist Nachlass. Munich: Staatliche Graphische Sammlung, 1926.
Obrist, Hermann. *Essays*. Leipzig, 1903.
Obschernitzki, Doris. *Der Frau ihre Arbeit! Lette-Verein: Zur Geschichte einer Berliner Institution 1866–1986*. Berlin: Hentrich, 1987.
Oelwein, Cornelia. *Max Littmann (1862–1931): Architekt, Baukünstler, Unternehmer*. Petersberg: Michael Imhof Verlag, 2013.
Oppler, Else. 'The German Dress Reform Movement'. *The Independent* 59 (July–December 1905): 487–93.
Osborn, Max. 'Ausstellungen für Frauen-Kleidung in Wiesbaden und Berlin'. *Deutsche Kunst und Dekoration* 11(1902): 165–6.
Österreichisches Biographisches Lexikon 1815–1850. Band 4, 364. Vienna: Verlag der Österreichischen Akademie der Wissenschaften, 2012.
Otto, Elisabeth. *Haunted Bauhaus: Occult Spirituality, Gender Fluidity, Queer Identities, and Radical Politics*. Cambridge: MIT Press, 2019.
Otto, Elisabeth and Patrick Rössler. *Bauhaus Women: A Global Perspective*. London: Bloomsbury, 2019.
Otto, Elisabeth and Patrick Rössler. *Bauhaus Bodies: Gender, Sexuality, and Body Culture in Modernism's Legendary Art School*. London: Bloomsbury Academic, 2019.
Ottomeyer, Hans. *Jugendstil Möbel*. Munich: Prestel, 1998.
Ottomeyer, Hans and Margot Brandlhuber. *Wege in die Moderne: Jugendstil in München 1896 bis 1914*. Munich: Klinkhardt & Biermann, 1997.
Paeslack, Miriam. 'Framing Progress: Ludwig Hoffmann, Ernst von Brauchitsch, and Berlin Architectural Photography, 1902–1912'. In *Constructing Imperial Berlin: Photography and the Metropolis*, 35–68. Minneapolis: University of Minnesota Press, 2019.
Panzer, Marita A. 'Zwischen Küche und Katheder: Bürgerliche Frauen um die Jahrhundertwende 1890–1915'. In *Frauenleben in Bayern*, 86–118. Munich: Bayerische Landeszentrale für politische Bildungsarbeit, 1993.

Parker, Rozsika. *The Subversive Stitch: Embroidery and the Making of the Feminine.* London: Women's Press, 1984.
Paul, Bruno. 'Der Münchner Jugendbrunnen'. *Simplicissimus* 10 (5 June 1897): 76.
Pecht, Friedrich. 'Aus dem Münchner Glaspalast'. *Beilage zur Allgemeinen Zeitung* (15 June 1876): 2551.
Peck, Clemens. 'Theodor Herzl and the Utopia of the Salon in *Fin-de-Siècle* Vienna'. Translated by Deborah Holmes. *Austrian Studies* 24 (2016): 79–93.
Pehnt, Wolfgang. *Die Mathildenhöhe: Ein Jahrhundertwerk.* Darmstadt: Justus Liebig Verlag, 1999.
Pekacz, Jolanta T. *Conservative Tradition in Pre-Revolutionary Franc: Parisian Salon Women.* New York: Peter Lang, 1999.
Penner, Barbara, Iain Borden and Jane Rendell. *Gender Space Architecture: An Interdisciplinary Introduction.* London: Routledge, 2000.
Pepchinski, Mary. *Feminist Space: Exhibitions and Discourses between Philadelphia and Berlin, 1865–1912.* Kromsdorf: VDG, 2007.
Pese, Claus. 'Biography of Else Oppler'. https://claus-pese.de/else-oppler/
Pevsner, Nikolaus. *Pioneers of the Modern Movement.* New York: Faber & Faber, 1936.
Pollock, Griselda. *Mary Cassatt: Painter of Modern Women.* London: Thames & Hudson, 1977.
Potvin, John and Marie-Ève Marchand. *Design & Agency.* London: Bloomsbury Visual Arts, 2020.
Powers, Martin J. 'Art and History: Exploring the Counterchange Condition'. *Art Bulletin* 77, no. 3 (September 1995): 382–7.
Pudor, Heinrich. *Die Frauenreform-Kleidung: Ein Beitrag zur Philosophie, Hygiene und Aesthetik des Kleides.* Leipzig, Seemann Verlag, 1903.
Pudor, Heinrich. *Dokumente zum Jugendstil: Modernes Kunstgewerbe 1902–1908.* Stuttgart: Arnoldsche Verlagsbibliothek, 2011.
Pytlik, Priska. 'Okkultismus und Moderne: Ein kulturhistorisches Phänomen und seine Bedeutung für die Literatur um 1900'. PhD Dissertation, Universität Paderborn, 2005.
Rall, Hans. 'Wie der König Max II die Kultur förderte,' *Das Bayernland* 55 (1953): 27–32.
Rammert-Götz, Michaela. *Das Abstrakte Ornament im Münchner Jugendstil: Theorien und Gestaltung.* Munich: Quick Druck, 1994.
Rammert-Götz, Michaela. *Richard Riemerschmid: Möbel und Innenräume von 1895–1900.* Munich: Tuduv Verlag, 1987.
Rappaport, Erika. *Shopping for Pleasure: Women in the Making of London's West End.* New Haven: Princeton University Press, 2001.
Rathke, Ewald. *Jugendstil.* Mannheim: Bibliographisches Institut, 1958.
Rawson, George. 'Francis Henry Newbery and the Glasgow School of Art'. PhD Dissertation, The Glasgow School of Art, 1996.
Rée, Paul Johannes. 'Richard Riemerschmid', *Dekorative Kunst* 9 (1906): 265–303.
Reeber, Sharon. 'What Hoelzel Learned from European Sacred Art'. *Zeitschrift für Kunstgeschichte* 76, no. 2 (2013): 243–60.
Reed, Eileen. 'Edward William Godwin (1833–1886): Towards an Art-Architecture'. PhD Dissertation, University of London, 1999.
Reiter, Cornelia and Robert Stalla. *Theophil Hansen: Architekt und Designer.* Weitra: Bibliothek der Provinz, 2013.
Renda, Gerhard. *Gertrud Kleinhempel, 1875–1948: Künstlerin zwischen Jugendstil und Moderne.* Bielefeld: Verlag für Regionalgeschichte, 1998.
Reuter, Gabriele. *Frau Bürgelin und ihre Söhne.* Berlin: Fischer Verlag, 1900.

Rhoden, Wilfred Jack and E. E. Snyder. *Poetry, Politics and Pictures in the Nineteenth Century*. Bern: Peter Lang, 2013.

Richardsen, Ingvild. 'Modern Sein 1894–1933'. In *Evas Töchter: Münchner Schriftstellerinnen und die modern Frauenbewegung 1894–1933*. Edited by Ingvild Richardsen, 20–32. Munich: Volk Verlag, 2018.

Richter, Andrea. *Hans Schmithals: Malerei zwischen Jugendstil und Abstraktion*. Regensburg: Schnell und Steiner, 2014.

Rinker, Dagmar. *Die Lehr- und Versuchs-Ateliers für angewandte und freie Kunst (Debschitz-Schule): München 1902–1914*. Munich: Tuduv Verlag, 1993.

Risley, Christine. *Machine Embroidery*. London: Studio Vista, 1973.

Rose, Clare. *Art Nouveau Fashion*. London: Victoria & Albert Museum Publications, 2014.

Rosenberg, Alfred. *Houston Stewart Chamberlain als Veründer und Begründer einer deutschen Zukunft*. Munich: Bruckmann Verlag, 1927.

Rossbacher, Karlheinz. *Literature und Bürgertum: Fünf jüdische Familien von der liberalen Ära zum Fin-de-Siècle*. Vienna: Böhlau, 2003.

Rössler, Patrick. *Vier Bauhausmädels*. Dresden: Sandstein Verlag, 2019.

Rowold, Katharina. *The Educated Woman: Minds, Bodies, and Women's Higher Education in Britain, Germany and Spain, 1865–1914*. London: Routledge, 2010.

Rudolf. 'Von-der-Tannstrasse 15: Zur Geschichte eines Hauses und einer Strasse'. In *Hof-Atelier Elvira, 1887–1928: Ästheten, Emanzen, Aristokraten*, 43–62. Munich: Stadtmuseum, 1985.

Sachova, Anna. *Fotografie als Hilfsmittel in der Malerei von Franz Lenbach, Max Slevogt, Franz von Stuck, Alfons Mucha*. Munich: GRIN Verlag, 2014.

Sachsse, Rolf. 'German'. In *Encyclopedia of Ninteenth-Century Photography*. Edited by John Hannavy, 581–6. London: Routledge, 2013.

Safranski, Rüdiger. *Romanticism: A German Affair*. Translated by R. Goodwin. Evanston: Northwestern University Press, 2015.

Salge, Christine. 'August Endell: Leben, Werk und Schriften'. In *August Endell, 1871–1925: Architekt und Formenkünstle*. Edited by Nicola Bröcker, Gisela Moeller and Christiane Salge, 35–66. Petersberg: Michael Imhof Verlag, 2012.

Salice, Alessandro. 'The Phenomenology of the Munich and Göttingen Circles'. In *Stanford Encyclopaedia of Philosophy*. https://plato.stanford.edu/entries/phenomenology-mg/.

Saxe, Cornelia. *Das gesellige Canapé - Die Renaissance der Berliner Salons*. Berlin: Ullstein, 1999.

Schatter, Debra. *The Order of Ornament, the Structure of Style: Theoretical Foundations of Modern Art and Architecture*. Cambridge: Cambridge University Press, 2003.

Scheffler, Karl. 'August Endell'. *Kunst und Künstler* 5 (1907): 314–24.

Scheffler, Karl. 'Hermann Obrist'. *Kunst und Kunsthandwerk* 8 (1910): 556.

Scheffler, Karl. *Die fetten und die mageren Jahre: Ein Arbeits- und Lebensbericht*. Leipzig: Paul List, 1924.

Scheu, Ursula and Anna Dünnebier. *Rebellion ist eine Frau: Anita Augspurg und Lida G. Heyman. Das schillernste Paar der Frauenbewegung*. Basel: Sphynx Verlag, 2002.

Schilling, Barbara. *Tischkultur in der bürgerlichen Gesellschaft des 19. Jahrhunderts: Die 'Gute Gesellschaft' ist, was und wie sie isst*. Munich: GRIN Verlag, 2008.

Schlief, Nina and Karein Beth. *Views on Europe: Europe and German Painting in the Nineteenth Century*. Ostfildern: Hatze Cantz Verlag, 2013.

Schlüter, Anne. *Pionierinnen – Feministinnen – Karrierefrauen? Zur Geschichte des Frauenstudiums in Deutschland*. Frauen in Geschichte und Gesellschaft, Band 22. Pfaffenweiler: Centaurus, 1992.

Schmalenbach, Fritz. *Jugendstil: Ein Beitrag zur Theorie und Geschichte der Flächenkunst.* Bern: Peter Lang, 1935.

Schmalhofer, Claudia. *Die Kgl. Kunstgewerbeschule München (1868–1918): Ihr Einfluss auf die Ausbildung der Zeichenlehrerin.* Munich: Herbert Utz Verlag, 2005.

Schmoll-Eisenwerth, Helga. 'Die Münchner Debschitz Schule'. In *Kunstschulreform 1900–1933.* Edited by Hans M. Wingler, 66–82. Berlin: Gebrüder Mann, 1977.

Schmutzler, Robert. *Art Nouveau-Jugendstil.* Stuttgart: Hatje, 1962.

Schorske, Carl. *Fin-de-Siècle Vienna: Politics and Culture.* New York: Knopf, 1980.

Schramm, Ingrid and Michael Hansel. *Hilde Spiel und der literarische Salon.* Innsbruck: Studien Verlag, 2011.

Schrick, Kirsten Gabriele. *München als Kunststadt: Dokumentationen einer kulturhistorischen Debatte von 1781 bis 1945.* Vienna: Holzhausen, 1994.

Schrott, Karin. *Das normative Korsett.* Würzburg: Königshausen & Neumann, 2005.

Schuette, Marie and Sigrid Müller-Christenen. *The Art of Embroidery.* London: Thames & Hudson, 1964.

Schuldenfrei, Robin. *Luxury and Modernism: Architecture and the Object in Germany 1900–1933.* Princeton: Princeton University Press, 2020.

Schultze-Naumburg, Paul. *Die Kultur des weiblichen Körpers als Grundlage der Frauenkleidung.* Jena: Eugen Diederichs, 1901.

Schulze, Otto. 'Jugendstil Sünden'. *Kunst und Handwerk* 52 (1901/1902): 198–202.

Schulze, Otto. 'Neue Stickereien von Margarete von Brauchitsch'. *Deutsche Kunst und Dekoration* 21 (1907): 30–1.

Schulze, Sabine. *Jugendstil: Die Grosse Utopie.* Hamburg: Museum für Kunst und Gewerbe, 2015.

Schumann, Paul. 'Die dritte deutsche Kunstgewerbeausstellung Dresden 1906'. *Kunstgewerbeblatt* 17, no. 9–11 (1906): 165–227.

Schuster, Peter Klaus. *Peter Behrens und Nürnberg: Geschmackswandel in Deutschland, Historismus, Jugendstil und die Anfänge der Industriereform.* Munich: Prestel, 1980.

Schwartz, Frederic J. *The Werkbund: Design Theory and Mass Culture Before the First World War.* New Haven: Yale University Press, 1996.

Seelig, Lorenz. 'The Art Collection of Alfred Pringsheim (1850–1941)'. *Journal of the History of Collections* 29, no. 1 (2016): 161–80.

Seibert, Peter. *Der literarische Salon: Literatur und Geselligkeit zwischen Aufklärung und Vormärz.* Stuttgart: Metzler, 1993.

Selle, Gert. *Jugendstil und Kunst-Industrie: Zur Ökonomie des Kunstgewerbes um 1900.* Ravensburg: Otto Maier Verlag, 1974.

Selig, Helmut. *Jugendstil: Der Weg ins 20. Jahrhundert.* Heidelberg: Keyser, 1959.

Seymour, Bruce. *Lola Montez: A Life.* New Haven: Yale University Press, 1996.

Shapira, Elena. *Style and Seduction: Jewish Patrons, Architecture and Design in Fin-de-Siècle Vienna.* Waltham: Brandeis University Press, 2016.

Siebel, Ernst. *Der großbürgerliche Salon: 1850–1918.* Berlin: Walter de Gruyter, 1999.

Simmel, Georg. 'Zur Psychologie der Mode: Soziologische Studie'. *Die Zeit: Wiener Wochenschrift für Politik, Volkswirtschaft, Wissenschaft und Kunst* 42, no. 12.10 (1895): 22–4.

Simmel, Georg. *Philosophie des Geldes.* Berlin: Duncker & Humboldt, 1900.

Slezkine, Yuri. *The Jewish Century.* New Jersey: Princeton University Press, 2004.

Smith, Woodruff D. *Politics and the Science of Culture in Germany, 1840–1920.* New York: Oxford University Press, 1991.

Sombart, Werner. *Kunstgewerbe und Kultur.* Berlin: Gurlitt, 1908.

Sparke, Penny. *As Long as It's Pink: Sexual Politics of Taste*. London: Rivers Oram Press/Pandora List, 1995.
Sparke, Penny. *The Modern Interior*. London: Reaktion Books, 2008.
Specht, Bruno. 'Die beiden neuen Warenhäuser in München'. *Deutsche Bauzeitung* 39, no. 54 (July 1905): 325–35 and *Deutsche Bauzeitung* 39, no. 56 (July 1905): 337–42.
Spelsberg, Helmut. *Thomas Manns Durchbruch zum Politischen in seinem kleinepischen Werk*. Marburg: N.G. Elwert, 1972.
Spener, Carl. *Die jetzige Frauenkleidung und Vorschläge zu ihrer Verbesserung*. Berlin, 1897.
Spindler, Max. *Bayerische Geschichte im 19. und 20. Jahrhundert*. Munich: C.H. Beck Verlag, 1978.
Spree, Reinhard. *Geschlechterverhältnis und bürgerliche Familie im 19. Jahrhundert*. Texte zur Sozial- und Wirtschaftsgeschichte. 2011. https://rspree.wordpress.com/2011/02/21/geschlechterverhaltnis-und-burgerliche-familie-im-19-jh/.
Stamm, Brigitte. 'Das Reformkleid in Deutschland'. PhD Dissertation, Technische Universität, Berlin, 1976.
Stamm, Rainer. *Farbwelten: Von Monet bis Yves Klein: Werke der klassischen Moderne aus den Kunstmuseen Krefeld*. Bremen: Kunstsammlungen Bottcherstrasse and Paula Modersohn-Becker Museum, 2009.
Starl, Timm. 'Das "Starfoto" im 19. Jahrhundert'. *Parnass* 2, no. 3 (März/April 1983): 60–4.
Stark, David. *Charles Rennie Mackintosh and Co. 1854 to 2004*. Mauchline: Stenlake Publishing, 2004.
St Clair, Cassia. *The Golden Thread: How Fabric changed History*. London: John Murray, 2019.
Steele, Valerie. *The Corset: A Cultural History*. New Haven: Yale University Press, 2001.
Steling, Helmut. *Jugendstil: Der Weg ins 20. Jahrhundert*. Heidelberg: Keyser, 1959.
Stern, Fritz. *The Politics of Cultural Despair: A Study in the Rise of the Germanic Ideology*. Berkeley: University of California Press, 1961.
Stratigakos, Despina. 'Women and the Werkbund: Gender Politics and German Design Reform, 1907–1914'. *Journal of the Society of Architectural Historians* 62, no. 4 (December 2003): 490–511.
Stratigakos, Despina. *Hitler at Home*. New Haven: Yale University Press, 2015.
Sturdza, Michael. 'Allgemeine Einführung über die Familie Cantacuzène'. In *Archiv für Sippenforschung mit praktischer Forschungshilfe, 35/36*. Edited by Hans Kretschmer, 257–67 (1969–1970): 257–67.
Sturken, Marita and Lisa Cartwright. *Practices of Looking: An Introduction to Visual Culture*. New York: Oxford University Press, 2001.
Sullivan, Louis. 'The Tall Office Building Artistically Considered'. *Lippincott's Magazine* (March 1896): 403–9.
Sutton, Peter T. *Reclaimed: Paintings from the Collection of Jacques Goudstikker*. New Haven: Yale University Press, 2008.
Teeuwisse, Nicolaas. *Vom Salon zur Secession*. Berlin: Deutscher Verlag für Kunstwissenschaft, 1986.
The Prophet: The World of Karl Wilhelm Diefenbach. Vienna: Wien Museum, 2011.
Thieme, Ulrich. 'Wilhelm von Debschitz'. In *Allgemeines Lexikon der bildenden Künstler von der Antike bis zur Gegenwart*, vol. 8, 510. Leipzig: E.A. Seemann, 1913.
Toepfer, Karl Eric. *Empire of Ecstasy: Nudity and Movement in German Body Culture, 1910–1935*. Berkeley: University of California Press, 1997.
Topp, Leslie. *Architecture and Truth in Fin-de-Siècle Vienna*. Cambridge: Cambridge University Press, 2004.

Ugolini, Laura. *Men and Menswear: Sartorial Consumption in Britain 1880–1939*. Aldershot: Ashgate, 2007.

Ullmer, Renate. *Jugendstil in Darmstadt*. Darmstadt: Eduard Roether, 1997.

Umbach, Maiken. *German Cities and Bourgeois Modernism, 1890–1924*. Oxford: Oxford University Press, 2009.

Van de Velde, Henry. 'Das neue Kunst-Prinzip in der modernen Frauen-Kleidung'. *Deutsche Kunst und Dekoration* 10 (1902): 363–71.

Van de Velde, Henry. *Die künstlerische Hebung der Frauentracht*. Krefeld: Kramer & Baum, 1900.

Van de Velde, Henry. *Geschichte meines Lebens*. Munich: Piper Verlag, 1962.

Vergo, Peter. *Ein moderner Nachmittag. A thoroughly Modern Afternoon*. Vienna: Böhlau, 2000.

Vickery, Amanda. 'Golden Age to Separate Spheres? A Review of the Categories and Chronology of English Women's History'. *Historical Review* 36, no. 2 (1993): 383–414.

Vogel, Rudolf. 'Moderne, wahre Baukunst'. *Deutsche Bauhütte* 6 (1902): 329–95.

Voit, Antonia. *Ab Nach München: Künstlerinnen um 1900*. Munich: Süddeutsche Zeitung Edition, 2014.

Von Poellnitz. 'Betrachtungen über den modernen Stil'. *Deutsche Kunst und Dekoration* 2 (1898): 301.

Wagner, Richard. *The Artwork of the Future and other Works* (1849). Translated by William Ashton Ellis. Lincoln: University of Nebraska Press, 1993.

Wagner-Rieger, Renate. *Die Ringstrasse: Bild einer Epoche*. 11 Vols. Wiesbaden: Steiner, 1969–1981.

Walker, Fred M. *The Song of the Clyde: A History of Clyde Shipbuilding*. Edinburgh: John Donald Publishing, 2011.

Wallach Scott, Joan. 'Deconstructing Equality-versus-Difference, or the Uses of Post-Structuralist Theory in Feminism'. *Feminist Studies* 14 (Spring 1988): 33–50.

Wallach Scott, Joan. 'Gender: Still a Useful Category of Analysis?'. *Diogenes* 57, no. 1 (October 2010): 7–14

Wallenberg, Louise and Andrea Kollnitz. *Fashion and Modernism*. London: Bloomsbury, 2018.

Weese, Arthur. 'Neue Wege im Münchner Kunstgewerbe'. *Kunst und Kunsthandwerk* 1 (1898): 367–79.

Weiss, Peg. *Kandinsky in Munich: The Formative Jugendstil Years*. Princeton: Princeton University Press, 1979.

Weiss-Sussex, Godela and Ulrike Zitzlsperger. *Das Berliner Warenhaus/The Berlin Department Store: Geschichte und Diskurse/History and Discourses*. Frankfurt: Peter Lang, 2013.

Weltausstellung in Paris 1900: Amtlicher Katalog der Ausstellung des deutschen Reichs. Berlin: Reichskommissariat, 1900.

Weltge, Sigrid. *Women's Work: Textile Art from the Bauhaus*. San Francisco: Chronicle Books, 1992.

Wertheimer, Max. *Experimentelle Studien über das Sehen von Bewegung*. Leipzig: Johann A. Berth Verlag, 1912.

West, Candace and Don H. Zimmerman, 'Doing Gender'. *Gender and Society* 1, no. 2 (1987): 125–51.

Whitaker, Jan. *The Department Store: History, Design, Display*. London: Thames & Hudson, 2011.

White, Gleeson. 'Some Glasgow Designers and their Work'. *The Studio* 11 (July 1897): 86–100.

Wichmann, Siegfried. *Jugendstil Art Nouveau: Floral and Functional Form.* Boston: Little Brown, 1984.

Widmer, Karl. 'Kleid und Wohnraum'. *Innendekoration* 20, no. 7 (1909): 237–41.

Wieber, Sabine. 'Between Invention and Tradition: In Search of a Modern Style'. In *Atlas of Furniture Design.* Edited by Mateo Kries, 26–50. Weil am Rhein: Vitra Design Museum, 2019.

Wieber, Sabine. 'Designing the Nation: Neo-Northern Renaissance Interiors and the Politics of Identity in Late Nineteenth-Century Germany, 1876–1888'. PhD Dissertation, University of Chicago, 2004.

Wieber, Sabine. 'German Art Academies and Their Impact on Artistic Style'. In *A Companion to Nineteenth-Century Art.* Edited by Michelle Facos, 103–21. Hoboken: John Wiley & Sons, 2017.

Wieber, Sabine. 'Martha Vogeler and the Worpswede Artists' Colony, 1894–1905'. In *Künstlerinnen: Neue Perspektiven auf ein Forschungsfeld der Vormodern.* Edited by Brigitte Munch and Andreas Tacke, 199–210. Petersberg: Michael Imhof Verlag, 2017.

Wieber, Sabine. 'The Warp & the Weft: Tradition and Innovation in Skærbæk Tapestries, 1896–1903'. *Journal of Design History* 28, no. 4 (2015): 331–47.

Wigley, Mark. *White Walls, Designer Dresses.* Cambridge, MA: MIT Press, 1995.

Wilhelmy-Dollinger, Petra. *Die Berliner Salons.* Berlin: Walter de Gruyter, 2000.

Willmann, Rainer and Julia Voss. *The Art and Science of Ernst Haeckel.* Cologne: Taschen, 2017.

Winiwarter, Verena, Gertrud Haidvogl and Michael Bürkner. 'The Rise and Fall of Munich's Early Modern Water Network: A Tale of Prowess and Power'. *Water History* 8 (2016): 277–99.

Wittmann, Reinhard. *Hundert Jahre Buchkultur in München.* Munich: Hugendubel, 1993.

Witzling, Mara. 'Quilt Language: Towards a Poetics of Quilting'. *Women's History Review* 18, no. 4 (2009): 619–37.

Wolf, Georg Jacob. 'Erinnerungen an Hermann Obrist'. *Deutsche Kunst* 31 (1927/8): 108 and 166.

Wolfgang, J. Mommsen, *Bürgerliche Kulture und politische Ordnung: Künstler, Schriftsteller und Intellektuelle in der deutschen Geschichte 1830–1933.* Frankfurt: Fischer Verlag, 1980.

Wolzogen, Ernst von. *Das Dritte Geschlecht.* Berlin: R. Eckstein, 1900.

Woolf, Virginia. *A Room of One's Own.* London: Hogarth Press, 1929.

Zacharias, Thomas. *Tradition und Widerspruch: 175 Jahre Kunstakademie München.* Munich: Prestel Verlag, 1985.

Ziegert, Beate. 'The Debschitz School, Munich: 1902–1914'. *Design Issues* 3, no. 1 (Spring 1986): 28–42.

Zils, Wilhelm. *Geistiges und künstlerisches München in Selbstbiographien.* Munich: Kellers Verlag, 1913.

Zola, Emile. *The Ladies' Paradise* (1883). Translated by John Calder. London: Alma Classics, 2013.

INDEX

Page references in italic refer a figure on the corresponding page.

1848 Revolutions 7, 75

Abelson, Elaine S. 172
abstract patterns 11
Academic Society for Psychology 59
Académie Julian 94
acculturation 133–4
Adamson, Glenn 46
Adler, Friedrich 91, 98
Aestheticism 149, 152
aesthetics 5, 11, 12, 15, 16, 27, 36, 39, 41–3, 65, 80, 81, 91, 112, 150–1, 153
Aglaia 161
Ahlers-Hestermann, Friedrich 69
Alexander, Zeynep Çelik 98, 101, 112
Allgemeine Verein für Verbesserung der Frauenkleidung (Association for the Improvement of Women's Dress) 163, 164, 173
Alte Pinakothek (1836) 6
Anderson, Harriet 81
Andreas-Salome, Lou 79
animal prints 65
Annual Art Exhibition (1898) 126
Anschauung 97
'anti-fashion dress' (*Anti-Modekleid*) 167
anti-Semitism 132, 133, 169, 189
Appadurai, Arjun 121
applied arts 5, 7, 10, 12, 15, 28, 29, 32, 34, 35, 44, 46, 48, 49, 62, 90, 91, 94, 98, 99, 105, 109, 149, 150, 159, 175
    exhibitions 33
    objects 37
    reform 10, 12, 16, 28, 32, 46, 91, 93, 95, 97, 149, 184, 185

Applied Arts Pavilion 38, 89
Applied Arts Seminar 97
applique work 28, 162
architecture 3, 6, 12, 17, 35, 60–2, 126, 150, 160, 169, 187, 191
Arendt, Hannah 3
Argyle Street Tea Rooms 129
Arnim, Achim von 136
Arp, Hans 80
art(s). *See also* applied arts
    economy 9
    exhibitions 9
    market 9
    publishing houses 124
    system 9
'Art and Revolution' (Wagner) 36
Art Museum Krefeld 148
Art Nouveau in Munich (1988) 11, 66
Arts and Crafts Exhibition Society 12, 34, 37
Arts and Crafts Exhibition Society's exhibition (1896) 130, 131
'The Artwork of the Future' (Wagner) 36
Ashbee, C. R. 37
As long as It's Pink (Sparke) 55 n.82
Ateliers und Werkstätten für Angewandte Kunst (Studios and Workshops for Applied Arts) 109
atlas stitch 40
Au bonheur des dames (The Ladies Paradise, Zola) 171
Au Bon Marché 172
Augenmass (visual measure) 102
Augspurg, Amalie 70

Augspurg, Anita   15, 48, 57, 59, 61, 62, 69–76, 78–82, 94, 99, 138, 164, 185, 189
Au Printemps   172
Ausschuss für Kunst im Handwerk (Committee for Art in Handicraft)   36–7
avant-garde   15, 34, 40, 61, 73, 80, 82

Bach, Alexander von   124
Bahr, Hermann   160
Bardt, Margarethe   102
Bartesch, Hermine   38, 53 n.44
Barthes, Roland   156
Bauausstellung (Trade Fair for the German Building Industry, 1931)   189
Baudelaire, Charles   156
The Bauhaus   18 n.16, 48
Bauhaus architecture   42
Bauhaus design   3
Bauhäuslerinnen/Bauhausmädels   48–9
Bauhaus women   49
Bäumer, Gertrud   77, 82
Bavaria   7–9, 77, 109
Bavarian Applied Arts, Trade and Industry exhibition (1906)   186
Bavarian Association for the Applied Arts   48
Bavarian Catholic Church   10
Bavarian National Museum   7
Bavarian State Library   130
Bavarian State Photography School (*Staatslehranstalt*)   82
Bavarian Trade Exhibition (1912)   111, 190
Bayerische Kunstgewerbe Verein (Bavarian Applied Arts Association)   7, 33, 44, 96, 98, 105, 186
Bayerische Landes-Gewerbe-, Industrie- und Kunstausstellung (Bavarian Trade, Industry and Art Exhibition, 1906)   89, *90*, 90–1
Beaudry, Mary C.   28, 43
Bebel, August   103
Beckmann, Bertha   72
'Bedroom Furniture' (Debschitz)   *96*
Beeg, Gunta   151
Behren, Peter   189
Behrens, Lili   164

Behrens, Peter   126, 167
Benjamin, Walter   1
Berenson, Bernard   94
Berlepsch-Valendas, Hans Eduard von   12, 13, 23 n.66
Berlin   6, 7–9, 59, 62, 63, 69, 70, 77, 78, 100, 136, 163, 166, 167, 173, 174, 189
Berlin Fashion Week   174
Bertsch, Karl   128, 141 n.43
Billroth, Theodor   124
Bilski, Emily   134
Bode, Wilhelm von   34, 36
Bonnaz, Antoine   45
Bourdieu, Pierre   138
bourgeois ideology   104
Brachvogel, Karoline 'Carry'   77
Brahms, Johannes   124
Brandl, Jakob   171
Brandow-Faller, Megan M.   108
Brauchitsch, Ernst von   28
Brauchitsch, Margarethe von   15–17, 27–30, *29*, 32, 34, 36–8, 45, 147, 153–5, 167, 189
  'Back Pillow'   *31*
  'Curtain for the Munich Schauspielhaus'   *27*
  early life   28–9
  embroidery and   29–30, 38–45, 49
  illustration in *Die Jugend*   *31*
  'Interior with Furniture and Embroidery Work: A Ladies' Toilette'   *39*
  'Interior with Furniture and Embroidery Work: Dressing Room'   *41*
  as Jugendstil woman   47–9
  Kunstsalon Littauer (1896)   34
  machine embroidery and   45–7
  'Two Embroideries on Linen'   *30*
  and United Workshops   30, 32, 36–9
Braun, Emily   134
Braun, Irene   44, 45
Braunmühl, Clementine von   106, 117 n.73
Bredt, Ernst Wilhelm   6
Brentano, Clemens   136
Breward, Christopher   156
Breysig, Kurt   61
Bridgerton (TV series)   1

INDEX   217

British Arts and Crafts movement   5, 12, 32, 37, 47, 130–2, 149, 165
Bröhan Museum   62
Bruckmann, Alphons   124, 125, 132
Bruckmann, Elsa (née Cantacuzènes)   16, 17, 35, 109, 119, 121–2, 124, 127, 129–37, 165, 184, 185, 189, 190
   debut as salonnière   132–4
   'enhanced independence'   137–8
   marriage   124–5
   in Todesco Palais   122–4
Bruckmann, Hugo   16, 119, 122, 124–6, 130–4, 137, 138
The Bruckmann's 'Publishing House for Art and Science'   124, 125
Bruckmann Villa Munich   *120*
Buchanan Street Tearooms   129
Bücher- und Lesestube (book and reading room)   34
Buddenbrooks: The Decline of a Family (Mann)   137
Bülow, Eva von   132
Bund deutscher und österreichischer Künstlerinnen-Vereine (Association of German and Austrian Women Artists)   107
Buschmann, Hedwig   162
Butters, Emilie   110–11, 185
Butters, Gerold   110
Butters, Lina   110
'By Georgian! Needlework and Piano Keep Lockdown Lizzies Busy'   1

Cabinets 24 and 25, Seventh International Art Exhibition   5, 6, 34–6, 59
Calvert, Robyne   149
Carl du Prel   14
Cartwright, Lisa   75
Catholicism   13
Cauer, Minna   74, 78, 164
censorship laws   10
ceramics workshop   111
Chamberlain, Houston Stewart   132, 133, 189
Christmas Story (Macdonald)   128
Clark, T. J.   191
Club der ehemaligen Schülerinnen des Lette-Vereins (Club of former students of the Lette Association)   72

Coco Chanel   174
Collective Exhibition, Munich Women Artists' Association (1900)   38
Cologne Werkbund Exhibition (1914)   187
consumer culture   172–3
contemporary art   6
contemporary art exhibitions   34
contemporary design   12
contemporary discourses and practices   4
Cornely Chain Stitch Machine Type K   45, 46
Correvont, Antonia   72
corsets   156–157, 161, 163
couso-brodeur   45
Covid-19 pandemic   1, 2, 17 n.2
craft practices   2, 46
Crane, Walter   131, 149
Craveri, Benedeta   133
cultural-political entanglement   15, 59
culture
   change   2, 3
   feminism   81
   German   3, 10, 11, 136
   history   4
   life   13
   vernacular   121
Culture of the Female Body as a Foundation of Women's Clothing (Schultze-Naumburg)   161

Dachau Painting School   10
daguerreotype studios   72
Damenabteilung für ornamentales Entwerfen (Women's Studio for Ornamental Design)   30, 37, 111
Damenakademie (Ladies' Academy)   107, 108, 111
Darwin, Charles   13
Das Eigenkleid der Frau (Woman's Own Dress, Muthesius)   16, 159, 165, 167
Dasio, Maximilian   107, 166
Das Kleid der Frau (Women's Dress, Mohrbutter)   159, 167
Davidson, Hilary   161
Debord, Guy   172
Debschitz, Kolmar von   96
Debschitz, Wilhelm von   15, 91, 95–6, 99–101, 108, 109, 111, 184

Debschitz School   15–16, 48, 61, 89, 91, 93, 184
  Butters and   110–11
  curriculum   98–102, 112
  Debschitz and   95–6
  as largest private art and design school   96–8
  Obrist and   93–5
  women at   102–3, 108–10, 112
decorative arts   5, 12, 125
decorative objects   47
Dekorative Kunst (Decorative Arts)   33, 49, 91, 101, 109, 119, 125, 132, 138, 185
de Lauretis, Teresa   2
dem Borne, Pauline von   96
Deneken, Friedrich   156, 147–50, 152, 153, 158, 175 n.3
Der Kunstwart   33
Der Münchner Jugend Brunnen (Munich's Fountain of Youth)   191
Der Ring der Nibelungen (Ring of the Nibelung, 1876)   8
'Der Tag der deutschen Kunst' (The Day of German Art)   57
design
  definition   5
  discourse   28
  reform   3, 5, 9, 28, 37, 44, 149
Deutsche Kunst und Dekoration (German Art and Decoration)   12, 29, 33, 39, 131, 147, 185
Deutscher Frauenverein Reform (German Women's Association Reform)   75
Deyseve, Yvette   107
Die Frauenbewegung (Women's Movement)   78
Die Frau: Monatsschrift für das gesamte Frauenleben unserer Zeit (The Woman)   75
Die Gartenlaube   65
Die Insel   33
Die Jugend: Illustrierte Wochenschrift für Kunst und Leben (The Youth)   10, 11, 30, 33, 184, 185
Die Kunst (Fine Arts)   38, 125
Die Künstlerin (The Female Artist, Märten)   183
Dietrich, Oskar   57, 59, 62

dilettantism   103
Dingelstedt, Franz von   124
dining-room-cum-salon   127–9, 134, 136–8
Dobeneck, Hedwig von   103
Doblhoff-Dier, Anton von   124
domestic interiors   42, 44
domestic space   159
d'Ora, Madame   73
Dresden Applied Arts Association   186
Dresdner Werkstätten für Handwerkskunst Karl Schmidt (Dresden Workshops for Handicraft)   187
dress. See also *Künstlerkleider* (Artistic Dress)
  contemporary   149
  and function   153–5
  styles   150
Dritte Deutsche Kunstgewerbe Ausstellung (Third German Applied Arts Exhibition, 1906)   186, 187
Dülfer, Martin   16, 35, 125–6, 137
Düll, Heinrich   171

Eckart, Friedrich   131
Eckmann, Otto   12
eclecticism   9, 13
Egidy, Emmy von   77
Einfühlung (empathy)   59–60
Einführungskurs (preliminary course)   100
Eisner, Kurt   78
Elferich, Christa   81
Ellenrieder, Marie   116 n.58
embroidery   16, 29, 30, 38–9
  exhibition   33
  floral   32
  and Jugendstil historiography   46–7
  machine   45–7
  materiality of Brauchitsch's   40–2
  modern   61
  practice   27
  silk on linen   34
Endell, August   15, 32, 35–6, 57, 63–6, 69, 70, 75, 76, 80–2, 94, 97, 126
  first commission   59–61
  and Munich Jugendstil   61–2
'*Endlich ein Umschwung!*' (At Long Last, a Turnabout!, Berlepsch-Valendas)   12

INDEX   219

English House, The (Muthesius)   130
English Pre-Raphaelite Brotherhood   149
ephemera   150
Ercole Cornely   45
Erste Deutsche Kunst und Kunstindustrie Ausstellung (First German Art and Art Industry Exhibition, 1876)   8
Erste Kunst- und Kunstgewerbe Ausstellung (First Art and Applied Arts Exhibition, 1898)   29
Europe   3, 7, 12, 36, 44, 70, 73, 76, 99, 103–5, 121, 124, 125, 129, 130, 138, 152, 158, 172, 188
experiential form   57, 60
experimentation   44, 65, 73, 79–82, 162
Expressionism   187, 191

Fachausschuss für Textil- und Bekleidungsgewerbe (Committee for the Textile and Garment Industry)   47
fashion/anti-fashion   155–7
Fashion System, The (Barthes)   156
femininity   43, 45
feminist movement   59, 70
Fichte, Johann Gottlieb   136
Fiedler, Konrad   132
Fiedler, Mary   132
fine arts   12, 32, 44, 48, 97, 99, 150
Fine Arts Pavilion   91, *92*
'Fire Lilies'. *See* 'Whiplash' (Ruchet)
First Hague Peace Conferences   78
First International Exhibition of Decorative Arts (1902)   166
First National Art and Applied Arts Exhibition (1876)   36
First Universal Exhibition (1851)   105
First World War (1914)   49, 111, 173, 183, 188, 189
Fischer, Theodor   35
folklore   121
formal dress   *154*, 155
Form-School   97
Förster, Ludwig Christian Friedrich   123
Foucault, Michel   2
Foundations of the Nineteenth Century, The (Chamberlain)   132
'The Four-Leaved Clover' (Bruckmann) 121–2

Franco-Prussian War (1870–1) 7, 20 n.38
Franz Joseph (king)   122–3
Frauenfrage (Women's Question)   185
Freistaat Bayern (Free State of Bavaria)   78
French Art Nouveau   38
French Enlightenment (1685–1815)   134
French fashion industry   174
French haute couture   173, 185
French hegemony   156
Freudenberg, Friedericke 'Ika'   75, 76, 78, 80
Fuchs, Georg   103

Ganghofer, Ludwig   124
Gaul, Gustav   123
Gebrauchskleider (functional dress)   153
Gedon, Lorenz   123
Gemütlichkeit (contentment)   10, 136–7
gender
  concept   4
  dynamics   2, 48
  equality   2, 108, 163
  identity   2, 19 n.21, 80, 173
  norms   15, 104, 106, 137, 150
  politics   59, 75, 76
  roles   4, 39, 43, 79, 80, 104, 184, 185
  salon culture and   137
gendered design values   28
geometric abstraction   65
geometric forms   11, 32, 41
George, Stefan   52 n.21, 61
George-Kreis   33, 61
German Applied Arts Reform   103
German Dressmakers' Meeting (1900)   147
German dress reform   2, 16, 150–3, 155, 158, 161, *162*, 163–5, 167, 173, 174, 175 n.9
German education   97, 103, 109
German Empire   2, 3, 5, 8, 9, 12, 30, 33, 34, 36, 37, 39, 44, 47, 48, 71–5, 77, 79, 80, 97, 98, 103, 106, 109, 130, 137, 138, 147–9, 155, 162, 163, 168, 173, 183–5, 190
German life reform   162–3
German-National Applied Arts Exhibition (1888)   8
German Romanticism   136, 155
German society   4, 99, 184

German Werkbund   17, 28, 38, 47, 48, 174, 187
German Werkbund Exhibition (1927)   189
German Women's Association Reform   75
German Workshops Hellerau   47
Germany   3–5, 7–12, 34, 36–38, 40, 46, 47, 49, 50, 59, 62, 72, 75, 80, 81, 91, 97, 130, 133, 137, 147, 149, 164, 184, 185
Gesamtarrangements (total arrangements)   36, 42, 138
Gesamtkunstwerk (total work of art)   12, 14, 36, 42, 159
Gesamtwirkung   38
Gesellschaft für Modernes Leben (Society for Modern Life)   76
Gesellschaftskleider (evening gowns)   153, 161
Gestalt-Psychology   99
Gestaltung   99
Gewerbefreiheit (freedom to trade)   72
Geyer, Michael   172
Gil Blas (1883)   171
Gizycki, Lily von   74
Gladius Dei (Mann)   9, 69
Glasgow Four   119, 125, 129, 130, 132, 165
Glasgow School of Art (GSA)   99, 165
Glasgow Style   132
Glaspalast exhibition (1897)   17, 94
Glyptothek (1830)   6
Godwin, Edward William   160, 152, 161
Goethe, Johann Wolfgang von   103
Golden Thread, The (St Claire)   43
Goodman, Nelson   4
Götz, Hermann   94
Goudstikker, Jacques   70
Goudstikker, Mathilde   73
Goudstikker, Sophie   15, 48, 57, 59, 61, 62, 69–75, 77–82, 94, 99, 138, 185
Grand, Sarah   2
Grant Duff, Alice Jane   77, 93
graphic arts   11, 33
Gropius, Walter   3, 39, 63
Guild of Handcraft   37
Gumppenberg, Hanns von   186

Habermas, Jürgen   134, 135
Habsburg Empire   122, 148, 160
Haeckel, Ernst   13, 14

Haeckel, Friedrich August   64
Hahn, Else von   167
hand-embroidery   28, 46
handicraft   37, 46, 48, 50, 105
handmade furniture   47
Hansen, Fritz   72
Hansen, Theophil   123
'Happiness' (Bruckmann)   121
Hartmann-Sapatka, Else   100
Hartwig, Josef   63
Haushofer, Marie   77
Haushofer, Max   76
health and beauty   161–2
Healthy and Artistic Dress Union   149, 152, 161
Heilemann, Ernst   104
Hellingrath, Marie von   132
Heymann, Lida Gustava   71, 78, 80–2, 189
Hiesinger, Kathryn Bloom   11, 28
Hildebrand, Adolf von   132, 133
Hirth, Georg   10
historiography   3, 4, 11, 45–7, 62, 150
Hitler, Adolf   82, 189, 190
Hoelzel, Adolf   10, 22 n.57
Hof-Atelier Elvira   15, 59, 71
Hofbräuhaus beerhall   25, *26*
Hoffmann, Josef   134, 166
Hofmannsthal, Hugo von   124
Hohenzollern Kaufhaus   167
Höhere Schule für Dekorationskunst   167
Horta, Viktor   66
Houze, Rebecca   148, 160
Huch, Ricarda   77
hunger strikes   78
Hunter, Clare   43
Hunterian Art Gallery   128

Illustrirte Frauen-Zeitung (Illustrated Ladies' Journal)   122, 132
Independent, The   167
industrialization   9, 162
Innendekoration   30, 33
interior decoration   12, 14, 25, 30, 36
interior design   39, 47, 123, 124
interiors and textiles   42–5
International Art Nouveau   3, 11–12, 39, 43, 165, 185
Internationaler Kongress für Frauenwerke und Frauenbestrebungen

(International Congress for
    Women's Work and Efforts) 163
International Modernism 48, 189, 191
International Union of Progressive
    Women's Associations 78
International Women's Congress 78
'intimate collaboration' 80–1
Isar-Athen (Athens on the River Isar) 7
Itten, Johannes 100

Jacquard looms 5
Jarausch, Konrad 172
Jaskolla, Else 106
Johnson, Julie 3, 103
John VI Kantakouzenos (king) 121
Jopling, Louise 149
Jugendstil 2, 3, 9–14, 43, 65, 94,
    121, 125, 191. *See also* Munich
    Jugendstil
  building 126
  design 5, 11, 14, 47–8, 57, 59, 73,
    121, 137, 138, 149, 152, 153, 161,
    162, 168, 184
  designers 7, 12, 17, 28, 42, 49, 147,
    150, 155, 159–61, 173, 174, 186, 187
  interiors 159–161
  objects 3, 16, 112, 192
'Jugendstil Sins' (Schulze) 185

Kammerspiele 50 n.4
Kandinsky, Wassily 65, 66, 80, 97
Kant, Immanuel 136
Kaufhaus Oberpollinger 25, 169–71, 173
Kaufhaus Wertheim 167, 168, 173
Keramischen Werkstätten 110, 111
Kermische Werkstätten München-
    Herrsching (Ceramic Workshops
    Munich-Herrsching) 109
Kettler, Hedwig 75
Khnopff, Fernand 128
kinaesthetic learning 102
Kirchner, Eugen 132
Kirsch, Reinhold 64, 66
Kleinkunst (minor arts) 34, 62
Kleist, Heinrich von 136
Klenze, Leo von 6
Klinger, Max 28
Knorr, Heinrich 96
Knorr, Julius 132

Koch, Alexander 12, 29, 30
Koebke, Otto 110, 111
Königliche Kunstgewerbeschule (Royal
    Applied Arts School/RAAS) 104,
    107, 111, 190
  Frauenabteilung 106, 108, 110
  weibliche Abteilung (women's
    department) 105–6
Königliches Kunstgewerbemuseum (Royal
    Applied Arts Museum) 40
Korn, Simon 63
Kraut, Gertrud 102
Krefeld exhibition (1900) 156, 148–50,
    152, 153, 158, 160
Krieger, Wilhelm 111
Krüger, Franz August Otto 32, 96, 148
Kuhnow, Anna 161, 178 n.56
Kunowski, Wanda von 96, 97, 100
Kunsterziehung (art education) 93, 95,
    97–9
'*Kunsterziehungstag*' (Conference on Art
    Education, 1901) 97
Kunstformen der Natur (Artforms of
    Nature, Haeckel) 14, 65
Kunst für Alle (Art for All) 124–5
Künstlergenossenschaft (Artists'
    Association) 34
Künstlerkleider (Artistic Dress) 147–8,
    153, 158–9, 165, 173, 185
  definition 149–50
  and department store 167–9
  and German dress reform 150–3
  and Jugendstil interiors 159–161
Künstlerkleid exhibition (1904) 166
Kunstsalon Littauer (1896) 33–4, 46,
    61, 94
Kunstschule für Mädchen (Art School for
    Girls) 105
Kunststickerei (art embroidery) 34, 38, 46
Kunst und Handwerk 33, 98
Kunstverein (Art Club) 6

Lampe, Marie-Louise 94
Lange, Emil 106
Lange, Helene 75
Lange, Laura 101, 103
Lasenby, Arthur 131
Laube, Heinrich 124
Läuger, Max 36

Lebensreform (Life Reform)
  movement   16, 162, 164
*Lehr- und Versuchs-Ateliers für
  angewandte und freie Kunst* (Studio
  for Teaching and Experimenting
  in Applied and Free Art). *See*
  Debschitz School
Lehrwerkstätte (workshop-school)   98
Leipzig Strasse   166
Lenbach, Franz von   69, 72, 124, 126
Lenman, Robin   9
Lesker, Elsa   45
Lesker, Hedwig   45
Lette, Wilhelm Adolf   72
Lette Verein   72
Levi, Hermann   132, 133
Liberty, Arthur Lasenby   149
Liberty & Co department store   152
Liberty fabrics   151
Lichtwark, Alfred   9
Life Reform movement   61, 148
Limited Company   32
Lipps, Theodor   59–60
Liszt, Franz   124
Littmann, Max   25, 169, 171
Lochner, Hermann   91
Logan, Mary (Mary Smith Costelloe)   94
Loos, Adolf   32, 66
Ludwig I (king)   6, 7, 10, 59
Ludwig II (king)   7–10, 63, 104
Ludwig von Hessen, Ernst   29
Luitpold, Regent Prince   9–10, 90

McBride, Theresa   172
Macdonald, Frances   119, 128, 165
Macdonald, Margaret   16, 119, 127–32,
  134, 138, 165
Mackintosh, Charles Rennie   16, 119,
  127–34, 136–8
McNair, Frances   165, *166*
McNair, Herbert   119
Madelaine Vionnet   174
Makart, Hans von   123
malerische (atmospheric/painterly)   36
Mann, Thomas   9, 69, 137
Marcus, Jane   49
Märten, Lu   183
Maschinenmöbel (machine-made furniture)
  5, 19 n.24, 47, 50, 187, 190

material culture   28, 43, 47
material integrity (*Materialgerechtigkeit*)
  162, 184
materiality   42, 112
Mathildenhöhe   29–30
Maximilian II (king)   7
Maximilians Strasse   25
Max Joseph (king)   104
mechanized loom   46
Meier-Graefe, Julius   34, 125
memory work   3
Merton Abbey Mills   5
Meskimmon, Marsha   4, 191
Messel, Alfred   166
Metal Workshop   100
Mey, Hermann   106
Meyer, Eugen   100
Meyer, Julius   132
Michel, Wilhelm   39, 41–3
Miller, Josephine   150
Mims, Martina   60
Möbius, Paul Julius   104
'Model XVI'   63
modern art   50
modern design   4, 5, 10–12, 28, 30, 32, 34,
  42, 47, 50, 63, 66, 91, 131, 132, 138
modern interior (*Wohnkultur*)   13, 34,
  35, 49, 62, 119
modernism   3, 10, 42–3, 49, 66, 80,
  111–12, 122, 153, 155, 160, 164, 191
modernity   44, 47, 75, 79, 81, 134, 138,
  148, 150, 156
modern movement   130, 132
modern style   3, 4, 9, 12–14, 32, 34, 36,
  37, 44, 48, 69, 95, 126, 131, 147, 155
modern women   2–5, 11, 12, 44, 153, 185
Mohrbutter, Alfred   148, 152, 158–9, 167
Monaco of Bavaria. *See* Isar-Athen
  (Athens on the River Isar)
monochromatic colour scheme   40, 44
Montez, Lola   7
Morris, William   5, 37, 130
Morris & Company   37
Moser, Koloman   28
'Mother's Woes' (Rezniček)   104
Mrs Bürgelin and her Sons (Reuter)   76
Müller, Adam   136
Müller, J.   64
multiple-plate photogravure   124

Munich   4, 7–10, 11, 13, 14, 28, 30, 48, 49, 57, 59, 61–63, 69–75, 81, 133, 155
  art and design education   104
  cultural geography   5–7
Munich Academy of Fine Arts   6, 63, 96, 99, 100, 104, 107, 108
Munich Applied Arts Association   36, 44, 76
Munich Building Authority (*Oberste Baubehörde*)   57, 62
Munich Glaspalast   5, 8, 12, 14, 17, 33–6, 137
Munich Jugendstil   9, 17, 28, 38, 59, 61–2, 70, 75, 126, 131, 185, 188, 191
  artists   11, 22 n.60
  designers   5, 11, 12, 91
Munich's Latest News   132
Munich Women Artists' Association (*Künstlerinnen-Verein*)   106–8, 111, 166
Münter, Gabriele   77, 80
Muthesius, Anna (Anna Trippenbach)   16, 130–2, 159, 165–8, 185, 189
Muthesius, Hermann   37, 130–2, 165, 187, 188

National Romanticism   121
National Socialism   189–90
National Socialists   63, 82, 163, 189
National Zeitung   100
Nazi Party   82, 163
Nazism   190
needlework   28, 38, 40, 43–6, 49
Neo-Baroque style   8
Neoclassicism   57
Neo-Northern Renaissance style   8, 36
Neo-Rococo style   8–9
Netflix   1
Neue Frau. *See* New Woman
Neue Pinakothek (1853)   6
Neue Sachlichkeit (New Objectivity)   191
Newbery, Elsie   165
Newbery, Francis Henry   100
Newbery, Mary   165
New Gallery, London   37
New Woman   2, 16, 18 n.10, 81, 82
Nochlin, Linda   3
Nostitz, Helene von   160

Nuremberg exhibition (1906)   91, *92*, 108
Nuremberg Laws (1935)   189
Nutzbau   25
Nutz-Keramik (functional ceramics)   110
Nutzkunst (functional art)   187

'An Oak Husk with Eight Different Effects' (Debschitz)   101
Obler, Bibiana   15, 80
Obrist, Carl Kaspar   93
Obrist, Hermann   11, 15, 32, 34, 36, 38, 46, 59, 61, 62, 70, 75–7, 91, 93–7, 99, 100, 102, 103, 108–10, 112, 184
Old and New Embroideries exhibition (1899)   44
'On Dilettantism' (Goethe and Schiller)   103
'On the Physiological Imbecility of Women' (Möbius)   104
Oppler, Elsa   148, 165–8, 173, 185
Oppler-Legband, Else   17, 189
organic forms   11, 38
ornamental design   27, 91

Pan   33, 34, 36, 121
Pankok, Bernhard   32, 36, 94, 97, 148
Paragraph 1354, German Civil Code   77
Parisian haute couture   156, 155, 159, 168
Paris Universal Exposition (1900)   185
Paris World's Fair (1900)   38, 39
Parker, Roszika   43
patriarchal ideology   43, 44
Paul, Bruno   11, 32, 126, 191
Pecht, Friedrich   125
Petersen, Frieda   167
Pevsner, Nicholas   66
Pezold, Georg   171
Phalanx-Schule   97
Photo-Studio Elvira   35, 57, *58*, 59, *60*, 62, 73–5, 77–82, 94, 126, 189
  building and its façade   62–6
  and Endell   59–61
  establishment   71
  interior   66, *67–8*, 69
  and Munich's women's movement   74–5
pictorialism   73
Pinagel, Alfred   94
Pioneers of Modern Design, The (Pevsner)   66

Poiret, Paul   174
political activism   70, 73, 82, 161, 183, 189
political advocacy   80–2
Polster, Dora   98, 102
Potvin, John   192
Princess Victoria Melita of Saxe-Coburg and Gotha   29
Prinzregenten era (1886–1912)   9, 10
The Priory   131
private art and design schools   97
Proelss, Sera   163
progressive design   28, 38, 39, 45, 46, 49, 130, 133, 138
   discourse   2
   practices   4, 11, 129, 185
Prussian Cadets Corps Lichterfelde   96
Putz-Architektur   126

race   132, 133
radical dress reform   158
radical feminism   81
Rahl, Carl   123
Rappaport, Erika   172
Rat der Volksbeauftragten (Council of People's Deputies)   188
Raumkunst   5, 44
Reform Dress   149–50, 160, 161, 165, 173, 174, 175 n.9, 191
Reich, Lilly   166
Reinhard & Fia Wille   148
Renaissance   42–4
Renaissance Italy   134
Reuter, Gabriele   76, 79
Reutlinger   148
Reynier, Olga   103
Rezniček, Ferdinand von   104
Riemerschmid, Carl   25
Riemerschmid, Richard   5, 25, 27, 32, 35, 36, 47, 50, 94, 111, 126, 148, 187, 190
Rilke, Rainer Maria   76
Ringstrasse (Ring Street)   122–3
Rinker, Dagmar   98
Robert Blair & Sons   128
Rodin, Auguste   94
'The Role of Woman in the New Civil Code' (Stritt)   77
Romeis, Leonhard   105
Ruchet, Berthe   34, 46, 61, 76, 94, 98, 112

Ruckteschell-Trueb, Clara von   102, 111

St Claire, Cassia   43
salon   9, 16, 121, 124, 125, 133, 138, 190
salon culture   16, 134–7
satin stitch   40
Schäuffelen, Irene   132
Schauspielhaus   25–7, *26*
Scheffler, Karl   61, 69, 94
Schiller, Friedrich   103
Schlemmer, Oskar   63
Schmalhofer, Claudia   104
Schmerling, Anton von   124
Schmidt, Balthasar   63
Schmidt, Karl   187
Schmithals, Hans   98, 100
Schmoll von Eisenwerth, Karl   91
School for Young Ladies   121
School of Applied Arts   94
Schorske, Carl   122
Schuldenfrei, Robin   42
Schultze-Naumburg, Paul   161, 162, 165
Schulze, Otto   45–7, 185, 186
Schwabinger Bohème   61
Schwartz, Frederic   5, 189
Schwind, Moritz von   124
Scott, Joan Wallach   108
Scottish Room, Vienna Secession's Eighth Exhibition (1900)   129
secondary school system   97
Second World War   57
Seidl, Julius   171
Semper, Gottfried   8, 23 n.66
Sèthe, Marie-Louise 'Maria'   147
Seventh International Art Exhibition (1897)   5, 12, 23 n.66, 33–6, 59, 126, 184
sewing machine   46
shopping   172–5
Simmel, Georg   157, 164
Simplicissimus   11, 22 n.60, 33, 104, 184, 191
Skærbæk weaving workshops   98
Social Darwinism   189
Society for the Promotion of Intellectual Interests of Women   75
Soeltl, Johann Michael   6, 7
soft furnishings   30, 42, 47
Sonder-Ausstellung moderner Damen-Kostüme nach Künstler-Entwürfen

(Special Exhibition of Modern Ladies Costumes made from Artists' Designs)   147
South Kensington System   99
Sparke, Penny   55 n.82, 138
Specht, August   65
Spener, Carl   163
Staatliche Bauhaus   3
State Applied Arts School   106–7
stereotypes   43, 45
Stilkunst   38
Stratigakos, Despina   28, 187
Stritt, Marie   74, 77
Structural Transformation of the Public Sphere, The (Habermas)   134
Stuck, Franz von   126
Studio, The   12, 40, 94, 130
Studio for *Kunststickerei* (art embroidery)   94
studio photography   71–4
Sturken, Marita   75
Sullivan, Louis   153
Symbolism   34

Taeuber-Arp, Sophie   80, 102
Tag der Deutschen Kunst parade (1937)   189
Taylor, Lou   150
Teaching Workshop for Applied Arts   97
tea gowns   151–3, 166
tech-free hobbies   1
technical education   71, 72
Technical University   126
textile(s)
    arts   44
    history   150
    industry   147, 158
    interiors and   42–5
Thieme, Carl von   50
Thieme, Else von   50
Thiersch, Friedrich von   126
Third Applied Arts Exhibition (1906)   91
Third German Applied Arts Exhibition (1906)   19 n.24, 47
Third Sex, The (Wolzogen)   77, 78
Threads of Life (Hunter)   43
Tilgener, Viktor O.   124
Times, The   1

Tischgesellschaften (table societies)   134, 136
Tischkultur (table culture)   136
Todesco, Eduard von   122, 123
Todesco, Sophie von   122–4
Todesco Palais (Todesco Palace)   122–4, 133
Toorop, Jan   128
Troost, Paul   189

'Überbrettl'   76
Uffizi Gallery   161
Uibeleisen, Emma   82
United Workshops   14–15, 28, 30, 32, 33, 34, 36–9, 45, 47, 48, 50, 59, 91, 96–8, 112, 132, 148, 184
'unity of all arts'   12
Universal Exposition (1851)   7, 89
University of Berlin   93
University of Glasgow   128
University of Heidelberg   93
urbanization   162
urban rejuvenation project (1857–1918)   123
utopian socialism   37

van de Velde, Henry   156, 97, 131, 147–53, 160, 164, 166, 174, 187
van de Velde, Maria   153, 158–60, 164
Venus de Urbino   161
Verein Bildender Künstler (Secession)   9, 34, 69
Verein für Fraueninteressen (Association of Women's Interests)   48, 59, 62, 70, 74–8, 81, 94, 99
Vereinigte Werkstätten für Kunst im Handwerk (United Workshops for Art in Handicraft)   27, 32–3, 61, 94, 184
vernacular forms   35
Victoria & Albert Museum   40
Vienna   3, 4, 73, 81, 122–4, 133, 134, 160, 166
'Vienna 1900'   122
Viennese Workshops   41
visionary feminists   81
visual arts   9, 49, 79
Voigt, Martin Heinrich   59, 62
Von-der-Tann Strasse   57, 59

Vorbilder system (learning by example)   98
Vorkurs   100

Waerndorfer, Fritz   134
Wagner, Richard   8, 12, 14, 36, 42, 132
Walker, Emery   131
Warenhaus Hermann Tietz   25, 169–71
Watts, George Frederic   149
Wearden, Jennifer   40
Weimar Republic   4, 104, 188, 190
Weiss, Peg   65
Weiss-Sussex, Godela   169
Werkbund Exhibition (1914)   111, 187
Werner, Anton von   20 n.39
Wersin, Wolfgang von   98
Westheim, Paul   174
We Weren't Modern Enough (Meskimmon)   191
'Whiplash' (Ruchet)   94, 95
White, Gleeson   130
Who's Who of German Jugendstil   32
'Why Have There Been No Great Women Artists?' (Nochlin)   3
Widmer, Karl   159
Wigley, Mark   164
Wilhelm I (king)   20 nn.38, 39, 137
Wilhelmine Germany   6, 79, 98, 190
Wille, Fia   167
Wille, Rudolf   167
Wisinger-Florians, Olga   123
Wittmann, Reinhard   34
Wolf, Georg Jacob   102
Wolzogen, Ernst Freiherr von   76–8
women
    artists   3–4, 106–8, 183, 184
    body shapes and liberation   156, 163, 165
    clothing   160, 147, 161, 163, 165, 173
    curricular choices   111
    at Debschitz School   102–3, 108–10
    designers   3, 28, 32, 37, 39, 45, 48, 49, 98, 103, 111, 184
    drawing instructors   106, 109
    education   15, 75–7, 106–8, 111, 112, 163
    German   2, 42, 69, 76, 77, 93, 104, 173, 174, 188
    photographers   72, 73
    rights and movement   15, 59, 73–9, 81, 99, 108, 150, 163–5, 173, 174, 188
    role in art and design   3, 27, 37, 99, 107, 108
    working in German photography studios   72
Women's Clothing from the Perspective of Hygiene (Kuhnow)   161
Women's Congress (*Allgemeiner Bayerischer Frauentag*)   77
Woolf, Virginia   49
workshop system   97, 110

Yellow Book   12
Youth Court   79

Zeichnungs- und Modellierschule (Drawing and Modelling School)   105
Ziegert, Beate   98, 100
Zinspalast   123
Zitzlsperger, Ulrike   169
Zola, Emile   171